THEY KNEW THEY WERE

RIGHT

THEY KNEW THEY WERE

RIGHT

THE RISE OF THE NEOCONS

JACOB HEILBRUNN

DOUBLEDAY

NEW YORK LONDON TORONTO SYDNEY AUCKLAND

PUBLISHED BY DOUBLEDAY

Copyright © 2008 by Jacob Heilbrunn

All Rights Reserved

Published in the United States by Doubleday, an imprint of The Doubleday Broadway Publishing Group, a division of Random House, Inc., New York. www.doubleday.com

DOUBLEDAY and the portrayal of an anchor with a dolphin are registered trademarks of Random House, Inc.

Book design by Diane Hobbing of Snap-Haus Graphics

Library of Congress Cataloging-in-Publication Data

Heilbrunn, Jacob.
   They knew they were right : the rise of the neocons / Jacob Heilbrunn. — 1st ed.
      p.   cm.
   Includes bibliographical references and index.
   1. Conservatism—United States—History. 2. United States—Politics and government—1945-1989. 3. United States—Politics and government—1989-
4. Political culture—United States—History—20th century. 5. United States—Foreign relations—Islamic countries. 6. Islamic countries—Foreign relations—United States. I. Title.
   E839.5.H44 2007
   320.520973—dc22

                                                                  2007017587

ISBN 978-0-385-51181-0

PRINTED IN THE UNITED STATES OF AMERICA

10 9 8 7 6 5 4 3 2 1

First Edition

To my grandparents

Contents

Acknowledgments

I started working on this book when the neoconservatives were at the zenith of their influence. Like the Iraq war, the movement has taken a somewhat different turn than I had anticipated. I would like to record my gratitude to various colleagues and friends who served as highly valued sounding boards.

Early on, over sumptuous lunches, Chris Buckley provided puckish wisdom and voiced doubts about the direction of the Iraq war and the GOP that proved to be quite prescient. William F. Buckley Jr. kindly devoted several hours to musing about the early years of the conservative movement with me. Norman Podhoretz and Midge Decter submitted patiently to my queries. I also profited from discussions with Kenneth Adelman. Douglas J. Feith and Peter Rodman were most generous with their time, even while serving in the Defense Department. Walter Berns, Mark Blitz, and Kenneth Weinstein illuminated aspects of Straussian thinking. Jeane Kirkpatrick, whom I first came to know at Georgetown University years ago, spent a long afternoon with me discussing Strauss, Syria, and various other topics. John Bolton of the American Enterprise Institute was affable, witty, and direct in discussing his career. Gary Rosen of *Commentary* offered astute remarks about the state of the conservative movement. So did the *National Interest*'s Nicholas Gvosdev.

Kukula Glastris of the *Washington Monthly* provided both scorching assessments and irreverent asides. Joan Wohlstetter generously corrected my misapprehensions about her father and provided me with some of his writings.

A media fellowship at the Hoover Institution allowed me to consult its archives as well as meet a number of its permanent fellows. In this regard, I must single out Peter Berkowitz, a most discerning neocon, for special thanks. At the *Weekly Standard*, William Kristol offered valuable insights. Melvin J. Lasky was his inimitable self on the phone from Berlin, and I fondly recall visiting him in his lovely apartment in the Mommsenstrasse, where he offered me a cocktail at eleven a.m. Daniel Bell tried to guide me through some of the thickets of the early years of the "New York intelligenty."

Steven C. Clemons and Michael Lind of the New American Foundation helped me formulate my thoughts about the persistence of the neocon movement. Jonathan Rauch prodded me relentlessly forward. Over several dinners, John Judis and Walter Laqueur offered very different perspectives on the neocons. Lawrence F. Kaplan's keen observations and second thoughts have left a deep impression on me. I would also be remiss if I did not thank Doyle McManus of the *Los Angeles Times* and James Mann for their encouraging words.

I owe a great debt to my editors at Doubleday, particularly Adam Bellow, who not only displayed saintly patience but also provided expert guidance.

I would also like to thank my parents for their great assistance over the years. In addition, John and Gina Despres provided indispensable support. Perhaps my greatest debt is to my wife, Sarah Despres, and our son, Oscar, whose political predilections remain undetermined. Needless to say, any errors are mine alone.

THEY KNEW THEY WERE

RIGHT

Prologue: Now It Can Be Told: Bush Looks Back

As George W. Bush prepared to leave office in January 2009, he was able to look back with profound satisfaction on his record in foreign affairs. Derided as a simpleton by liberal elites in 2000, he had pulled off stunning victories in Afghanistan and Iraq. In particular the Iraq war, by common consent, had turned Bush into one of the most popular and revered presidents in American history. Though a few lonely critics on the left continued to complain that preventive war was illegal, most Americans hailed Bush's toppling of Saddam Hussein's tyranny as a noble action. Even many Europeans, who had fervently hoped that the United States would stub its toe in Iraq, had come around to acknowledge Bush's sagacity. To their amazement, the Iraq war had not only been a "cakewalk," as Bush's champions predicted, but also vindicated their vision of spreading democracy in the Middle East and elsewhere.

For one thing, U.S. troops rapidly secured the numerous weapons of mass destruction that Saddam had been secreting, including, most sensationally, centrifuges that suggested he was well on his way to constructing a nuclear weapon that would have allowed him to threaten Israel. Pacifying Iraq itself had proven relatively easy; like the Germans after World War II, most Iraqis greeted the U.S. troops not as occupiers but as liberators. Simply by establishing depots where Iraqis could voluntarily hand in their weapons, the United States reestablished order. To be sure, a few last-ditchers among Saddam's former Sunni officials occasionally took potshots at U.S. troops, but they were easily mopped up by the few remaining soldiers. Within months, most American and foreign troops had returned home. Ticker-tape parades greeted U.S. troops in New York and Washington, D.C., reminding old-timers of the reception that soldiers had received upon returning home from World War II. The dreaded Vietnam syndrome had apparently been put to rest for good.

Nor was Iraq experiencing any problems with its economy. Within months, it had begun to prosper. As Paul Wolfowitz—since promoted to secretary of defense—had predicted in congressional testimony, oil revenues were paying for the reconstruction of Iraq, which was taking place at a rapid pace. Foreign workers poured in from around the Middle East, Indonesia, Pakistan, and Europe, while outside contractors eagerly vied for lucrative contracts. The multinational Halliburton, which was supervising much of the work, stated that Iraqis were so eager to rebuild their country that much of the work would be completed several years ahead of schedule. Baghdad itself was flourishing, and the tourists who arrived were astounded by how rapidly the country had recovered from Saddam's depredations. The only real reminder of the reign of terror that Saddam had presided over was a few vendors outside the American embassy in Baghdad hawking trinkets like watches that bore the former president's image.

At his trial for war crimes, which had gone quickly, as numerous

Iraqis testified about his atrocities, Saddam was only able to fume impotently. Just as the Nuremberg war crimes trials had helped inoculate Germans against a repetition of the ghastly deeds of Nazism, so Iraqis made a permanent break with terror and violence. Saddam's hanging was itself conducted by the Iraqi government with great restraint and solemnity. Across the Arab world jubilant throngs gathered and rejoiced that a malevolent tyrant had been convicted and executed by a free and democratic Iraqi government.

Politically, Iraqis had rapidly established a thriving constitutional democracy, headed by the former exile Ahmed Chalabi. Chalabi, the scion of a distinguished Iraqi family, proved as capable in setting up a new political order as he did in drawing upon his economics training at the University of Chicago to revive Iraq. Despite some grumbling from hard-line Shiites, Chalabi established close ties with Israel, which was grateful for an Arab ally, and ensured that Iraq formed a bulwark against Iranian ambitions. Iran, flanked by two democracies, had announced that it was terminating its nuclear program, to the relief of Europe and the United States, though the French said it wasn't a significant matter and that they would trade with Tehran regardless of what it did. So popular was Chalabi that even many Sunnis hailed him as the George Washington of Iraq.

As a result of these momentous changes, U.S. popularity was at an all-time high around the globe. During his last trip as president to Western European capitals, Bush had basked in the applause of the locals. In Berlin and London crowds swarmed outside the American embassy and hoisted placards praising Bush's tenacity and courage. Politicians vied to be photographed with him. In England, former prime minister Tony Blair was now seen as rivaling Gladstone in historical significance.

In the United States itself, the controversial group of policy intellectuals and administration officials known as the neoconservatives were being hailed as hitherto neglected geniuses by much of the press. The *New York Times Magazine* featured flattering profiles of

Richard Perle, who had recently delivered the National Endowment for the Humanities' annual Jefferson Lecture, and Douglas J. Feith. The article included numerous favorable assessments from former critics such as the Brookings Institution's president, Strobe Talbott, and the *Newsweek* reporter Michael Isikoff, who admitted that they had been dead wrong about the perils of invading Iraq.

Perhaps the figure who enjoyed vindication most was Vice President Dick Cheney. It was Cheney who had pushed Bush to embrace the war. It was Cheney who poured scorn on the foreign policy "realists" who warned of dangers in attacking Iraq. Instead, just as Bush and Cheney had predicted, the Middle East was transformed almost overnight from an incubator of terrorism into a bastion of democracy. Syria's autocratic regime was quickly toppled by popular protests led by freedom-loving locals, as was Iran's, just as a "Bletchley II" conference at the American Enterprise Institute, convened on the eve of the war, had prognosticated. In Lebanon, Hezbollah, deprived of its former patrons, was a shadow of its former self. The Israeli-Palestinian conflict, too, had all but expired. Hamas, like Hezbollah, was unable to obtain outside support and had reluctantly agreed to abandon the Palestinian right of return and fully recognized Israel. The wall that Israeli prime minister Ariel Sharon had been constructing to seal off the West Bank from Israeli cities was demolished. As Wolfowitz and other neoconservatives had stated, the road to peace for Israel ran through Baghdad. In retrospect, it was inevitable, a number of American and European pundits and historians agreed, that democracy would spread in the Middle East.

———

Something along these lines, it seems safe to say, was what the neoconservatives envisioned when they were plotting the future of foreign policy at the Project for the New American Century, the *Weekly Standard,* and the American Enterprise Institute during the late

1990s. Instead, the opposite occurred. Iraq is a quagmire. Iran has been emboldened and Syria empowered. Terrorism is up, not down.

To all appearances, then, neoconservatism is on the outs. Donald Rumsfeld, a patron saint of the Defense Department neoconservatives, is gone from government, as are his aides Paul Wolfowitz and Douglas Feith. The realist camp in the GOP seems to be making a comeback, led by Senator Chuck Hagel of Nebraska, who warns that the administration is committing the greatest foreign policy blunder since Vietnam in Iraq. A host of other commentators, including George F. Will and William F. Buckley Jr., decry what they see as the administration's Wilsonian utopianism. The allegations against Canadian tycoon and prominent neoconservative Conrad Black and his wife, Barbara Amiel Black, who had neocons such as Richard Perle on the board of Hollinger International, have further tarnished the movement and robbed it of one of its main financial backers. The Cato Institute's Michael D. Tanner, in his recent book, *Leviathan on the Right*, complains that the neoconservatives introduced liberal principles into the GOP by sanctioning big government programs and national greatness conservatism. Patrick J. Buchanan, exiled to the fringes for his attacks on the Bush Doctrine and on Israel, can only chortle as he looks forward to the wholesale expulsion of the neocons from the Republican Party. Web sites such as Right Web are devoted to tracking the neoconservatives. The *Christian Science Monitor* Web site has a section called "Empire builders" that is devoted to the neoconservative movement and includes an interactive quiz called "Are you a 'neocon'?"[1]

Why, then, another look at the neoconservatives? After all, a number of fine works have already examined the neocons, starting with the former *New York Times* reporter Peter Steinfels's analysis in 1979, which depicted them as a movement of former liberals run amok who were catering to the worst instincts of the right. Then Sidney Blumenthal, in his deftly written *The Rise of the Counterestablishment*, scrutinized the network of organizations on the right, including the neoconservatives, that emerged in the 1970s and 1980s. In *The Rise of Neoconservatism* John Ehrman praised the neoconservatives as maintaining the faith of cold war liberalism. A few years later Jay Winik provided a thoroughly researched and upbeat assessment of neoconservatism in the 1980s in *On the Brink.* The gifted historian and Trotskyist Alan M. Wald more critically examined neoconservatism in his book *The New York Intellectuals.* Stefan Halper and Jonathan Clarke have decried the neoconservatives from the realist perspective in their scholarly *America Alone.* Other efforts include Gary Dorrien's *Imperial Designs,* Douglas Murray's *Neoconservatism: Why We Need It,* and Francis Fukuyama's *America at the Crossroads.*

No one, however, has ever really succeeded in precisely defining neoconservatism. Is it a Jewish cabal? Is it a bunch of misguided idealists? Or is it a gang of conniving zealots who believe that it's acceptable to lie to the people for their own good? Is there even such a thing as "neoconservatism"? The neoconservatives themselves have been quite divided on these questions; indeed, once the Iraq war went south, a number began to claim that no such thing as neoconservatism existed.

The closest attempt at a self-definition came from Irving Kristol, who, writing in his son William's *Weekly Standard,* called it a "persuasion," one aimed at bringing the GOP into modern times on domestic and foreign policy issues. In Kristol's words, "One can say that the historical task and political purpose of neoconservatism would seem to be this: to convert the Republican party, and American conservatism in general, against their respective wills, into a new kind of conservative politics suitable to governing a modern democracy."[2] But Kristol's remarks only triggered new disputes.

Why are there so many conflicting theories about neoconservatism? A simple taxonomy of the different schools of thought may help answer that question. Over the decades the neoconservative political journey, from youthful Trotskyists to confreres of the Bush administration and the Christian right, has inspired what literature professors these days like to call competing master narratives. These narratives, each of which embodies a different view of the neoconservatives as historical actors, might be called heroes, renegades, and traitors.

The "heroes" school is the most congenial to the neoconservatives because they created it. It goes something like this: As staunch liberals, they were mugged en masse by the realities of the 1960s. Having seen the descent into totalitarianism in Nazi Germany and the Soviet Union, they were horrified as student radicals on the New Left went down the same path. Unwilling to turn to the GOP, they initially hoped to save the Democratic Party, but the hard left turn the party took in the late 1960s and early 1970s, followed by Jimmy Carter's fecklessness in foreign affairs, forced them to embrace Ronald Reagan, who, to their pleasant surprise, turned out to be a reincarnation of Harry Truman. Since then, George W. Bush, in leading the war on terrorism, has proven to be even more aggressive than Reagan and a stalwart friend of Israel. The only place a neoconservative can feel comfortable today is in the GOP, not the Democratic Party, which has abandoned any pretense to the cold war liberal principles that it began shedding during the Vietnam War.

This school of thought has most recently been propounded by the British writer Douglas Murray in *Neoconservatism: Why We Need It.* "With confidence in its power, knowledge of a just cause, and the myth of inevitable decline banished, the American people can reaffirm their instinctive ambition and hope, and the conservative revolution can truly begin," concludes Murray.[3] The columnist Charles Krauthammer has been even more sweeping:

> This conservative alternative to realism is often lazily and invidiously called neoconservatism, but that is a very odd name for a school whose major proponents in the world today are George W. Bush and Tony Blair—if they are neocon-

servatives, then Margaret Thatcher was a liberal. There's nothing neo about Bush and there's nothing con about Blair. Yet they are the principal advocates of what might be called democratic globalism, a foreign policy that defines the national interest not as power but as values, and that identifies one supreme value, what John Kennedy called "the success of liberty." As President Bush put it in his speech at Whitehall last November: "The United States and Great Britain share a mission in the world beyond the balance of power or the simple pursuit of interest. We seek the advance of freedom and the peace that freedom brings." Beyond power. Beyond interest. Beyond interest defined as power. That is the credo of democratic globalism.[4]

The "renegades" narrative, which comes from the liberal camp, is somewhat less flattering. It views with nostalgia the ideological disputes of the 1930s, when great men tested their intellectual mettle at the City College of New York by occupying Alcove 1 in the smelly college cafeteria to argue against the communists in Alcove 2. The golden age of the New York intellectuals ends abruptly in the 1960s, when neoconservatism emerges and the intellectuals, so the story goes, sell out their principles. In this narrative the neoconservatives are (insincerely) mourned as renegades who have abandoned the true faith. As Steinfels somewhat melodramatically concluded in his account of neoconservatism in 1979:

> Antibodies which overreact can destroy the organism. The great danger posed by and to neoconservatism is that it will become nothing more than the legitimating and lubricating ideology of an oligarchic America where essential decisions are made by corporate elites, where great inequalities are rationalized by straitened circumstances and a sys-

tem of meritocratic hierarchy, and where democracy becomes an occasional, ritualistic gesture.[5]

The third, and most radical, narrative is the "traitors" school of thought. It comes from Republican conservatives who view the neoconservatives as threatening outsiders, ex-Trotskyists who have infiltrated the GOP to smuggle in dangerous heresies on both the domestic and the foreign policy fronts. Whether it's Brent Scowcroft or James Baker, they fear the crusading spirit, the wish to export democracy to troubled lands that would benefit from U.S. tutelage.

A subdivision of the realist branch comes in the form of paleoconservatism. The paleoconservative wing of the GOP has the purest pedigree in what has become a mongrelized conservative movement: it stands, by and large, for the original belief in small government and isolationism. The paleoconservatives loathe the neoconservatives. As the paleoconservative Stephen J. Tonsor declared at a 1986 meeting of the Philadelphia Society convened to discuss the neoconservative menace:

> It has always struck me as odd, even perverse, that former Marxists have been permitted, yes invited, to play such a leading role in the Conservative movement of the twentieth century. It is splendid when the town whore gets religion and joins the church. Now and then she makes a good choir director, but when she begins to tell the minister what he ought to say in his Sunday sermons, matters have been carried too far.

The paleoconservatives view neoconservatism as a kind of Jewish ideology on behalf of Israel. Russell Kirk, for example, declared at the Heritage Foundation on December 15, 1988, in a lecture titled "The Neoconservatives: An Endangered Species," "Not seldom has it seemed as if some eminent neoconservatives mistook Tel Aviv for the capital of the United States."

What none of these narratives captures is the fact that neoconservatism isn't about ideology. It isn't about the left. It is about a mindset, one that has been decisively shaped by the Jewish immigrant experience, by the Holocaust, and by the twentieth-century struggle against totalitarianism.

It has frequently been suggested, especially in recent debates about the Iraq war, that the foreign policy pushed by the neoconservatives is a reflection of "Jewish" concern with the survival of Israel. These suggestions have been vociferously denied by the neoconservatives and attacked by them in turn as prima facie evidence of anti-Semitism. Some criticisms are perfectly legitimate. Anatol Lieven, writing in the *London Review of Books*, asserted that the neoconservatives "and their allies in Israel would indeed like to see a long-term imperial war against any part of the Muslim world which defies the US and Israel."[6] Others are not. According to the *Chicago Defender*, the Nation of Islam's Louis Farrakhan ranted in 2006: "You can't be a Jew and not love the law of Moses and the prophets. I'm warning America. You'd better get rid of those neocons. They're making America weak."[7]

Nevertheless, one cannot avoid the fact that these accusations of Jewish "dual loyalty" point not to traitorous behavior but to something else—a conflation of America's and Israel's interests. After all, it is quite true that while not all neoconservatives are Jews, the majority of neoconservatives were, and are, Jewish; it is also true that they tend to propose foreign policy goals that support and favor Israel. The fact that they argue, and sincerely believe, that Israeli and American interests are closely aligned only makes them look more "ideological" in the eyes of their critics.

The neoconservatives have tried, in a form of political jujitsu, to brand any criticism of Israel (not to mention themselves) as anti-Israel. A good instance of this practice came in a February 2007 exchange between the scholar Mark Lilla and the *Commentary* editor Gabriel Schoenfeld, who upbraided Lilla for having the temerity to point to self-defeating actions by American Jewish organizations. The anti-Israel charge functions as a substitute for addressing legitimate questions and problems about the U.S.-Israel relationship. In this regard, neoconservatives have invested the Holocaust with a contemporary political significance that warrants caution. The scholar David Biale's observation about the Holocaust remains pertinent: "There is a difference between remembrance and constructing a collective identity around an event and an experience alien to the realities of American Jewish life."[8]

The neocons claim to be an intellectual movement with no ethnic component to speak of. But neoconservatism is as much a reflection of Jewish immigrant social resentments and status anxiety as a legitimate movement of ideas. Indeed, however much they may deny it, neoconservatism is in a decisive respect a Jewish phenomenon, reflecting a subset of Jewish concerns. One of the few members of the movement willing to address this has been the British neoconservative Melanie Phillips (herself the author of a controversial book which asserts that radical Muslims have overrun London and turned it into a base of worldwide operations). Phillips has observed that "neo-conservatism is a quintessentially Jewish project: a re-sanctification in everyday life of the core values of western civilisation, and the achievement of human potential through virtuous practice. The neo-cons' crucial insight is that public signals through law, custom and tradition are the key to getting people to behave well. And that is a Jewish insight."[9]

As the children of immigrants who came to the United States from Central and Eastern Europe, the original neoconservatives were steeped in the ideological feuds of the past and present. As Jews, they were exquisitely attuned to the social exclusion and WASP snobbery that their fathers experienced in the early part of the twentieth century—an attitude they carried with them through the debates of the cold war and into the halls of power after 9/11. The neoconservatives were also haunted by the failure of liberalism in the 1930s, when the Weimar Republic was destroyed by the twin forces of communism and Nazism and the Western democracies failed to stand up to totalitarian forces. As a result, its members see new Munichs everywhere and anywhere. (Douglas Feith told me in an interview that because of his family history he understands the true nature of foreign policy, unlike the "WASPs in the State Department.")

At the same time, the neocons are apoplectic about the allegiance of American Jews to liberalism. Irving Kristol made a useful distinction in 1979, trying to account for why so many American Jews, as he saw it, retained lingering socialist sympathies. His explanation was that they were drawn to the prophetic mode of Judaism rather than the rational one that emphasized adherence to the orthodox laws. Socialism became a secular prophecy, the new civic religion of American Jews, who embraced secular humanism. Kristol believed that this peculiar disposition was paving the way for the extinction of Judaism in America itself. But Kristol's conceit can also be turned on the very movement that he himself has headed for several decades. The neoconservatives themselves have veered between the prophetic and the rational schools. A good case could be made that they have now gone astray in indulging their own prophetic tendencies.

This book divides the remarkable odyssey of the neoconservatives into three parts that broadly recapitulate the ancient biblical narrative: exodus, the wilderness years, and redemption, followed by a return to exile. This narrative scheme has been adopted less in a spirit of irreverent impiety than as a way to capture the peculiar nature of the neoconservative saga, which is made up of recriminations, flip-flops, recklessness, and courage. While their story does not follow its ancient model point for point, and while it can be difficult to tell at any given time whether they are in exile or have reached the promised land, this approach may illuminate certain recesses of the neoconservative mentality. That mentality is ineluctably Jewish, immigrant, and conditioned by a highly selective and moralistic view of history as a drama of salvation and idolatry.

The neocons started out in a position of self-imposed Olympian exile within the left itself. At this point their prophet—their Moses, you might say—was Leon Trotsky. Trotsky, who remains a figure of admiration to some today, including the latest defector to the neoconservative cause, Christopher Hitchens, was the warrior-intellectual par excellence, a crusader, a fighter for freedom and truth against both the capitalists and the betrayer of the Bolshevik Revolution Joseph Stalin. His American votaries—Max Shachtman, Sidney Hook, James Burnham, Irving Kristol, and Irving Howe—aspired, at one time, to reshape the United States as a socialist utopia. No sooner did World War II end, however, than they abandoned radicalism to go from being anti-Stalinists to being anticommunists. But their political peregrinations were not over. Decades later many wound up in the GOP. Now they are back in exile, where they belong—and where they are, in some respects, most content.

The neoconservatives, one might say, have experienced a series of exiles without ever reaching the promised land. First they abandoned Judaism, trading it in for a cosmopolitan brand of Marxism, before fleeing it for liberalism. Then they turned against liberalism and embraced conservatism. Now they may be on the outs with the conservative movement. Why does this keep happening? Why does this history recur with what almost seems like a fatal—dare one say—Marxist inevitability?

The reason is that the neoconservatives are less intellectuals than prophets. They tend to be men (and women) of an uncompromising temperament who use (and treat) ideas as weapons in a moral struggle, which is why the political class in each party regards them with a mixture of appreciation and apprehension, even loathing.

That temperament is hardly confined to Jews, and it is often objected that not all neocons are Jewish. This is, of course, quite true.

Catholics, as the late Michael Joyce—a moving force behind the Olin and Bradley foundations and a friend of Irving Kristol's—pointed out to me, are attracted to neoconservatism. Part of it may be the emphasis on traditional values and even, in the case of the political philosopher Leo Strauss, premodern ones. Leading Catholic neoconservatives like Daniel Patrick Moynihan, Michael Novak, and William J. Bennett shared a critical view of liberalism, or at least liberal complacency, when it came to social issues and a number of foreign policy ones. Moynihan himself was emblematic of the neoconservative penchant for flipping between political parties, starting his career in the Kennedy administration and serving as Gerald Ford's ambassador to the United Nations.

Anyway, the New York Family, as it was known, was always capacious enough to contain various religious and political persuasions. No doubt the family thought of itself as Jewish, but it contained non-Jews such as Mary McCarthy. By the 1980s the neocons would welcome the evangelicals for their backing of Israel. This was an offshoot of the kind of WASP philo-Semitism that is the flip side of WASP anti-Semitism. The very fervor with which the neocons would champion this alliance may hint at some suppressed unease about it. Still, the delight the neoconservatives, Jewish or otherwise, felt in shocking and tormenting their erstwhile liberal brethren should never be underestimated.

Despite the fervent protestations of its founders and adherents, then, it is anything but an anti-Semitic canard to label neoconservatism a largely Jewish movement. I hope it's clear, however, that I am talking about a cultural proclivity specific to American Jews of a certain generation, not about something that is "essentially" Jewish in either a religious or a racial sense. The best way to understand the phenomenon may be to focus on neoconservatism as an uneasy, controversial, and tempestuous drama of Jewish immigrant assimilation—a very American story. At bottom, it is about an unresolved civil war between a belligerent, upstart ethnic group and a staid, cautious

American foreign policy establishment that lost its way after the Vietnam War. The neoconservatives always had an uneasy relationship with the WASPs who had launched the cold war but lost their will to wage it during Vietnam. Their initial impulse was to remonstrate with the patricians such as McGeorge Bundy for losing their will to confront communism; ultimately they sought to replace them with their own counter-establishment, much like their counterparts in the worlds of finance, law, and entertainment.

But if the neoconservatives have always targeted the left, they have also battled another adversary. The neoconservative ascendancy has been accompanied by a struggle within the ranks of the right (and to some extent within the neoconservative milieu itself) between the tendencies of realism and those of Wilsonian internationalism. These tendencies are represented in the neoconservative pantheon by two figures: Leo Strauss and Henry Kissinger—both refugees from Weimar Germany. From World War II, Strauss drew the lessons that totalitarianism must be confronted and that liberalism has a proclivity for appeasement; his ideal statesman was Churchill, a democratic philosopher-king who stood up for Western civilization in its darkest hour. Kissinger drew the different lesson that it is necessary to engage in cynical, cold-blooded realpolitik in order to manage the inevitable decline of the West. The war between these two men (or their disciples) has shaped much of neoconservatism—and American foreign policy itself. And the neoconservatives, in turn, have shaped a romantic narrative for themselves in which they are the new Churchills staring down the forces of evil.

—————

I myself was once attracted to neoconservatism. As a teenager and adult, I found that it supplied me with a beguiling but ultimately artificial clarity about the world that was hard to shake. And part of it, as with so many neoconservatives, is personal.

As a little boy fleeing Nazi Germany, my father, Gunther, sailed on a Jewish children's transport to America from Italy in May 1940. His father, Kurt, a doctor, felt that it was his obligation to remain in the city of Kassel to aid other Jews; after 1938, when it became all too clear that there was no future in Germany for Jews, he applied to emigrate. His application was refused. My father grew up in Chicago. My grandfather and my grandmother, Margaret, and many relatives were murdered by the Nazis.

After he saw a brochure from the University of Chicago with the title "Learn How to Think," my father skipped his senior year in high school. At Chicago he studied with Leo Strauss. As with so many students, he was initially captivated by Strauss, who seemed to personify dedication to learning, bringing only original texts in three or four different languages to his lectures and seminars.

There were other early influences on me. Magazines flooded into our house—*Encounter*, the *New Republic*, the *Reporter*, the *New Leader*, and, not least, *Commentary*. I compulsively read all the articles. *Commentary*'s sweeping verdicts seemed irrefutable, and its essays would end, more often than not, with some condemnation of the West's irresolution and flaccidity, not to mention its failure to heed the lessons of Munich. In the tenth grade I was debating Richard Pipes's controversial article "Why the Soviet Union Thinks It Could Fight and Win a Nuclear War." It was exciting to participate, in however attenuated a form, in the battle of ideas. My heroes were George Orwell, Melvin Lasky, Irving Kristol, and Norman Podhoretz. I still own and cherish a used, battered paperback copy of Arthur Koestler's *The God That Failed* that I bought in high school for $1.25. I remember the eagerness and shock with which I read a series of probing interviews by the BBC's Michael Charlton that were featured in *Encounter* the summer before I went to college. The interviews were with the remaining participants at the Yalta Conference and various Eastern European dissidents and former communists. They were revelatory about the almost willful naïveté of American perceptions of Stalin during World War II. How could Roosevelt and company have been so deluded? Why didn't anyone care that General George Patton had been only forty-five miles outside of Prague but wasn't told to liberate it? Why was General Dwight D. Eisenhower so indifferent to beating the Soviets to Berlin?

A different kind of surprise came when I attended Oberlin College. I can't claim that any gods failed me. What I discovered at Oberlin was something else: a hamlet steeped in the acrimonious politics of the 1960s with a dose of political correctness and identity politics coming on strong. It wasn't unusual for students and professors not just to defend but to praise the Bolshevik Revolution as a valiant workers' uprising. In retrospect, I should probably have taken this less seriously than I did. I didn't quite realize it at the time, but it was a rarefied experience, like wandering into an untouched village that had never experienced civilization. Back then, however, I was enraged by the historical falsehoods, the indifference to the suffering of those swept into the Gulag. Why was the Soviet Union any less reprehensible than Nazi Germany, Stalin less evil than Hitler? Forget moral equivalence; I wasn't being told that the United States was just as bad as the U.S.S.R.; I was being told that it was worse. No one could ever give me a straight answer about how he or she arrived at these conclusions; instead, I was surfeited with absurd apologetics about the Soviet Union representing a better hope for the future that recapitulated the nonsense that the fellow travelers spouted in the 1930s.

Determined almost single-handedly to expose these illusions—the campus conservatives, at least those willing to out themselves, numbered in the single digits—I headed the college Republican club, even though I was a card-carrying Democrat: a quintessential baby neocon. The college's president, S. Frederick Starr, a gifted scholar of Russian history, encouraged our efforts to stir up debate, at least as much as he could given the general environment. Of course, we also engaged in our own kind of radical chic, which involved wearing suits, trench coats, collar bars, and cuff links for those momentous occasions when an outside speaker would show up or when we just felt like creating a stir on campus.

Still, I couldn't quite bring myself to vote for Ronald Reagan. I dutifully pulled the lever for Walter Mondale in 1984. At Oberlin, I invited numerous neoconservatives to speak, including Carl Gershman, the head of the National Endowment for Democracy, and the Russian scholar Richard Pipes. Clarence Thomas, then the head of the Equal Employment Opportunity Commission, also showed up and engaged in a lengthy dispute with the outraged students over affirmative action. "Get a job!" he shouted when asked how the black underclass was supposed to pull itself up.

On the side I oversaw the construction of a replica of the Berlin Wall to counter the erection of a "shanty town" that student protesters had built in front of the president's office to protest apartheid and demand divestment from South Africa. When I mentioned this to Midge Decter, a neoconservative writer married to Norman Podhoretz, whom I had also invited to Oberlin, she laughed happily and said that it was the appropriate response. Then there was my correspondence with Sidney Hook, who sent me a letter denouncing the left's apathy about World War II.

Probably my biggest event was "Ronald Reagan Appreciation Day," which was supposed, among other things, to feature a twenty-one-gun salute in front of Finney Chapel by the Veterans of Foreign Wars. Protesting students made it impossible to hold the salute; the American Civil Liberties Union denounced this as a suppression of free speech. The event made the campus paper with the title "Students Stop Gun Salute, Disrupt Reagan Day Rally"; in looking at it the other day, I was amused to see that it read, "The crowd attacked Heilbrunn on issues such as Libya, abortion, the arms build-up, and aid to the contras in Nicaragua. Most of the comments were along the lines of 'White male power,' 'Ronbo,' and 'Murderer'; however some members of the crowd did get excited enough to throw melon rinds at one of the College Republicans." The day's activities also were mentioned in Cleveland's *Plain Dealer* and on National Public Radio. I believe that Lorain County was debating a mental health bill at that time; a local deejay observed that they should quit focusing on it and take a closer look at Oberlin College.

My entrée into the neoconservative world came in 1985 when I attended a symposium in New York at the Lotos Club headed by the right-wing astrophysicist and scientific popularizer Robert Jastrow, who was plumping for Ronald Reagan's Star Wars initiative and had formed a think tank called the George C. Marshall Institute, which now apparently devotes its efforts to debunking global warming. I see now that the letter from the Marshall Institute inviting me portentously declared, "In the morning period, Dr. Jastrow will present a report on the scientific progress of strategic defense and other new developments in this area. The agenda for the afternoon will include Soviet and American ASAT tests and the Nuclear Winter. The meetings will conclude with an open discussion of methods for communicating important facts in these areas to the campus population." For an undergraduate, this was heady stuff—the Reagan revolution was advancing. America was being defended from the Soviet threat. The second time I saw Jastrow, he was ranting about the "threat to the Republic." An editor at the *Harvard Salient*, then a fledgling conservative student newspaper, voiced some of our doubts about such apocalyptic language. Were the lunatics taking over the asylum?

One thing attending that seminar helped me understand firsthand was the web of connections that constitute the neoconservative world. The intercession of a friend I met at that conference helped me land my first job at the *National Interest*, where I worked for its publisher, Irving Kristol, and its editor, Owen Harries.

When Harries interviewed me, his first question was whether or not the United States could follow a realist foreign policy. I gulped and repeated something about Norman Podhoretz saying that it was necessary to bang the patriotic drum to get Americans mobilized on any foreign policy issue. Fortunately, my answer seemed to pass muster. Harries himself was a staunch realist and cold warrior who would end up a fierce critic of U.S. foreign policy under George W. Bush. Ironically, when I was at the *National Interest*, he published Francis Fukuyama's famous article, "The End of History?" which served as a trumpet blast for the triumphalist brand of cold war history that landed the neocons in Iraq. By then, Fukuyama, too, had jumped ship, claiming (in an ironic inversion of the standard neoconservative line) that he hadn't changed but that neoconservatism had morphed into something unrecognizable and horrifying.

But in the 1980s the neoconservatives were already quite sure of themselves, cozying up to Reagan and the Christian right, which they were intent upon giving a veneer of scholarly respectability. Along with Michael Lind, who staged a dramatic break, as these things go, with neoconservatism over its embrace of the Christian right, anti-Darwinism, and culture war rhetoric, I wrote a piece for the *New York Review of Books* examining the anti-Semitic sources that the evangelist Pat Robertson had used for his book *The New World Order.* Norman Podhoretz, writing in *Commentary*, acknowledged that my ferreting out of these sources spoke volumes, but then went through contortions to try to exonerate Robertson from the charge of anti-Semitism.

Lind himself had worked as executive editor at the *National Interest*—a sign of Harries's intellectual tolerance. In retrospect, Lind was the first insider in the 1990s to point to the debility of the neoconservative movement, namely, that it had become a partisan cause dedicated to advancing the Republican Party's electoral fortunes rather than an independent collection of thinkers. Irving Kristol said in 1979, "When two neoconservatives meet they are more likely to argue with one another than to confer or conspire." That was no longer the case in the 1990s.

Meanwhile, the *New Republic* beckoned. Thanks to the generosity of its literary editor, Leon Wieseltier, I wrote a series of reviews on American foreign policy leaders and on the cold war. At the *New*

Republic I took some swipes at the neoconservatives, but the magazine, by and large, subscribed to the neoconservative foreign policy worldview—taking an inflexible stance on Israel, pushing for missile defense, and so on—minus the overtures to the Christian right and the conservative domestic agenda.

The distinction is important. The Christian right, with its pretensions to support Israel, was never part of the foreign policy armamentarium of the liberal hawks. (There was, and remains, a kind of aesthetic revulsion to the Republican Party among liberal hawks.) But much of the rest of the neocon foreign policy agenda was popular, whether it was democracy promotion or an aggressive military buildup. It was no surprise to me later to see that the magazine lustily championed the Iraq war. It had, in any case, hired the talented writer Lawrence F. Kaplan to elucidate the Bush view of the world, which, when it came to foreign policy, was also that of my former patrons. Now Kaplan is something of a disillusioned neoconservative, lamenting the collapse of what he sees as the ideals of the movement. In truth, neoconservatism has become a rather lonely credo. The longer the Iraq war goes on, the faster even neoconservatives seem to be rushing to disembarrass themselves of the label, whether it's Richard Perle or Kenneth Adelman. Like the Marxism they once denounced, they now declare that the neoconservative vision was a beautiful dream but bungled in execution.

Most recent accounts have focused on how the neoconservatives flubbed up once they entered the Bush administration. This book takes a different approach. It is an attempt to look at the mental world the neoconservatives have inhabited for decades. Many observers remain perplexed that the Iraq war ever occurred. But this is looking at it backward. The neoconservatives had been agitating for something on these lines for decades. Indeed, it would have been more surprising if the war had not occurred. In like manner, the foes of neoconservatism continue to underestimate the movement's influence. They act as though neoconservatism were something new, but it isn't. Neoconservatism has always existed in some form, and in every society. The Athenian general and student of Socrates, Alcibiades, who pushed for the ill-fated invasion of Sicily, was probably the first neocon. Like today's neocons, he was, so Plutarch says, eloquent and spurned the philosophical path of true wisdom to engage in political scheming and imperial dreams. Tsar Nicholas II had his set of neocon advisers who decried reforms that might have saved his rule. And the nationalist claque in pre–World War I Germany baying for war eerily resembles today's American neoconservatives; switch the impetuous Kaiser Wilhelm, who tried to outdo his cautious father, for George W. Bush, and you have what seems like a perfect match.

Today the neoconservatives are responsible for three wars: the crusade in Iraq, the struggle against liberalism at home, and the battle against the realists in the GOP. As the Bush administration hews to the neoconservative battle plan for Iraq, and potentially Iran, the 2008 election will be fought on the terrain mapped out by the neoconservatives. My friend Melvin Lasky, the irrepressible editor of *Encounter* magazine who attended the City College of New York in the 1930s, mused to me in a phone conversation shortly before his death that there was a search for "a dogma, a line" in America, a quest for "a coherent intellectuality." He was right. The neoconservatives exemplify that quest for coherence. But their self-confidence derives as much from their inherent need to be in opposition, like prophets in the wilderness, as it does from their belief in the rightness of their own ideas.

As Norman Podhoretz recently put it, in the course of a rousing defense of George W. Bush and the war in Iraq, "I have learned from experience that the more a given idea gets to be accepted as a self-evident truth by my fellow intellectuals, the more likely it is to be wrong."[10] To understand how the neoconservatives have become conditioned to thinking in this manner, we must begin by examining their past.

Exodus

And you, stand here by Me and I shall speak to you all the commands and the statutes and the laws that you will teach them, and they will do them in the land that I am about to give them to take hold of it.

—Deuteronomy 5:28

It's the same with all you comfortable, insular, Anglo-Saxon anti-Communists. You hate our Cassandra cries and resent us as allies—but, when all is said, we ex-Communists are the only people on your side who know what it's all about.

—Arthur Koestler, The God That Failed

I call them utopians ... I don't care whether utopians are Vladimir Lenin in a sealed train going to Moscow or Paul Wolfowitz. Utopians, I don't like. You're never going to bring utopia, and you're going to hurt a lot of people in the process of trying to do it.

—Lawrence B. Wilkerson, chief of staff to former secretary of state Colin Powell in GQ

In the spring of 2003, shortly after the liberation of Iraq, Irving Kristol and Gertrude Himmelfarb attended a party in Washington, D.C., for Melvin Lasky. They hadn't seen one another since a conference in Berlin in 1992 celebrating the end of the cold war. Now they were enjoying a sentimental reunion at which these eighty-year-olds reminisced about their years at the City College of New York in the 1930s. As Lasky held forth, Kristol waspishly intervened to tell the room that "none of you know what the first magazine" was that he had published an article in—an obscure Trotskyist publication called the *Chronicle*. After Kristol observed that the then-eighteen-year-old Lasky "rewrote every sentence in the piece," Lasky responded, "That was the last recorded moment your prose needed help."

It was a telling moment. For all the joviality, their reminiscences weren't about going out for sports or their old professors. Instead, they were about the intensely political sectarianism of the left. Decades later, the passions that had first impelled them into politics had hardly dimmed; as Lasky later recounted to me, "The memories are very sharp, it's not like an old man who says, 'Who? What college were you in?' "

Their saga began in Russia. At the turn of the twentieth century, Jews, overrepresented in left-wing and revolutionary movements, intent on creating a utopia, went on the attack against capitalism and imperialism. As one Yiddish newspaper put it, "With hatred, with a three-fold curse, we must weave the shroud for the Russian autocratic government, for the entire anti-Semitic criminal gang, for the entire capitalist world."[1]

So pronounced was this phenomenon that in a 1927 study titled "The Jew as Radical," the Russian historian (and apologist for Stalin) Maurice Hindus maintained that Jews had an innate propensity to radicalism dating back to their biblical origins. Indeed, the Menshevik exile Simeon Strunsky, who would end up on the editorial board of the *New York Times*, sardonically recalled the intensity of Marxist debates that had been transported from Europe to the United States: "I remember quite well those pioneer Yiddish labor papers of the '90s with their learned editorialettes of six or seven columns and five thousand words about what Werner Sombart thought of what Boehm-Bauwerk said about how Karl Marx slipped up in a footnote on page 879."[2]

Of the avatars of world revolution, no one beckoned more alluringly to a new generation of young Jewish radicals than the Russian exile Leon Trotsky. As Jews, they were deeply influenced by their parents' flight from czarist oppression and the rise of fascism in the 1930s, but they also sought to transcend the religiosity of their elders. Some joined the American Communist Party, at least until the 1939 Molotov-Ribbentrop pact dividing up Poland and the Baltic States between the Soviet Union and Nazi Germany. A much smaller segment became Trotskyists, attacking both Stalinism as a perverted form of communism and New Deal liberalism. The Trotskyist intellectuals saw themselves as martyrs, a kind of aristocratic intelligentsia.

According to their own prolific writings, they started out purely as an intellectual response to events such as the Spanish civil war, the Moscow show trials, the Hitler-Stalin pact, and the New Deal. Frequently scanted, or even missing altogether from this tale of brilliant and ambitious young intellectuals, is their Jewishness, which enters into the story as an over-the-shoulder glance at the vanishing "world of their fathers." In their seemingly inexhaustible stream of memoirs and autobiographical essays, the Jewish intellectuals who became the core of the neoconservative movement present themselves as fully secularized, their ideas and attitudes bearing little, if any, relation to the Jewish past or, in some cases, even to the immigrant milieu of their youth. Their Trotskyist past appears as a minor episode, paling in comparison to the supposed real emergence of neoconservatism in the late 1960s. One exegete of neoconservatism says that "despite its current popularity, the 'Trotskyist neocon' assertion contributes nothing to our understanding of the origins, or nature, of neoconservatism."[3] Another, Joshua Muravchik, maintains that hardly any neoconservatives have been interested in Trotskyism, let alone sincere believers.

But as the sons of Jewish immigrants, they undoubtedly had a special perspective, one torn between tradition and assimilation, buffeted by radical winds, in love with ideas, consumed with ambition to participate in the great doings of the world outside the immigrant ghetto. Contrary to some of their critics, the neoconservatives hardly remain political Trotskyists in any meaningful sense. Their fling with Trotskyism did, however, endow them with a temperament as well as a set of intellectual tools that many never completely abandoned—a combative temper and a penchant for sweeping assertions and grandiose ideas.

Some of that grandiosity was rooted in the generational tensions between Jewish immigrant fathers and their Americanizing sons, which often took the form of disagreements about religion and politics. Put otherwise: the religiosity of the fathers was sublimated by the sons in radical politics. Trotsky, as a literary critic, a historian, a politician, and a warrior, captured their youthful imaginations. But on a deeper, unconscious level, they appear to have identified with Trotsky as a way of breaking with the paternal religion while maintaining the radical faith of their parents. They saw Trotsky as a kind of secular Jewish prophet who had been betrayed by the murderous "bureaucrat" Stalin.

The young radicals could hardly have grown up in a more intensely Jewish world. Yiddish theater, journalism, and literature flourished on the Lower East Side of Manhattan. The social reformer Jacob Riis dubbed it "Jewtown," while Henry James referred to it more delicately as "The New Jerusalem." Whatever Lower East Side Jewish life was called, the children, desperate to Americanize, sought first to escape it, then to memorialize it. According to Irving Howe, the Jewish socialist intellectual who did more than anyone to re-create it in *World of Our Fathers*, "Often enough it was the purity of their vision—the moral firmness induced by religion or set free by radicalism—that provided the energies for realizing their personal ambitions."[4] The literary critic Alfred Kazin recalled in his own memoir that he was expected to shine by his immigrant parents: "I was the first American child, their offering to the strange new God; I was to be the monument of their liberation from the shame of being— what they were."[5]

Though the parents hoped for careers in medicine, law, and business for their sons, or as musical and intellectual prodigies, Marxist radicalism was the most common route of escape. As teenagers, they would stand on soapboxes in New York—known as the most interesting city in the Soviet Union—and demand a more just society. They didn't have to be told about the grinding, carking poverty created by capitalism; they saw people living in hovels all around them and foraged themselves for fruits and vegetables on the Lower East Side docks. As a sixteen-year-old freshman at City College, for example, Sidney Hook helped create the Social Problems Club, an organization made up of socialists, syndicalists, and communists that saw itself as part of the world revolution emanating from Moscow. In a number of stories and novels Saul Bellow, who grew up in a working-class milieu in Chicago and traveled to Mexico in August 1940 to meet Trotsky, captured the febrile intellectualism of the young immigrant Jews lecturing their elders on the fine points of Hegel and Marx while still in their knickers.

In America the Jews would no longer be downtrodden and contemned. But for a number of radical children, this was not enough. They didn't want in. They wanted out. They saw themselves as the avatars of a secular movement that would overturn the old order in America as well. After all, no matter how hard they worked, there were still quotas at the Ivy League universities. Then there were the fancy clubs, the legal and financial firms that saw Jews as interlopers who would soil their proud escutcheons and were to be kept at bay. Smarting with unsuppressed social resentment, the young Jews viewed themselves as liberators, proclaiming a new faith. They embraced a cosmopolitan creed that supposedly left behind the stifling religious customs of their elders as well as the warring nationalisms that perpetually dragged Europe into strife and combat.

Even as they nursed these illusions, however, the radical generation of intellectuals serenely ignored the mounting threat to their brethren in Central Europe and Russia. On the whole, the Jewish intellectuals have given themselves a pass on this question. They rarely talk about it. Indeed, it is telling that amid all the panegyrics to the moral seriousness of these intellectuals, one of the few critical notes was sounded only decades later by the neoconservative literary scholar Ruth Wisse in *Commentary.* As she shrewdly noted, "So great was the distance these Jews felt between themselves and their community that they voiced no sense of special responsibility toward the fate of their fellow Jews in Hitler's Europe."[6] Even during World War II, these Jewish radicals saw the struggle against German and Japanese fascism as a sideshow, an imperialist plot, while ignoring the destruction of European Jewry. They were too busy searching for a prophet, a political Moses to lead them out of the wilderness, to focus on the actual threat to world civilization.

The Prophet Unarmed: Max Shachtman

No one exemplified these impulses better than a Jewish immigrant from Poland—and founding father of neoconservatism—named Max Shachtman. Shachtman wasn't physically commanding. He was short and had a high-pitched voice and a pencil mustache. But he more than made up for it with his exuberance, zaniness, irony, and zest for polemics: put him up on a rostrum or podium and he could speak for hours about the fate of the world and socialism—in Yiddish, English, German, and French. He was a fiery presence—a Trotskyist who went from denouncing U.S. participation in World War II to embracing the Vietnam War and George Meany's AFL-CIO.

Shachtman inculcated a hatred of liberalism in his protégés: he taught them how to organize an obscure political movement, he hammered away at the idea of Trotsky's belief in a Fourth International global democratic revolution, and he set forth the lineaments of what would become the idea of an exploitative, postbourgeois "new class." He remains an object of fascination: it was no accident that Christopher Hitchens, himself now far along the road from youthful Trotskyism to neoconservatism, recently declared in the pages of the *Atlantic* that a biography of him would constitute an "intellectual Rosetta Stone" for the cold war. His protégés included everyone from Carl Gershman, the current head of the National Endowment for Democracy, to the neoconservatives Irving Kristol and Joshua Muravchik, the longtime head of the American Federation of Teachers Albert Shanker, Irving Howe, and the African-American leader Bayard Rustin.

Shachtman, who was born in Warsaw on September 10, 1904, grew up in a working-class Eastern European Jewish neighborhood in East Harlem that was filled with synagogues, coffee shops, and religious schools. His father transmitted his hatred of the Russian, German, and Austro-Hungarian empires to him. Though his parents hoped he would enter a middle-class profession, Shachtman dropped out of City College to become a radical organizer in 1921. His mentor was a humorless, hard-nosed American Bolshevik named James P. Cannon. Born in Rosedale, Kansas, in 1890, Cannon was a founding member of the American Communist Party, serving as party secretary from 1919 to 1928, when he, along with Shachtman, was expelled for supporting the Trotskyist heresy. Unlike Shachtman, however, Cannon didn't engage in abstruse theoretical debates; instead, he simply repeated what the grand old man Trotsky dictated from exile.

At the time of his expulsion Shachtman was twenty-four years old. Together with Cannon and Martin Abern, the young firebrand founded the rival Communist League of America, which was quickly dubbed "Three Generals Without an Army." Shachtman became editor of the party newspaper, the *Militant*, and focused on winning the support of young radicals. Under Shachtman's influence, young educated Jews would transfer their innate hostility toward the WASP establishment to the cause of the working class. The labor movement was supposed to serve as a kind of petri dish where radicals of all stripes could mingle. It was a place where ideas and politics intersected, allowing intellectuals to forge schemes to bring the working class to power. To many of his followers, Shachtman seemed to exemplify the union of theorist and politician.

In 1930 Shachtman visited Trotsky, then in exile on the Turkish island Büyükada. He quickly became an international figure in the Trotskyist movement, corresponding with comrades around the globe. But his main work was at home. Shachtman saw radicalism as synonymous with youth. He started the Young Workers League and denounced Citizens' Military Training Camps as well as the Boy Scouts and Girl Scouts. They were tools for molding young people into the slaves of big industry. "In America," he said, "the minds of the youth are filled with a greater proportion of capitalist poison per square brain cell than in any other country."[7]

In a not untypical schism within the communist ranks, Shachtman and Cannon were expelled from the Socialist Party in August 1937. This time, however, they took along many members, including the party's youth division, the Young People's Socialist League. The YPSL served as a training ground for several generations of neoconservatives, ranging from Irving Kristol in the 1930s to Jeane Kirkpatrick in the 1940s to Joshua Muravchik in the 1960s. This glittering prize would allow the Trotskyists to swell their future ranks, capturing the best and brightest among the New York Jewish intellectuals. The result was that in January 1938 they founded the Socialist Workers Party.

Prominent among Shachtman's youthful followers was Irving Howe, who went on to become a famous critic and editor, not to mention a mentor in his own right to several generations of Jewish writers and socialists. Like Trotsky, Howe was a tremendous rhetorician who took an almost sadistic pleasure in eviscerating his opponents in debates. But Howe did his most lasting work as a literary critic. He would eventually reconcile himself to his Jewish heritage, partly by editing several volumes of Yiddish poems, short stories, and essays. He would contrast the communal world of the shtetl with the avaricious capitalism that he believed prevailed in the United States. But Howe recoiled at the New Left and its consequences: in the early 1990s he berated his younger English department colleagues at the City University of New York as "gutless" for failing to condemn multiculturalist fads that pooh-poohed high culture and the literary canon as being made up of "dead white males."

Howe, born Irving Horenstein in 1920, was what Daniel Bell, not entirely flatteringly, calls the "commissar" of the Shachtman group. The failure of his father's grocery store at the onset of the Great Depression forced the family to leave the middle-class West Bronx for the working-class East Bronx. Howe never forgot the searing experience of being shoved to the bottom of the heap. He joined the YPSL and, like many of his contemporaries, saw in it, as his biographer Gerald Sorin writes, "a secular version of the Judaic prophetic tradition."[8] Again and again, the young Jewish radicals would seek to paper over the generational conflict inherent in their abandonment of Judaism by worshipping the idea of a secular, socialist utopia. The fact that the first attempt had been sullied by Stalin and his camarilla only made their efforts seem more precious and pristine by comparison.

In 1938 Howe inducted Kristol into Trotskyism, an act he would subsequently regret. The only one who resisted (as he has continued to resist orthodoxies on the left and right throughout his long, distinguished career) was Daniel Bell. Bell, who was born in 1919 and joined the Young People's Socialist League in 1932 at the precocious age of thirteen, had always opposed the communists. (Today he calls himself a liberal in politics, a socialist in economics, and a conservative in culture—an example of dialectical thinking in the service of rationality.) A cousin of Bell's had handed him a book called *The Bolshevik Myth* that laid bare Trotsky's role in ordering the shooting of sailors at Kronstadt who had demanded food supplies and free elections in 1921. It was a shattering experience for Bell, one that prompted him to speak up in passionate indignation at debates with members of the Young Communist League. "What happened at Kronstadt?" he would shout in fury.[9]

Others were more susceptible to the lure of a hermetic sect. A sociology student and Trotskyist renegade named Philip Selznick, who took the party name "Sherman," organized his own little Trotskyist corpuscle, which was known as the Shermanites, that ended up quarreling with Shachtman. There were dozens of such groups. But according to Bell, "The Sherman group was coherent." It included Kristol, his future wife, Gertrude Himmelfarb, and Melvin Lasky. They also published an earnest little magazine called *Enquiry*—the first of many such. They even adopted underground code names— Kristol wrote under the nom de guerre "William Ferry."

No one has done more than Howe to evoke and, at times, to romanticize this era. A lifelong socialist, he felt nostalgia and wistfulness for a past that he knew (and showed) was suffused with illusions and false hopes. Howe deftly evoked the sense of superiority that he and his chums felt to the common ruck of humanity. They were an exalted elite whose radicalism gave them a purchase on events that others could only dream of. They became Trotskyists because of the fervor for absolute answers, for revolutionary purity, for the tragic aura of a fallen leader who had been betrayed by an inferior. They learned to read with Talmudic care, to master Marxist doctrine, to reproduce axioms—a very similar approach, as we shall see, to the followers of Leo Strauss. As with Strauss, some profited from but others were crippled by this intellectual atmosphere. To be a Trotskyist was to be a member not of an inclusive party but of an exclusive sect. Howe would eventually break with Trotskyism, but his steadfast insistence on intellectual independence and on retaining socialist ideals, in theory if not practice, and his lively interest in literature and history independent of contemporary politics made him a justly admired figure—and alternately befuddled and enraged the neoconservatives.

The intellectual arena in which Howe and his compatriots conducted their duels with the Stalinists was the City College of New York. City College was seen as the poor man's Harvard. Situated on the Lower East Side, where the children of poor Jewish immigrants lived, it was supposed to open the portals of American society to the young Jews whose parents slaved away in the sweatshops of the garment industry. The offspring of these immigrant Jews burned with ambition, fueled in part by a double humiliation—first at the hands of the WASP establishment (not to mention other immigrant groups), and again at the hands of the upper-class German Jews who lived uptown and looked down their noses at the teeming hordes from Eastern Europe that had invaded New York. For some, City College genuinely served as the gateway into America; for many others, the snubs they received from their various class and ethnic enemies—including their fellow Jews—rankled for the rest of their lives.

The intensity of Jewish feeling about this secular shrine can hardly be exaggerated. According to Abraham Cahan, the founder of the Jewish *Forward*, education was a surrogate religion for Jewish immigrants: "It was a symbol of spiritual promotion . . . University-bred people were the real nobility of the world." City College was "the synagogue of my new life . . . the building really appealed to me as a temple, as a House of Sanctity, as we call the ancient Temple of Jerusalem."[10] The student body was made up almost exclusively of Jews.

William Barrett, a writer for *Partisan Review* (and one of those gentiles who seems to have been attracted to Jewish intellectual intensity), described his bemusement at the ructions at City College in his memoirs: "It was something of a shock for me at first to be thrown into an almost completely Jewish environment . . . Now I was suddenly thrown, like Daniel in the den of the lions, into a swarm of intense, squabbling, and noisy young Jews."[11] When Paul Weiss, who became a noted Yale philosophy professor, was the first City College graduate to be accepted by Harvard (where he studied with Alfred North Whitehead), he disconcerted everyone in his first class by raising his hand when the professor asked, "Are there any questions?" It was considered "ungentlemanly" to do so.[12]

Nowhere was the tone less "gentlemanly" than in the slugfests that took place at the City College cafeteria between the Trotskyists in the horseshoe-shaped Alcove 1 and the Stalinists in Alcove 2. Alcove 1 had about thirty members; the Stalinists were able to muster about five hundred students for rallies. Daniel Bell, a lifelong social democrat, remained immune to these sectarian quarrels. Bell was accorded special status; although he resisted the appeal of Trotskyism, his knowledge of Marxist texts made him a kind of honorary member. According to Kristol, ever the ironist, "It was between these two alcoves that the war of the worlds was fought, over the faceless bodies of the mass of students, whom we tried desperately to manipulate into 'the right position.' "

For Shachtman, City College was prime recruiting territory. Howe would reminisce that in 1937 he was thunderstruck the first time he heard Shachtman debate a wooden Stalinist English instructor named Morris Schappes, who was defending the Moscow show trials. Shachtman seemed to possess an encyclopedic knowledge of the Bolshevik Revolution, tearing through names, dates, and places. After Schappes clumsily referred to the defendants as a bunch of Benedict Arnolds, Shachtman declared that the more apt analogy was with Benedict Arnold managing to hijack the American Revolution and murder George Washington, Thomas Jefferson, and Benjamin Franklin. "Max's boys," as his acolytes were known, were mesmerized by his performance. This wasn't simply debate; it was guerrilla theater.

Shachtman's influence reached its high-water mark after he split with Cannon himself over the Soviet invasion of Finland on November 30, 1939. Trotsky had implausibly defended the invasion by defining the Soviet Union as a "degenerated workers' state." It was essential to defend the Soviet Union, no matter what actions it might take. The cause of socialism transcended the mistakes of its leaders. Cannon agreed. Shachtman did not. He established his own Workers' Party in 1940 and developed a theory of Stalinism as the ideology of a parasitic bureaucratic class that had corrupted true socialism. This theory would later be transmuted by Irving Kristol into the idea of a "new class" of intellectuals that emerged in the 1960s and that contributed nothing productive to society. Indeed, Kristol's argument would form the basis for neoconservative theory.

There is something more than a little touching about the fervor with which these young radicals debated the Spanish civil war, the Nazi-Soviet pact, and the implications of the New Deal. Philip Selznick, who went on to become a professor of law at Berkeley, reminisced decades later, in an American Enterprise Institute volume dedicated to Irving Kristol, that "we could retain, even to this day, a certain nostalgia for the Trotskyist days—days of high political passion and, especially, of extraordinary intellectual stimulation. In retrospect, we would say that we had great fun; luckily, we were too insignificant to do much harm; and we learned much that stayed with us long after we in our turn had said 'goodbye to all that.' "[13]

———

While Shachtman provided the political, theoretical, and organizational underpinnings that the young radicals would draw upon in coming decades, their ambition was also nourished by the embrace of Trotskyism on the part of such literary and cultural lions as Lionel Trilling, Philip Rahv, and William Phillips. Indeed, it's important to remember that Kristol, Himmelfarb, Martin Diamond, Seymour Martin Lipset, Howe, and others were never simply political operatives; they were deeply interested in sociology, philosophy, history, and literature. They saw themselves as dissidents on the ramparts, defying the easy and cheap orthodoxies of both the Stalinists and the liberals. This intensely personal struggle ended up reverberating in the outside world, which is why it continues to be viewed with such nostalgia. The notion that they count, that they aren't simply shouting into the wilderness, that their independence has never been compromised but serves as a goad and inspiration to others remains deeply attractive to sedentary intellectuals who are, more often than not, habituated to obscurity rather than renown.

One important source of intellectual stimulation came from the magazine *Partisan Review*. Originally a Marxist publication that was produced by the John Reed Club and competed with the *New Masses*, *PR* broke with the party in 1937. In what its editors saw as a bold act of emancipation from Stalinist dogma, they reached out to Trotsky and at the same time embraced the new "modernist" spirit in literature and art.

Many tributes have been written to *Partisan Review*. In some respects it was the quintessential little magazine. More than just a political organ, it was also a means of advancing a "Jewish" critique of American culture, whether or not the editors wanted to acknowledge it explicitly, which they usually didn't. *PR*'s editors and writers reveled in upending the WASP hierarchy of cultural values, bringing what might somewhat anachronistically be called their street sensibility into the grotto of the Graces. William Phillips recalled, "We were cocky kids, driven by a grandiose idea of launching a new literary movement, combining older with younger talents, and the best of the new radicalism with the innovative energy of modernism."[14] They published appreciations of movies and pulp fiction alongside interviews with André Malraux and letters from London by George Orwell. The poet Randall Jarrell complained that the editors saw the United States as "a backward Europe" and that *Partisan Review* was "barely an American magazine, and always sinks with a sigh of joy into the friendly harbor of Sartre, Camus, Silone, the great European writers."

An article in the magazine served as an entrée into the glittering and ferocious world of the New York intellectuals. The editors, whose names—Philip Rahv, Dwight Macdonald, and William Phillips—have become a kind of intellectual honor roll, often seemed to spend more time fighting with each other than their Stalinist opponents. The veneration they have been posthumously accorded sometimes sits uneasily with the outlandish political stances they adopted, but the magazine published and boosted the careers of everyone from Lionel Trilling to Sidney Hook, from Saul Bellow to Delmore Schwartz, and from Hannah Arendt to Susan Sontag. Gertrude Himmelfarb later recalled in the *Weekly Standard:*

> I was . . . a faithful reader of Partisan Review, which was,
> in effect, the intellectual and cultural organ of Trotskyites
> (or crypto-Trotskyites, or ex-Trotskyites, or more broadly, the
> anti-Stalinist Left). Many years later I remembered little
> about [Lionel] Trilling's essay except its memorable title,

"Elements That Are Wanted," and the enormous excitement it generated in me and my friends.[15]

But the skepticism of the neoconservatives about liberalism, as well as their literary ambitions, was perhaps fired even more by a gnomic, jovial, and obsessive little man named Elliot Ettelson Cohen, the legendary editor who influenced both Lionel Trilling and *his* protégé Norman Podhoretz. Cohen probably has not received as much attention as he deserves, but he is one of those curious figures who had an outsize impact via the magazines he ran and the disciples he cultivated. Cohen was a *Schwätzer*, a compulsive talker who could discourse on everything from great books to manners, from comedians to the social sciences. He anticipated the kinds of novels Philip Roth would write, with their emphasis on the Jewish demotic—sexual, tormented, witty, gossipy.

Unlike many of the other Jewish radicals, however, he did not grow up in New York. Cohen was born in Des Moines, Iowa, in 1899 and grew up in Mobile, Alabama. His father, Henry Cohen, was a haberdasher, but early on Elliot showed signs that he would embark on a different career. At age three, he could read and understand newspaper headlines. When he was fifteen, he entered Yale, where he became president of the Menorah Society and compiled an impressive academic record, particularly in the English department. But he was told that only someone of Anglo-Saxon descent could properly understand English literature. All his life Cohen was embittered by this event—one that was experienced by many other Jews of his generation who felt collectively blocked and humiliated by the WASP establishment in business, law, the academy, the arts, and many other areas in which the Jewish immigrants aspired to distinguish themselves.

Long before *Partisan Review* first appeared, Cohen was grappling with the issue of Jewish identity in the United States. He became the managing editor of the *Menorah Journal* at age twenty-five, and in 1925 he declared,

> [T]here is a restlessness, a confusion, an inner sense of instability about our communal existence that augurs a fundamental unsoundness at its roots . . . [O]ur buildings in stone rest on no deep and abiding Jewish values. We are a people who desire intensely to live, but can find no rationale for their continued existence . . . [W]e are a people who have come a long way and are at last lost.

Like many other Jewish intellectuals, Cohen became a Trotskyist in the 1930s. Though unable to produce much writing himself, he drove his disciples relentlessly; indeed, he and his circle of acolytes were parodied in a slim but potent novel called *The Unpossessed* by the gifted writer Tess Slesinger, who decamped from New York to Hollywood. She depicted Cohen as a kind of *Luftmensch* who feared seeing his brilliant ideas actually put into action: "But it was the Idea that Bruno was in love with. As he saw his Idea tampered with, taken up, exposed, filling cabinets ordered to put it into action, it became less clear, less dear to him." Bruno declares, "To the future this era will be known as the great age of panaceas, of patent medicines, of Little Magazines."[16]

How right he was! The magazines that drove the fevered intellectual life of the radical avant-garde were essentially (like so much else in their surprisingly Anglophile outlook) an imitation of English literary culture, which has been chronicled by John Gross in *The Rise and Fall of the Man of Letters*, and the great tradition of radical pamphleteering. Little magazines also drove the radical currents of the socialist movement and the literary movement known as modernism. The idea was that an article read by a few dozen people could have an outsize effect as long as they were the *right* people—people with power and influence. The strategy never really changed, whether the intellectuals were on the left or the right.

What's more, it was remarkably successful. In either their radical or their neoconservative incarnations, the Jewish intellectuals never controlled any votes nor could they exert any political pressure. They were never able to persuade American Jews to vote for the GOP. They had no battalions and little money. What they did have were pens and magazine platforms that helped make them useful, even indispensable, to a series of tactical allies who wielded the power and influence that they coveted. Leafing through the yellowed pages of these magazines today, one is struck by their grandiosity and the conviction of self-importance on the part of a tiny group of obscure critics and intellectuals who never doubted their own wisdom, insight, and above all, prescience. Their strategy succeeded. The seemingly endless succession of magazines and ad hoc committees the Jewish radicals formed over the next fifty years served their purposes very well, lending a patina of legitimacy to their propositions and creating a kind of counter-establishment.

Cohen was key. Like the *Partisan Review* crowd, Cohen wanted to influence the intersection between Jewish and American culture, but he was embittered at having to work as a fund-raiser for Jewish organizations during the Great Depression. He wouldn't get his own magazine until the advent of *Commentary* in 1945 (when it was founded by the American Jewish Committee as the successor to the *Contemporary Jewish Record*).

Probably Cohen's most significant protégé was Lionel Trilling, in many ways a surrogate son. But the son outstripped the father in terms of worldly reputation and achievement. Trilling's success—he was the first Jewish professor to receive tenure at Columbia, which had maintained strict quotas on Jewish undergraduates—was symbolically important for his circle, but its members never completely lost their sense of being trapped between the world of their fathers and America. Trilling thus became a kind of representative man for the New York intellectuals.

Trilling was born into a middle-class Jewish family. His father was a furrier; his mother—who had been schooled in London's East End, spoke of her own "little English mother" in a manner that suggested a resemblance to Queen Victoria, and was an incessant reader of English literature—molded him. When he was four years old, she announced that he would take an Oxford Ph.D. According to his wife, Diana, Trilling would always feel vaguely discomfited that the closest he came to fulfilling his mother's dream was to become Eastman Professor at Oxford in 1964.

Trilling graduated from Columbia in 1925 and, like several other Columbia graduates, honed his writing and editing skills by working for Cohen at the *Menorah Journal.* Cohen left a deep impression on Trilling. According to Trilling, "He taught the younger men around him that nothing in human life need be alien to their thought, and nothing in American life, whether it be baseball, or vaudeville, or college tradition, or elementary education, or fashions in speech, or food, or dress, or manners."[17]

Unlike Cohen, Trilling became an academic mandarin. Appointed an instructor at Columbia in 1932, he labored for several years on a dissertation on Matthew Arnold that seemed to be going nowhere. In 1936 the Columbia English department informed him that "as a Freudian, a Marxist, and a Jew," he was no longer welcome. Abandoning his habitual reserve, Trilling confronted several members, including his mentor Mark Van Doren, and told them that they were making a terrible mistake. They reconsidered. Trilling received a one-year extension, and work on his dissertation now went smoothly, but he could never quite escape the concerns of the WASPs about letting in too many Jews. After Trilling received tenure in 1939 through the direct intervention of Columbia's president, Nicholas Murray Butler, his colleague Emery E. Neff visited him to express the hope that he would not use his position to insinuate more Jews into the English department. Trilling said nothing, but he disavowed any particular interest in Jewish topics and initially refused to join the board of *Commentary*, partly because he feared it would be preoccupied with parochial Jewish concerns.

Trilling equivocated on many issues, which is why he was respected but never embraced by the neoconservatives. He felt a certain skepticism about the pieties of liberalism and tried, as much as possible, to question it from the inside. Sidney Hook recalled, "One sensed in him an inner reserve, a certain distance from total commitment. He had a distrust of strenuous displays of virtue . . . of crusades of any kind."[18] Though he would never have publicly endorsed the neoconservative outlook—his wife, Diana, a skillful polemicist in her own right, was horrified by Kristol's endorsement of Nixon for the presidency in 1972—he privately sympathized with it on narrow cultural grounds. He never lived to see the rise of multiculturalism and deconstruction, but intimations of it in the early 1970s left him aghast. Like the Yale literary critic Harold Bloom, he was the kind of Jewish academic liberal who would become a fellow traveler of neoconservative opponents of these trends.

Indeed, it is not difficult to find in him a certain proto-neoconservative strain. In his finely rendered essays, he subtly implied stands that were subversive of the dominant liberalism. All along, Trilling had an acute sense of the political problems that assailed the left, in no small part from personal experience. In one of those typical New York feuds, he had, for example, been denounced in the Communist Party organ *New Masses* in 1934, along with Elliot Cohen, as a "loop-de-looper from Zionism to internationalism" for signing a letter in the *Modern Monthly* lamenting that Communist Party thuggery was destroying a united front against fascism in Europe.[19]

Trilling, however, quickly realized that Trotskyism was not an escape route but a blind alley. (In his only novel, *The Middle of the*

Journey, he traced the intellectuals' disenchantment with Trotskyism.) As he observed in a December 1937 letter to Sidney Hook, "The superbly single-minded commitment of the intellectual to an ethics of power is really quite a spectacle to watch. And that goes, it seems, not only for literary Stalinists but for our intelligent Trotskyist friends as well . . . maybe there's a chance that what you call the basic moral problem of our time—or *any* moral problem—will yet be forced upon our intellectuals."[20] No statement captures the problems of Trotskyism then, and of neoconservatism now, more acutely than this prescient diagnosis. Trilling never lost the commitment to an independent mind, as did so many of his contemporaries, whether they called themselves Trotskyists in the 1930s or neoconservatives today. The difference is simple but profound. He never fell into an overt hostility toward liberalism, but always maintained an aloof, questioning stance toward the dominant pieties.

That aloofness was emblematic of the stance that the New York intellectuals took toward their identity as American Jews and (a fortiori) toward the Holocaust. Throughout the 1930s, as Europe moved inexorably toward war, they were consumed with sectarian infighting. Fascism was on the rise. Hitler and Stalin were carving up Europe. FDR seemed helpless to stop the Great Depression. But the Jewish intellectuals, in many ways, fled inward. They were trapped in their insular Manhattan disputes.

Despite their grand pronouncements about fascism and capitalism and liberty, the intellectuals failed to make any meaningful distinctions between Roosevelt and Stalin, Churchill and Hitler. It was liberalism that would unite the United States and lead it to victory. But the New York intellectuals didn't see it that way. Instead, they reveled in their hatred of capitalism and their snobbish alienation from American society. Writing about Hitler's annexation of Czechoslovakia, for example, the editors of *Partisan Review* mordantly declared: "If the Czech crisis did not come to war, it was certainly not the fault of the intellectual left . . . It would almost seem that the peculiar function of the intellectuals is to idealize imperialist wars when they come and debunk them after they are over."[21]

Not until the 1939 Hitler-Stalin pact carving up Poland did American intellectuals begin to appreciate that there might be a difference between Roosevelt and Stalin, between Churchill and Hitler. The change started to come in the pages of *Partisan Review.* To be sure, Dwight Macdonald, writing with Clement Greenberg, clung to the notion that little distinguished the Western powers and Nazi Germany in their foreign policy aims. In "Ten Propositions on the War" they argued that entering the global conflict would only lead to fascism inside the United States. "The lesser evil policy meant toleration of the existing system," they declared, and "capitalism is *intolerable.*" Predictably enough, this kind of principled opposition to capitalism would fade with time as the intellectuals made their peace with American bourgeois society; and in the case of the neoconservatives, they would wholeheartedly embrace it.

In the late 1930s and early 1940s, however, many Jewish Trotskyists remained so consumed with their dual hatred of Stalin (the betrayer of Trotsky) and Roosevelt (the betrayer of the working class and savior of capitalism) that Hitler almost seemed to be a sideshow. The strange thing is that even though Trotsky himself was warning about the danger of Nazism, his American intellectual followers were somewhat blasé about it. Even when storm troopers and hooligans destroyed Jewish shops and synagogues in an orgy of violence on November 9, 1938, the cataclysmic event was viewed through the spectacles of cosmopolitan Marxism.

One notable exception was Sidney Hook. A former Marxist who had dabbled in Trotskyism, Hook had been a rebel since his years at Boys High School in New York, where he opposed American entry into World War I. He studied philosophy at City College and taught in the New York public school system before taking up graduate studies under the leading American pragmatist, John Dewey. In the

New Leader in November 1938, Hook declared (in an article on the "tragedy of German Jewry"), "Let us bear in mind that in protesting against Hitler's anti-Jewish brutalities we are also protesting against the hounding of other religious and political minorities ... Stalin has killed more Jews in the last two years than Hitler has since coming to power." According to Alexander Bloom, "It is ... remarkable that Hook's article was almost the only discussion of the topic during prewar years—a period in which the *Partisan* writers kept busy attacking the Stalinists, proletarian literature, and the Popular Front."[22] Max Shachtman was no better. *Labor Action* declared that the only issue of World War II was "who is going to get the major share of the swag. The blood stains all of their hands alike."[23]

To date there has been very little confrontation with this aspect of the Jewish radical past. One of those who, shortly before his death, did address the topic was Melvin Lasky. The scholar and rabbi Albert Friedlander said Lasky was "the paradigm of the New York Jew; he would accept this as an encomium as long as it did not contain the dimension of religion." Lasky, who grew up in the Bronx, was born in 1920. He attended City College, was a Trotskyist as a youth, landed a job as a junior historical archivist at the Statue of Liberty, and later became editor of the British journal *Encounter*—the best of the cold war journals. According to Lasky,

> The most shameful, embarrassed, masochistic moment of
> all came, at least for me, in the late summer of 1941. Arguing
> in Lewisohn Stadium (we all attended the outdoor concerts
> in CCNY's backyard) I was suddenly paralyzed with outrage
> when I noted the general glee in most of our Trotskyite cir-
> cles that the German Army was cutting through (like a-hot-
> knife-in-butter was the horrific phrase) the Soviet Russian
> resistance. All they could think of was how they had taken
> the correct position on Stalin's purges! ... Who devoted a

single thought to the onset of all the mass murders of East European Jewry in all the ghettoes and shtetl of Eastern Europe? . . . Who cried havoc?

Lasky continued:

> The whole subject was, as I remember, utterly taboo. Did anyone in our crowd ever write a line about it? It would only have been a first waning of a romantic youthful enthusiasm for utopia and revolution—but it would have been important as a record of egregious intellectual folly . . . I don't believe the two Irvings [Kristol and Howe] ever documented their mid-War abandonment of the Trotskyite 4th International Party Line.

But Lasky himself, writing in 1943 in the *New Leader*, where he was a young staffer, would denounce the passivity of Franklin Roosevelt in the face of the destruction of the Jews—one of the few who decried what was transpiring in Europe.

Even after Pearl Harbor, many Trotskyists saw the United States, not Nazi Germany, as the real problem. After the Japanese attack, for instance, Irving Howe declared that the rush by numerous intellectuals to support the war showed they were fake radicals. Like their predecessors who had been gulled into supporting Woodrow Wilson's new order, a new generation was conniving with Rooseveltian capitalism. According to Howe,

> The liberals have so lost themselves in their uncritical attitude toward the imperialist war that they do not even attempt to distinguish their aims and purposes in the war from those of, say, the *Herald Tribune* . . . It is this undiluted chauvinism, this two-penny jingoism which is the sole pro-

gram of *The Nation.* Remember, it writes these words of American imperialism, the shining star of altruism in a world of gangsters.[24]

In February 1943, Shachtman declared that "England, France and Poland were not fighting for democracy or against fascism, but for imperialist gain and power; and that, in this decisive respect, they differed not at all from the equally predatory Axis." The editors of *Enquiry,* including Irving Kristol, were similarly deluded. In "The Dilemma of Social Idealism," Philip Selznick declared that the "concrete social influences representing an anti-democratic trend are far more extensive than the Nazi legions."[25]

Kristol took a similarly blinkered view. In 1944, as Jews were being herded into ghettos and gassed in concentration camps, he attacked Hook for supporting the war. Hook, Kristol said, was a demagogue:

In his near hysterical insistence upon the pressing military danger . . . we recognize not only a common academic reaction to events, but also an ominously familiar political weapon. It is the exact technique of the Communist-liberal coalition during the days of the Popular Front and Collective Security. One element is seized from its context as the receptacle of all political significance, and crucial political disagreements based on a broader perspective than "licking the villain" are condemned as malicious and irresponsible criticism.

Dripping with scorn for the war effort, Kristol declared:

The war in Asia clarifies brutally the activating war aims of the United States, Britain, and the Netherlands as far as the vital questions of empire and freedom are concerned. Professor Hook busies himself with an abstract war against Hitler rather than handle the less attractive reality of a completely reactionary crusade against "those yellow b——s." It's always the other fellow's nerve.[26]

Kristol was indulging in an abstract crusade for a better world.

Articles did occasionally appear in the radical press about the plight of the Jews. Jessie Kaaren wrote in *Labor Action* that "hundreds of Jews die daily in the concentration camps of Poland, in the labor battalions of the Nazis, in the barracks of Hungary, Siberia, Rumania and other countries, because there is no place for them to escape to."[27] Alfred Kazin declared in the *New Republic* that liberals, radicals, and reactionaries were all ignoring the tragedy taking place in Europe.

This did not change after World War II. For the Jewish intellectuals it was America, not Israel, that remained central. The neocons (though they did not yet own the name) had spent most of their lives in the wilderness. With prophetic austerity they had opposed capitalism and were equally contemptuous of both major political parties. Now they were confronted with a profoundly transformed situation—the United States had won the war. Socialism was defeated. The American economy was thriving. Harry Truman, against the almost unanimous advice of the foreign policy establishment, recognized a Jewish state. Except among the diehards, the socialist dream had already expired. Now the Jewish intellectuals made their spiritual way back from Moscow or Barcelona to New York. They had always been anti-Stalinists. Now, somewhat to their own surprise, they became anticommunists *tout court.* But while they were now ostensibly ex-radicals in political terms, they never really ceased to be radicals in temperament and style.

———

At the dawn of the cold war, there were basically two possible postures toward communism—two paths out of the wilderness for the Jewish radicals. One was the path of containment of communism set out by the Truman administration. This was the point of view that came to be associated with the tradition of "liberal hawks," embodied by such figures as Arthur Schlesinger Jr., George F. Kennan, and Reinhold Niebuhr—a party that went into steep decline after the Vietnam debacle. The other was a more militant path that hewed closer to their Trotskyist roots and was championed by the formerly isolationist right. This path—of rollback, confrontation, and liberation—was blazed by James Burnham and William F. Buckley Jr. at the *National Review*, later adopted by Reagan, and finally given intellectual credibility by the neocons.

Burnham's influence on the neoconservative movement should not be discounted. A Roman Catholic who was born in 1905, he grew up in wealthy circumstances in the Chicago suburb of Kenilworth. Burnham, who became a philosopher, was a colleague at New York University of Sidney Hook's. Hook converted Burnham to the Marxist faith. In 1932 Burnham wrote a review of Trotsky's *History of the Russian Revolution* and was bowled over by it, becoming a staunch Trotskyist. He became coeditor of the *Militant* along with Max Shachtman, but went furthest in distancing himself from Trotsky during World War II. In 1941 he wrote *The Managerial Revolution*, a famous polemic which argued that a "new class" of technocrats was taking over in Russia and the United States.

In 1945 Burnham caused a furor with an article in *Partisan Review* called "Lenin's Heir," in which he depicted Stalin, not Trotsky, as the true successor to Lenin. Far from betraying Lenin, Burnham argued, Stalin had in fact fulfilled his vision. This came to be conventional wisdom during the cold war until revisionist historians began to argue, in Great Britain and the United States in the 1970s, that Lenin had been betrayed by Stalin—an updated version of the Trotskyist argument, purveyed most prominently by the historian and *Nation* contributor Stephen F. Cohen. Burnham had it right, but as George Orwell perceptively noted, he seemed to derive an unseemly and gleeful pleasure from the rise of Stalin, not to mention the prospect of the demise of the intellectually flaccid West. As Orwell put it:

> The real aim of the essay is to present Stalin as a towering, super-human figure, indeed a species of demigod, and Bolshevism as an irresistible force which is flowing over the earth and cannot be halted until it reaches the outermost borders of Eurasia. In so far as he makes any attempt to prove his case, Burnham does so by repeating over and over again that Stalin is "a great man"—which is probably true, but is almost completely irrelevant. Moreover, though he does advance some solid arguments for believing in Stalin's genius, it is clear that in his mind the idea of "greatness" is inextricably mixed up with the idea of cruelty and dishonesty. There are curious passages in which it seems to be suggesting that Stalin is to be admired *because of* the limitless suffering that he has caused.[28]

Burnham also set the stage for neoconservative melodrama about the fate of the West resting on decisive action. He lurched from declaring that there was nothing worth saving in the West and that totalitarianism would prevail (in his 1941 book, *The Managerial Revolution*) to calling for all-out preventive war against the Kremlin (in his 1947 book, *The Struggle for the World*). He failed to consider that the Soviet Union might, as George F. Kennan predicted, mellow as a result of a vigilant containment policy. Instead, everything had to be solved in a grand burst. This mind-set of boredom with a patient foreign policy would come to dominate both conservatism and neoconservatism. In fact, when William F. Buckley Jr. founded the *National Review*, it was heavily influenced by ex-Trotskyists, down to its founding language about battling elites in the media and academia.

It was a dilemma that the neoconservatives would never really resolve: Was the Soviet Union an implacable and irresistible force, or could it be stopped? Was it necessary to ape the methods of totalitarianism to defeat it? Once he developed his strategy for the "rollback" of communism, Burnham seemed to want it both ways. The triumph of communism was inevitable, but it nonetheless had to be halted.

Initially, many of the ex-radicals took a more moderate path than that counseled by Burnham. It was shown to them by another set of Jewish exiles from Russia. The postwar marriage between the Trotskyists and the liberal centrists began at a magazine called the *New Leader,* which was founded in New York in 1924 by the socialist and labor leader James O'Neal. The magazine has never really gotten its due in the chronicles devoted to the liberal anticommunist movement. Unlike *Partisan Review*, the *New Leader* was never a Marxist publication, and it focused on politics as opposed to cultural matters. In 1940 the magazine cemented its liberal credentials by creating an alliance with Reinhold Niebuhr's Union for Democratic Action, a precursor of the cold war organization called Americans for Democratic Action. Both Sidney Hook and Daniel Bell would later write that the magazine was the crucible in which liberal anticommunism was forged.

From the outset, the magazine took an appropriately skeptical view of the Soviet Union. Once Samuel M. "Sol" Levitas, a Menshevik refugee from Russia who had escaped disguised as a police officer, became the business manager and executive editor, he turned it into a prominent part of what was known as the noncommunist left. The magazine warned that the Soviet Union had betrayed socialism, predicted the signing of the Molotov-Ribbentrop pact that carved up Poland and the Baltic States in 1939, popularized the word "totalitarian," and exposed Soviet concentration camps in 1947.

As an editor and mentor, Levitas was revered by Bell, Kristol, and

Lasky. Bell, who, of course, had never succumbed to Trotskyism, played a key role in bringing Kristol and Lasky on board in his capacity as managing editor. For Sidney Hook, who, along with James Burnham, had abandoned Trotskyist drivel, the magazine was a "vital center of anti-Communist thought and activity" years before the cold war had ever begun.[29] The social democrats of the *New Leader* weren't crusaders; they were realists about what could, and could not, be accomplished in the struggle against communism. Had Kristol and others hewed to this path, neoconservatism might never have been born and a social-democratic anticommunism might have prevailed. It would end up being a road not taken, or, better put, abandoned.

One of the most significant acts of the *New Leader* was to support an anti-Stalinist organization called the Committee for Cultural Freedom, which was founded in 1939 by Sidney Hook. It disseminated a bulletin, organized monthly radio broadcasts, and held large public meetings to expose Soviet totalitarianism, featuring speakers like the Soviet defector Walter Krivitsky. It also issued a report that attempted to classify the cultural and social organizations under the direct or indirect control of the American Communist Party. Hook's organization was a precursor of the CIA-sponsored Congress for Cultural Freedom (CCF), which would emerge after World War II, as well as the Committee on the Present Danger, the Committee for the Free World, and, most recently, the now-defunct Project for the New American Century.

The origins of the American intellectual cold war can be traced to a Soviet peace conference at the Waldorf-Astoria hotel in 1949. Eight hundred literary and artistic figures, including Lillian Hellman and Aaron Copland, gathered there to denounce "U.S. warmongering." Sidney Hook, Dwight Macdonald, and other former Trotskyists were determined to expose the conference as a Stalinist affair. Accordingly, they formed a counter-organization called Americans for Intellectual Freedom.

Hook and his comrades heckled and badgered the participants in the Soviet conference, including a member of the Soviet Writers' Union, Aleksandr Fadeyev. Hook and company successfully disrupted the conference and also staged a counterprotest at Bryant Park. Fired by his success, Hook would go on to somewhat grandiosely declare in Berlin in 1950, "Give me a hundred million dollars and a thousand dedicated people, and I will guarantee to generate such a wave of democratic unrest among the masses—yes, even among the soldiers—of Stalin's own empire, that all his problems for a long time to come will be internal. I can find the people."

Perhaps the greatest accomplishment of the early anticommunists was to stage a conference in Berlin in 1950 sponsored by the Congress for Cultural Freedom, where American and European intellectuals joined forces to demonstrate their solidarity in the face of communism. The Congress for Cultural Freedom came into bad odor in the 1960s, when its CIA subventions became public knowledge; the Berlin conference had been secretly supported by the CIA's fledgling covert action arm—the Office of Policy Coordination. But in the 1950s the CCF had been an impressive international organization whose headquarters were in Paris and whose European guiding spirits included Arthur Koestler, Ignazio Silone, Stephen Spender, and Raymond Aron. It was supposed to function as a kind of cultural NATO. The congress held numerous conferences in Berlin, Bellagio, and Paris and sponsored dozens of magazines, including *Encounter, Quadrant*, and *Preuves.*[30]

If the CCF had not existed, the left would have had to invent it. To some extent, it did this by magnifying the amount of control that the CIA had over the CCF. The purpose of the mythmaking about the CCF is to create a moral equivalence between East and West. But intellectuals, an ornery lot, can seldom be ordered around.

The congress's biggest success came early on in West Berlin, which had barely survived (via the Allied airlift) the Soviet attempt to starve it out in the exceedingly harsh winter of 1949 by blockading it to land traffic. For Kristol, Lasky, Hook, and Arthur Schlesinger Jr., it was an important opportunity to take a very public stand and to sound the alarm about Soviet advances in Europe. Lasky's role in organizing the conference was decisive. His recent experiences in Germany had only confirmed to him the importance of facing down tyranny.

Lasky, who had been drafted into the army and became a combat historian with the U.S. Seventh Army, was one of the first soldiers to enter Dachau. He was demobilized in Berlin (there were always rumors that he was really working for the Office of Strategic Services). Short, stocky, sporting a goatee, and always prone to making fiery statements, he helped shape postwar European culture. He became friends with Social Democrats like the mayor of Berlin, Ernst Reuter. He also edited for fifteen years a wonderful magazine called *Der Monat* that translated Orwell and other leading antitotalitarian thinkers into German. His cultural influence in a Germany shattered morally as well as physically by World War II was considerable. He single-handedly disrupted a German writers' conference in 1947 convened in East Berlin by dramatically standing up and paying homage to dissident Russian writers, insistent that the passion for freedom had to unite all intellectuals:

> The writer, the publisher and the reader have certain inviolable civil rights, and all three have responsibility for vigilant protection and uncompromising maintenance of these rights and this freedom. If they fail—that is, if you and I fail, here in Europe, or in America, or anywhere in the world—slavery has come again. Manuscripts will be banned, books will be burned, and writers and readers will once again be sitting in concentration camps for having thought dangerous ideas or uttered forbidden words.

The Soviets tried to get the U.S. military governor of Germany, Lucius D. Clay, to expel him. Clay ended up hiring Lasky as an adviser.

At the 1950 CCF conference in Berlin, some of the speakers got carried away. North Korea had just invaded the South. Burnham mused about the efficacy of dropping atomic bombs on the Soviet Union. Arthur Koestler, another prominent ex-communist, stated that "McCarthyism represents the wages of the American liberals' sins ... they were found wanting on the most crucial issue of our time"—a precursor of Irving Kristol's later statements on McCarthyism.

This wasn't the kind of language that George F. Kennan or Arthur Schlesinger Jr. would indulge in. In short, there were already latent tensions between the future neoconservatives and the mainstream liberals. The neoconservatives' radicalism and aggressive temperament always rubbed genuine cold war liberals the wrong way. Some of those differences emerged at the Berlin conference: thus the British historian Hugh Trevor-Roper denounced ex-communists like Koestler and Franz Borkenau in a famous article in the *Manchester Guardian* as fanatics. Trevor-Roper, writing to Bernard Berenson in a letter dated July 28, 1950, recorded that "I haven't been abroad except for four days in Berlin for a so-called 'Kongress für Kulturelle Freiheit,' where I misbehaved. . . . [A]ided by my English colleague A. J. Ayer . . . I led a resistance movement against the organisers of the Congress, which in fact was a totally illiberal demonstration dominated by professional ex-communist *boulevardiers* like Arthur Koestler & Frank Brokenau, confident in the support of German ex-Nazis in the audience." They had, he thought, traded one ideology for another—an accusation that would be leveled at the neoconservatives throughout their careers. In the 1960s, for example, Christopher Lasch, in the *New York Review of Books* and in his book *The Agony of the American Left,* depicted the Congress for Cultural Freedom as a bunch of CIA-backed zealots who brought into question the desirability and efficacy of anticommunism more generally. Most recently, the British writer Frances Stonor Saunders has damned the members of the CCF as lackeys of the CIA in her book *Who Paid the Piper?*

These were differences that went beyond mere tone. Schlesinger and Kennan argued for the containment of communism, but they did not see an internal threat from it in the United States. They essentially took a sober view. Kristol and company did not. They remained zealots.

Consider *Partisan Review*. William Barrett had already made waves in 1946 with an article in *PR* denouncing a "liberal Fifth Column." The article was supposed to expiate the magazine's own prior sins and keep it on the offensive. He accused liberals of selling out millions into Stalinist slavery: "Whether those who march always know where they are going, whether they are confused about their purposes or really taken in by sham purposes, they are not any the less a Fifth Column. Political positions are weighed by objective consequences and not by subjective intentions."[31] Subjective intentions? This phrase itself was redolent of Stalinism with its talk about "objective" class enemies, whether they had actually conspired against the state or not. There is something a little breathtaking, then and now, about how quickly intellectuals can turn on the position they once so passionately maintained. Having denounced war against Hitler as imperialist, *Partisan Review* now championed it against Stalin.

Another sign of the excesses to which the former radicals were prone came in Kristol's 1952 article on Senator Joseph McCarthy. Kristol ignored Daniel Bell's warnings and, at the bidding of the editor Elliot Cohen, who wanted to show that the Jews could be relied on in the fight against the Red menace (he need hardly have worried: Senator Joseph McCarthy's two sidekicks were named Cohn and Schine), made a name for himself by savaging liberals in the pages of *Commentary*. The liberals, he said, looked with a kindly eye on communists, but the same could not be said of Senator McCarthy. The American people, Kristol suggested, knew which side McCarthy was on. Such nonsense bedeviled Kristol for the rest of his career. Kristol was no supporter of McCarthy, but he was already succumbing to a populist tone that he would increasingly cultivate in coming decades, when he would, in effect, espouse a "no enemies to the right" policy.

Kristol's career took another fateful turn when he accepted a post offered by the Congress for Cultural Freedom to found a version of *Commentary* in England called *Encounter*. He was supposed to act as a highbrow agent on behalf of spreading the democratic and capitalist creed among English intellectuals, who tended, more often than not, to view the United States with ill-concealed loathing and contempt. In 1952 he and his wife, Gertrude Himmelfarb (as a distinguished historian in her own right, she kept her maiden name), left New York for England, where he became a founding editor, along with Stephen Spender, of *Encounter*.

In London the Jewish slum kid gained an entrée to the British upper class that did little to suppress his budding conservative instincts. The former Shermanite now wore a bowler hat and spent a good deal of time with conservatives like the historian Herbert Butterfield, who had debunked the "Whig interpretation" of history, or the idea that history was one long march of progress. Kristol himself was starting to find the idea of liberal progress rather boring. He had become skeptical of such illusions in the 1940s, and his time in England helped cement the conviction that great leaps forward were not in the offing when it came to the working class. The historian Walter Laqueur says that Kristol became something of a "Henry James" kind of "snob." Sir Peregrine Worsthorne reminisced that Kristol encouraged him to write a lament for the passing of the aristocracy and to "enjoy it while you have it." The sociologist George Lichtheim told Kristol in 1953, "You will end up a supporter of Nixon."

Kristol was annoyed, but Lichtheim was, of course, right. Kristol would end up supporting Nixon and condemning the radicals as new Bolsheviks intent on overthrowing the Republic, which, of course, in some ways they were. Kristol had thrived in opposition and had contempt for those, like Sidney Hook, who (as he used to see it) were insufficiently hostile to the American empire. Now he himself was becoming a charter member of the establishment.

This conflict in some sense reflects the divided sensibility of Jewish radicals between their social and their political attitudes. There was, on the one hand, a deep resentment of the social exclusion experienced by Jews at the hands of the WASP elite. On the other, their cultural Anglophilia (widely shared by immigrant Jews who named their sons for English lords—Lionel, Seymour, Norman, Irving, and so on) caused them to harbor an abiding respect for the cultivation and values of this transatlantic elite. Kristol and Himmelfarb were witnesses to the destruction of old England, which they saw as the passing of a golden age that could only be viewed with nostalgia and pity. There was also an awareness, perhaps unconscious at this point but still deeply significant, that in the crucial hour the defense of democracy and resistance to fascism had rested precisely on the traditional virtues of duty, honor, and patriotism that in their long phase as Trotskyist radicals they had despised.

The neoconservatives would play a surprising role in propagating nostalgia for the English aristocracy, supposed by them to be a kind of benign ceremonial caste that might have been stuffy and hidebound but had never frozen out the Jews the way the WASPs back home had. More than a hint of Straussian influence may be seen in their new appreciation for the specific virtues bred by aristocracy. Watching the disintegration of this class helped strengthen their conviction that an increasingly vulgar democratic culture, and the rise of the postwar welfare state, were inimical to a stable bourgeois society. They also became decidedly hostile to any social or cultural force that threatened to undermine, discredit, or attack those "English" virtues on which a strong liberal order depended.

Indeed, the political dimension of Himmelfarb's impressive and numerous books about the Victorian era is quite marked. Her Anglophilia was far more pronounced and influential than Kristol's and contributed greatly to the later conservative emphasis on moral values. In a sense she was fighting the culture war of the 1980s and 1990s, in book after book about Victorian values, decades before it had even begun.

Certainly Himmelfarb, who was born in 1922, embodied those values. She came from a middle-class family: her grandfather was a Hebrew teacher and her father a glass manufacturer. Her brother, Milton, became a prominent commentator on Judaism as well as an acidulous critic of liberal American Jews. She flirted with socialism, attending the Brooklyn chapter of the Young People's Socialist League at age eighteen with Irving, but her real passion was scholarly. She attended both Brooklyn College and the Jewish Theological Seminary. Her hard work won Himmelfarb a graduate fellowship in history at the University of Chicago (Irving followed her there and worked as a railroad freight handler before he was drafted into the U.S. Army). In England she researched and wrote a graduate dissertation on that high priest of classical liberalism, Lord Acton.

As with the Julio-Claudian clan of ancient Rome, the power and importance of the neoconservative matriarchs must not be overlooked. Himmelfarb exerted an austere, almost stoic authority in the neocon milieu—and one that was much to the good, insofar as she was a serious historian and set a high standard for scholarship. Indeed the intellectual standards of the founding generation as a whole were very high, leading to a quality of work that made their books and magazines respectable even when they were ideologically heterodox.

Himmelfarb's particular bête noire was the Bloomsbury group—Lytton Strachey, Virginia Woolf, and other aesthetes—which formed an effete and promiscuous elite that, so the neoconservatives believed, set the cultural climate for appeasement of Hitler, as much in their social attitudes (read: homosexuality) as in their fashionable Fabianism. They were wimps compared to the stalwart Victorians they so cruelly mocked. Under Queen Victoria, by contrast, England had been a self-confident empire, the very model for the United States as it entered its own phase of global dominance. For Himmelfarb, in closely researched books like *The Idea of Poverty* and *Poverty and Compassion*, it was the bourgeois capitalist virtues—thrift, industry, self-abnegation—that produced the class that ruled an empire. Himmelfarb's political message in praising the virtues of the Victorian era was that they should be emulated in the United States, where welfare programs had created a shiftless hereditary underclass permanently dependent on government handouts. It was not too great a stretch to see the self-indulgent and hedonistic Bloomsbury types as precursors of the modern New Left.

Like other neoconservatives, Himmelfarb found a special place for the Jews in her ideological pantheon. Far from being an alien element relegated to permanent exclusion in the majority Christian societies of England and America, the Jews, in her view, embodied the bourgeois capitalist virtues on which these countries rested. She has even said that she sees the Jews who emigrated from Poland and Russia to England as the quintessential Victorians. Jews shunned the dole, embraced education and the entrepreneurial spirit, and took pride in working their way up. Also counting in Victorian England's favor was its tolerance of Jews. The great historian Thomas Macaulay famously argued for abolishing restrictions excluding Jews from Parliament. Benjamin Disraeli had climbed the greasy pole to become prime minister. The Rothschilds joined the peerage. The British were also friendly to Zionist aspirations. George Eliot's novel *Daniel Deronda* extolled the idea of a Jewish homeland and featured an exemplary Jew named Mordecai as a benevolent prophet (which Lionel Trilling would perceptively criticize for presenting an idealized version of Jews). And of course it was Lord Balfour who engineered the famous, eponymous document that authorized the birth of Israel.

Still, the Kristols were avatars of the American way. For the first issue of *Encounter*, Kristol commissioned a mischievous essay by the literary critic Leslie Fiedler about the convicted atomic spies and heroes of the left Julius and Ethel Rosenberg that dispensed with liberal pieties about a saintly couple hounded to death by the FBI. Fiedler not only endorsed the verdict but also mocked the Rosenbergs' low-rent apartment, which was the "visible manifestation of the Stalinized petty-bourgeois mind," and the sentimental claptrap contained in Ethel's "death-house letters." Fiedler's fulgurations ensured that all ten thousand copies sold out within a week. Whatever his critics might say, Kristol always had a nose for controversy.

Leftists such as the historian A. J. P. Taylor, who loathed capitalism and America, saw *Encounter* as a Trojan horse for the expansion of U.S. hegemony. Consistent with his blasé attitude toward alliances with unusual partners—from McCarthy to the Christian right—Kristol didn't bat an eye at the exposure of CIA funding for the magazine, and always claimed he was unaware of it. But the Western intelligence agencies had learned from the prewar radicals—to the extent of hiring them. The irony was that the CIA, which was staffed by WASPs (William F. Buckley Jr. was one of its first recruits along with many other Yalies), was now funding the activities of the formerly radical New York Jews.

The CIA's main link to the intellectuals was a brilliantly talented Estonian émigré named Michael Josselson. Josselson was a fascinating figure and a linguistic polymath—he spoke English, German, Russian, and French fluently. In 1943 he was inducted into the U.S. Army. Three years later he, like Lasky, stayed on in Berlin. Josselson was an American cultural affairs officer and became friends with numerous leading German cultural figures, including the controversial conductor of the Berlin Philharmonic, Wilhelm Furtwängler. Josselson had the thankless task of trying to corral the perpetually bickering and feuding intellectuals into a semi-coherent force capable of opposing Soviet communism. The double life that he led, promoting intellectual freedom while dissembling about what was actually supporting it financially, took its toll. By the end, his life had come to resemble something out of a John Le Carré novel: at his funeral Josselson's wife spurned a medal and citation from an attending CIA officer. But in the 1950s the New York intellectuals were delighted to have such a talented and munificent sponsor. In the space of a few years Kristol and others had gone from denouncing the U.S. government to trumpeting its virtues and, incidentally, accepting its largesse.

This was a huge cultural shift. Indeed, so pronounced was it that in June 1956 *Time* magazine took note in a cover story called "America and the Intellectual: The Reconciliation." Everyone from Irving Kristol to Reinhold Niebuhr to Jacques Barzun made a cameo. It ratified the new role and importance of the intellectuals in postwar society. Lionel Trilling, who cultivated a deliberately opaque style, ironically declared, "An avowed aloofness from national feeling is no longer the first ceremonial step into the life of thought . . . For the first time in the history of the modern American intellectual, America is not to be conceived of as a priori the vulgarest and stupidest nation of the world."[32] That *Time* would devote an issue to intellectuals shows how important they had become as a symbol of the American liberal consensus.

The radical Jews had taken their first "ceremonial step" into the promised land of American bourgeois society, with all of its temptations and rewards. They had become the boosters of American exceptionalism and champions of middle-class values. Most of the New York radicals had left behind the Pharaonic mental and moral wasteland of Marxism. (The Marxist faith that once looked like the way to the promised land of socialist equality came to look more like Egyptian slavery as they began their move into the American middle class.)

A small remnant, led by Irving Howe, remained in the desert. Indeed, in a famous 1952 essay, "This Age of Conformity," Howe asserted that the intellectuals had sold out. The *Partisan Review*'s

"Our Country, Our Culture" symposium in 1952 represented a capitulation, he believed, to middlebrow culture. The intellectuals were no longer critics, Howe thought, but unquestioning celebrants of American exceptionalism. It was better to be a freelance writer for magazines or even to subsist on family assistance, he suggested, than to enter the wider world and become a domesticated intellectual.

These claims were bogus. As the British academic Stefan Collini tartly observes:

> At the heart of all such claims is an unrealistic or exaggerated idea of "independence," of being free to be critical because not in the pay of, or dependent upon the good favor of, a patron or constraining institution . . . The truth surely is that no one can escape "attachment" in this sense: freedom from one kind of dependence (patron or a government) is only achieved by another kind of dependence (on a family or a public).[33]

Howe later softened his critique, especially when the New Left accused him and his colleagues of timorousness. But he founded his own magazine, called *Dissent*, in 1954 to carry on the socialist tradition of moral purity and independence from the capitalist spirit. Just why intellectuals would be more free and independent writing for a mercurial magazine editor than enjoying the security of tenure, Howe did not explain—unless, of course, they were the editor.

Still, the intellectuals continued to commit doctrinal heresy as the American establishment beckoned. Nathan Glazer, Seymour Martin Lipset, Gertrude Himmelfarb, Daniel Bell, and even Kristol would all go on to careers in the university. To argue that their ideological shift was, in fact, nothing more than a reflection of their new class interest, as Howe implied, was, however, a kind of moral vanity. Bell left *Fortune* magazine to become an academic. A stand of alienation and permanent opposition to the American system implied a moral superiority to the very masses that Howe purported to represent. Years later he would mock students at Stanford University by telling them that they would end up as dentists. This was a kind of socialist reverse snobbery. (Didn't he need to have his own teeth cleaned from time to time?)

The rise of the neoconservatives had begun in the 1950s, when the ex-radicals embraced liberalism. For them, the key to the survival of the West lay in the survival of a robust liberalism founded firmly on the virtues of bourgeois capitalism. The fate of the West (and, not coincidentally, the fate of the Jews) hinged on a firm grasp in theory and practice of these virtues. It is what led the neoconservatives first to ally themselves with the liberal hawks. These allies in time would disappoint them, but in the late 1940s and the 1950s it seemed that liberalism had triumphed and that they had signed up with the winning side. They had traded in antinomianism and messianic dreams for a celebration of America.

But while their exodus may have ended, their wanderings had not. This fractious contingent was still searching for its Moses. Initially they were a Marxist vanguard leading the working class to a socialist utopia. In that period, liberalism was the enemy, and they sought to destroy it. After World War II they decided that American liberalism was the only bulwark against the triumph of a totalitarianism as evil as the Nazis'. In this period, liberalism was a noble but wavering faith that needed to be saved from the liberals themselves. During the 1960s the new "Jews" that they were trying to lead into the promised land were the Democrats. But the Democrats demurred, and the neocons entered the wilderness again, a political no-man's-land.

In the end, their only followers were their progeny. Indeed, it was the second generation that would ultimately lead the way into a new promised land—the Republican Party—and they would, in turn, despoil it.

Wilderness

Over Labor Day weekend in 1967, several thousand leftists gathered in Chicago to launch a new American revolution. The gathering, billed as the "Convention on 1968 and Beyond," was held by a small organization called the National Conference for New Politics. The group's executive director, William F. Pepper, told the delegates, "It may well be that what you begin here may ultimately result in a new social, economic and political system in the United States." Meanwhile, a bongo group outside the auditorium put a damper on the festivities as it began chanting, "Kill Whitey, Kill Whitey!"

The idea had been to create a third-party presidential ticket led by Martin Luther King Jr. and Dr. Benjamin Spock. But black hoodlums, whom the New Politics leaders called "ghetto psychotics," broke up the meeting. "Thus was conceived," reported the *New York Times*'s Walter Goodman, "the Black Caucus that was to rule the convention from tumultuous beginning to fatigued end.["] By the end of the conference, black radicals were demanding, among other things, that the convention condemn the existence of Israel.

The conference had been partly funded by a young Harvard lecturer named Martin Peretz, who was also a financial backer of the far-left magazine *Ramparts*, edited by Warren Hinckle III (who, on the side, hosted "rockdance-environment happenings" to benefit the CIA, or Citizens for Interplanetary Activity). Peretz had grown up in New York, attended the Bronx High School of Science, and earned his B.A. at Brandeis University, where he studied with Max Lerner, Irving Howe, and Herbert Marcuse. He then earned a Ph.D. at Harvard, where he subscribed to numerous radical causes, including signing a letter to the *New York Times* with the sociologist Barrington Moore denouncing American policies toward Brazil. Peretz, who was married to the Singer sewing machine heiress Anne Farnsworth, cut a wide swath at Harvard, where he was something of an enfant terrible. But like many Jewish liberals, his overriding commitment to the survival of Israel soon put him at odds with the left.

After the debacle in Chicago, Peretz—up to that point a fairly typical Jewish radical—was dismayed. His close friend Michael Walzer observed in 1969, "The new left for a while had a healthy growth, and Marty was involved in that growth. Then, things went sour."[2] In a passionate essay in the "God that failed" tradition for *Commentary,* he hotly denounced the left's hostility to the Jewish state. Peretz was revolted by the notion that

> Israel and Israel alone must bear the blame for the past and the responsibility for the future. Not, it should be clear, only for the plight of the Arab refugees, but for the behavior of the Arab regimes as well, and even (how powerful little Israel must have become!) for the policy of the Soviet Union, its sycophants (at least when Jews are in question), and virtually the entire Third World.[3]

Peretz did not shed his radical convictions all at once. A year later, at an international conference of intellectuals held at Princeton University, which included such members of the foreign policy establishment as George F. Kennan, Peretz would complain about American imperialism in Central America; Peretz was portrayed in an unflattering light in the *New York Times Magazine.* But as publisher of the *New Republic,* which he took over in 1974, Peretz would become a major force in the mainstreaming of neoconservative ideas. Though he has never accepted the label, he was—like many others who would become neoconservatives—profoundly shaken by the reaction of the New Left to Israel's triumph in the 1967 war, and by the rise of a militant and pro-Palestinian black nationalism.

Until the 1960s most of the intellectuals who would become neoconservatives had not really paid Israel all that much mind. But with the trial of Adolf Eichmann in Jerusalem, the 1967 war, and the rise of black anti-Semitism in the United States, neoconservatism was born.

By their own account, the older generation of neoconservatives was panicked by the 1960s. In 1965 in *Beyond Culture,* Trilling diagnosed an "adversary culture" of smug intellectuals who believed that the United States contaminated everything it touched. Now that class seemed to be in the driver's seat, as the left captured the Democratic Party, the antiwar movement flourished, and bourgeois values—the thing that Kristol and others cherished most as the bulwark of civilization—came under assault. In neoconservative mythology, the 1960s became a proving ground like the 1930s, especially for the younger generation, which wished (just like the radical children of the Old Left) to reenact the rituals that its elders had experienced. Ironically, the young neoconservatives would become a new generation of prophetic Jews, returning, in their own fashion, to the messianism that their parents had abjured.

When the neocons entered the decade, they were Democrats. This in itself represented a significant move to the right, and as we have seen, they were attacked for it by purists like Irving Howe. The events of the 1960s—first the failures of the Great Society, then the issues of Israel and communism—pushed them to the right. At the time the neoconservative claim was, as it has been ever since, that they weren't leaving the Democratic Party; rather, the party had left them. And there is a good deal of truth in this familiar story of how the McGovern forces seized control of the party's nominating process and disenfranchised the bosses and the white working class. But the fact is that the neocons were temperamentally predisposed to seek extremes. Confronted with extremists on the left, they entered into a kind of codependent relationship in which each side nursed the other's grievances.

The move didn't occur all at once. Nor did it happen as early as one might think. Throughout the 1960s and well into the late 1970s the neoconservatives remained Democrats and devoted themselves not to attacking liberalism but to saving it from the liberals. It wasn't until the debacle of the Carter administration that they began to move en masse into the GOP. During this long transitional period, when they were shifting their political allegiances, and in some ways had already entered the wilderness between the two parties, they also began to build or take over the network of institutions and publications that would sustain them whenever they were in exile—as they would be again and again in the coming years. This network would prove even more enduring than its founders could imagine and made it possible for the movement to reconstitute itself after it had seemingly been shattered. In this way, neoconservatism slowly became a self-perpetuating elite, much like the hated WASP establishment, though one that was based not on wealth but on ideas.

Neoconservatism was turned into an actual movement by Kristol and Norman Podhoretz. Even today, the neoconservative movement is best described as an extended family based largely on the informal social networks patiently forged by these two patriarchs. But as with any such movement, there were many other figures who contributed to its emergence, both as a movement and as a school of thought. Not all of them were Jews—a fact that has been frequently pointed out by the neoconservatives themselves to refute the contention that neoconservatism is a Jewish movement. Fair enough. Yet the movement's non-Jewish members were largely bound to the group by a shared commitment to the largest, most important Jewish cause: the survival of Israel.

What quickly became known, or, to put it more precisely, deplored, as neoconservatism would take two forms: a trenchant social and political critique of the Great Society and a vigorous, Israel-centered anticommunist foreign policy. The first was promulgated in the *Public Interest*, founded in 1965 by Irving Kristol and Daniel Bell. The magazine focused on domestic issues and cast a gelid eye on Great Society programs like affirmative action and the expansion of the welfare state.

It's important to remember that the neoconservatives did not oppose the idea of welfare itself. Instead, they wanted to reform it. Their skepticism about its unintended effects, however, made them anathema to the New Left as well as a thorn in the side of the federal welfare and civil rights establishment. It was only a matter of time before this opposition would lead to a permanent rift. Writing in 1966, for example, Kristol shrewdly observed:

> A great many people would like to think that the New Left and the New Right are passing eddies on the mainstream of American politics, and that after a while we shall all happily return to politics-as-usual . . . I do not believe this will happen . . . Though I approve, on the whole, of the various programs for a Great Society, I too am full of doubt about their potentialities for a good life in a good society.[4]

But Kristol's radical temperament, honed in the obscure, sectarian battles of the late 1930s and early 1940s, would soon push him to reject much of the Great Society. Like other neoconservatives, he was aghast at what he saw as the abandonment of morals among the youth—a degradation of the general culture that welfare programs helped promote among the underclass.

The moralism of the neoconservatives also manifested itself in their preoccupation with Israel and the Soviet Union. In the 1960s these two issues became closely linked. While many Jews had been antipathetic to American involvement in Vietnam—"a bunch of rabbis came to see me in 1967 to tell me I ought not to send a single screwdriver to Vietnam," Lyndon B. Johnson said, "but, on the other hand, said that I should push all our aircraft carriers through the Straits of Tiran to help Israel"—the neoconservatives started to champion a more aggressive stance. It was the good fortune of the neoconservatives that in the late 1960s and the 1970s these two causes would become intertwined as Israel became the focus of a superpower proxy war. The neoconservatives did their utmost to promote it, foreshadowing their roles as the high priests of the Reagan coalition.

Inevitably, the neocons' two-sided struggle against communism and for Israel also embroiled them in a confrontation with their old nemesis, the State Department. The "Arabists" at State (many of them scions of old-line diplomatic and mercantile families) had never cottoned to the existence of Israel. The neocons in contrast would demand that the United States take up the cause of the Jews as a fundamental plank of its foreign policy. They would assert that in the struggle with the Soviets—a struggle as much for global opinion as for military and economic advantage—the morality of U.S. policy was a vital strategic asset. That morality could partly be appraised on the basis of America's stance toward Israel.

The neocons pushed this argument relentlessly, trying to make it the consensus view in American politics. By the time of the George W. Bush administration, they had largely succeeded. A peculiar mixture of prophetic bravado and savvy street-fighting skills allowed them to maneuver their way from the fringes of American society to the White House.

Norman Podhoretz: Intellectual Street-Fighting Man

Perhaps no one has sounded the prophetic note longer or more fervently than the prolific and pugnacious Norman Podhoretz. As the longtime editor of *Commentary*, he probably did more than anyone else to keep the survival of Israel and the plight of Soviet Jews at the forefront of public debate. He was a central figure in the effort to make the defense of the Jews a pillar of American foreign policy in the cold war. Above all, however, he offers a fascinating study in the psychology of the neoconservative movement, with its fevered intellectualism, its immigrant class anxieties, and its intense father-son dynamics.

A half generation younger than Kristol, Podhoretz was distinctly junior to the older Jewish radicals; later, he became an elder to the younger generation. Suiting his in-between status, he also veered from center to left to right during his long career. Podhoretz faithfully reflects the peculiar amalgam of intellectual rigor and ethnic resentment that lies at the heart of the neoconservative outlook. He longed for acceptance and inclusion while making himself all but impossible to embrace. A compulsive truth teller, he was, from the outset, an obvious and self-confessed social climber. His reward was social ostracism. Neither a plotter nor a devious personality nor an ironist like Kristol, he was, and remains, a moralist and a street fighter par excellence. He never tried to mask his immigrant background or his resentment of the WASP establishment and of the assimilated Jews who sought to emulate it. Instead, he wore it as a badge of honor.

Podhoretz was born in 1930 into a lapsed Jewish-Orthodox family. His father, Julius, was a sixty-dollar-a-week mailman. Podhoretz's truculent character can be traced back to his childhood in the 1940s in Brownsville, New York, where he belonged to a gang called Club Cherokee. A group photo shows the diminutive Norman as the only member who refuses to smile.

Podhoretz grew up speaking Yiddish at home. So pronounced was his accent that as a five-year-old entering P.S. 28, which would in 1967 become the center of a Jewish-black confrontation over schooling, he was placed in a remedial English course. Had he not effaced his accent, Podhoretz later wrote, he would never have won scholarships to Columbia and Cambridge University.

The remaking of Podhoretz did not occur overnight. As a high school student, he was molded by his teacher "Mrs. K," who chided him for his slum manners. She took him out for dinner and taught him how to use silverware properly. Her dream was that he would enter Harvard, but Podhoretz attended Columbia. Like other Jewish students who had managed to make it in under the Jewish quota, he worked like a fiend, getting off the subway at 8:00 a.m., heading straight for the library, and studying every minute he could. According to one former professor, "Most of Norman's friends were the sons of New Jersey dentists; at least they looked like the sons of dentists. They had crew cuts, and they talked about 'breaking Keats' and were terribly aggressive and got very good grades . . . I believe Norman wore two-toned shoes, brown and white, and he brought his lunch in a spattered brown paper bag."[5]

Charles Peters, the former editor of the *Washington Monthly,* was a classmate of Podhoretz's. Peters recalled that they were both in a course taught by a tweedy professor named Harrison Ross Steeves:

Since the lures of life in New York often left me less than prepared for the morning's discussion, I sat in the back of the room. Podhoretz sat in the front and was always prepared. He was constantly waving his hand, constantly talking, constantly trying to impress the professor. The problem was that Podhoretz was a Jew from Brooklyn and Steeves was a snobbish old WASP with little patience for the upwardly mobile. However brilliant Podhoretz might be, Steeves would not give him the recognition he so avidly sought.[6]

Podhoretz had the classic Jewish experience with the WASP elite. There were those like Mrs. K who through a sense of noblesse oblige sought to groom and civilize the brash Yiddish-speaking youth. More prevalent, however, was the snobbery of the Columbia English department, where Jews were seen as interlopers. This attitude, which also prevailed on Wall Street and at the State Department, produced a lifelong antipathy toward the patrician class among the neocons and prompted them to create their own parallel establishment.

Fortunately for Podhoretz, Lionel Trilling recognized in him an ambitious and talented young critic, and the two formed a very close bond. It was very much the sort of father-son connection that would characterize the neocon milieu. But Podhoretz would eventually rebel against the Freudian-influenced Trilling, not just once but twice—first from the left, then from the right—in what amounted to a kind of double patricide. It was exciting, made for good fun, and became second nature to Podhoretz. Small wonder that he ended up writing a book called *Ex-Friends*. He had what amounted to a professional talent for alienating his intellectual superiors; it was a way of indulging his colossal ego and attracting some publicity.

Columbia further developed Podhoretz's sense of social exclusion. Sure, he was on the make. But he split the difference between Columbia and his Jewish heritage, studying for a degree in Hebrew literature at the Jewish Theological Seminary. He envied and disliked not only the WASP elite but also the wealthier Jews he encountered at Columbia. The feeling was apparently mutual. In his controversial memoir *Making It*, Podhoretz rhetorically asked,

Is it any wonder that I aroused so much hostility among certain Columbia types: the prep school boys, those B students who rarely said anything in class but who underwent such evident agonies over the unseemly displays of pushiness they had to endure from the likes of me; the homosexuals with their supercilious disdain of my lower-class style of dress and my brash and impudent manner; and the prissily bred middle-class Jews who thought me insufferably rude. All of them were lumped indiscriminately together in my mind as "snobs."[7]

Podhoretz, inasmuch as he was politically inclined, wanted to become a member of the bourgeoisie, not the radical set.

Podhoretz hoped to become a literary critic and write a history of the American novel. From the outset, however, his combative personality prompted him to follow the path of the culture warrior. He lacked Trilling's detachment and exquisitely developed sense of irony. Podhoretz wanted not to loftily observe the fray but to lead the charge against complacency and fashionable liberal thinking.

The turning point came after a visit to England—arranged by Trilling—to study with the critic F. R. Leavis. In 1950 Podhoretz won both a coveted Kellett Fellowship and a Fulbright at Columbia that allowed him to spend three years at Clare College, Cambridge, where he also got to publish in Leavis's magazine, *Scrutiny.* This was to have been the final stage in his finishing process. But rather than adopting the Anglophilia of his elders, Podhoretz rebelled. He was stunned at the hostility of English intellectuals not just to Jews (which he expected) but to the United States itself. It foreshadowed his full-fledged rebellion against the elites in the 1970s, when he became a neoconservative.

Podhoretz went on to serve as a lecturer on democracy and communism in the army in Germany, from 1953 to 1955. Upon his return to New York, Trilling arranged a job for him at *Commentary*, which was edited by Elliot Cohen. It was Trilling's early career all over again. In 1953 Podhoretz made his name as a critic with a blistering attack on Saul Bellow's *The Adventures of Augie March.* The novel had been loudly hailed by the Jewish intellectuals around *Partisan Review*, who embraced it as a rebuke to the WASP professors who had said that Jews could not comprehend, let alone write, English novels. (Bellow himself had been told by the head of the Northwestern English department that Jews could not grasp the subtleties of English literature.) Podhoretz declared that far from surpassing his early novels, Bellow had forfeited discipline and grace in his attempt to infuse English with Yiddish patterns of speech. Bellow was livid. The young novelist on the make had been one-upped by an even younger critic.

Whatever the merits of his argument, Podhoretz showed from the outset that he had an instinct for the jugular and, more important, a knack for self-promotion by going against the grain of tribal opinion. He went on to carry out hit jobs on Bernard Malamud and William Faulkner and deputed Irving Howe, in 1972, to assail and ridicule Philip Roth's oeuvre—an essay so personal and wounding that Roth retaliated by writing a novel (*The Anatomy Lesson*) ridiculing Howe. These were classic New York Family feuds—Podhoretz had discovered and promoted Roth, only to turn on him once he became more successful than his erstwhile editor; Howe and Podhoretz themselves would later break over *Commentary*'s move to the right.

Podhoretz's wife, Midge Decter, is another neoconservative matriarch, and a formidable figure in her own right. Born in St. Paul, Minnesota, in 1927, she chronicled her journey to neoconservatism in *An Old Wife's Tale.* Her parents had met in the Zionist movement. She recalled that as a small child, she had been terrified by listening to radio broadcasts of Hitler's rantings against the Jews. After the war she was so enraged by the Holocaust that "I literally did not know what to do with myself ... You might say I became a concentration-camp junkie." Decter, who had started out as a secretary to Robert Warshow at *Commentary*, left the magazine when she married her first husband, Moshe Decter; after they divorced, she returned as secretary to the editor in chief, Elliot Cohen. Decter did not pull her punches in describing him: "My boss was a manic depressive who would one day land in a hospital and subsequently take his own life, and he was famous in the intellectual world for being impossible to deal with."[8] But like Podhoretz, Decter was overjoyed that *Commentary*, under Cohen, was not interested in indicting the new American suburban life that arose in the postwar era. Besides, it was anticommunist.

Perhaps no passage better conveys the ferocity of Decter's and, by extension, Podhoretz's anticommunism than the following:

> [*Commentary*'s] true animating passion was a deep hatred for Communism in any and all of its manifestations, whether the policies of and the conditions in the Soviet Union or the political and cultural behavior of European and American Communists or the liberal fellow travelers of the Communists or even the liberals whose mind-set had unknowingly been influenced by the Communists.[9]

A year after Podhoretz returned from Germany, in 1956, Decter married him.

Podhoretz displayed his craving for bourgeois respectability when he denounced the Beat generation in a famous article in *Partisan Review* in which he maintained that they were dangerous to family values. Very much in the august Trilling mode, he attacked the freewheeling, improvisational Beat aesthetic as a "conglomeration of attitudes suitable only to the naïve, the callow, the rash: in short, the immature." The Beat poet Allen Ginsberg had been his classmate and chum at Columbia, and Podhoretz later wrote touchingly of their friendship in his volume of remembrances *Ex-Friends*. Yet it is revealing that although Podhoretz attacked Ginsberg, he always expected somehow to remain on good terms with him and blamed the demise of their relationship on Ginsberg's extreme sensitivity.

The contrast with a Tory conservative such as William F. Buckley Jr. is striking. Buckley didn't have ex-friends. He never saw political differences as tantamount to personal betrayal. He was best friends, for example, with the legendary journalist Murray Kempton, who was at the other end of the political pole. This is not necessarily to Podhoretz's discredit. There is something to be said for the almost willful, naive ferocity of his political passions. But ultimately, they ended up being intellectually stultifying.

In short, Podhoretz, longer on fulminating language than on insight, was a true prophetic type. Throughout his political peregrinations his basic personality and modus operandi remained the same: he was a warrior who could never, in all innocence, understand why his critical insights were rewarded with ostracism rather than praise. Yet in such opposition he also found not cause for self-doubt but confirmation of his righteousness. Indeed, the more universally he was contradicted, the more unanimous his critics, the more confident he felt of his position. In this unfailing certainty of being always right—no matter how many times he changed his own views over the years—he was perhaps the quintessential neocon.

———

In 1959 Elliot Cohen, convinced that he was being stalked by communists and suffering from depression, committed suicide. After several candidates, including Daniel Bell, turned down the job, Podhoretz accepted the American Jewish Committee's offer to become editor of *Commentary*, a post he would not relinquish until 1995. He was thirty years old. The magazine would be his private Sinai, where he would rail against his foes on left and right.

Podhoretz started out in Trilling's mold as a centrist defender of bourgeois values. But in the early 1960s he moved sharply to the left. Indeed, it should be remembered that Podhoretz helped to shape the 1960s counterculture—before he turned against it. Why?

For one thing, Podhoretz saw his friend Norman Mailer continuing to make waves. Mailer, fiery, coruscating, and brilliantly inventive, was getting all the ink. Podhoretz had been promised by Trilling that he would be the leader of his generation. Instead, he looked like a fuddy-duddy. But it was also a rebellion against Cohen, who had been an editorial tyrant, and Trilling, who was a father figure. Podhoretz promptly moved left, breaking with both Cohen's anticommunism and Trilling's condemnations of the "adversary culture." To Podhoretz, they were the adversaries.

Podhoretz's impulse, whether on the left or the right, was to scold, hector, and denounce. But it's also the case that his shift was based on a shrewd assessment that American culture was moving left. Podhoretz liked to think of himself as speaking inconvenient truths, but he had an astute feel for politics and culture. His later move back to the right was just as timely as his earlier shift to the left.

Podhoretz made no secret of his intentions once he became editor of *Commentary.* The uncompromising moralism of the New Left appealed to his own prophetic instincts. According to Podhoretz, "This left movement will be a moral criticism of all existing social institutions." Podhoretz courted it with zeal, publishing Paul Goodman, Norman O. Brown, George McGovern, and Richard N. Goodwin as well as extensive criticisms of American foreign policy. In essence, he helped develop the left-wing critique of American imperialism as being culpable for the cold war. Soon it would come into vogue, when the Vietnam War became a fiasco. In the eyes of the left, America, not the Soviet Union, was the international bad guy. Perhaps one of Podhoretz's most amusing effusions from this time, in light of his later support for George W. Bush, was his declaration in a *Partisan Review* symposium that "Kennedy makes himself more and more vulnerable by pretending that he is indomitably holding the line instead of explaining that he is trying to effect a series of necessary strategic retreats."[10]

Podhoretz helped set the stage for what became a more general cultural shift. He was, you might say, promoting anti-Americanism. He was repudiating everything that Elliot Cohen had stood for. By 1967 John Leo could report in the *New York Times* that "some American historians and other intellectuals are rewriting the history of the cold war, assigning much if not all of the blame to the United States."[11] Indeed they were. The truth was that Stalin, not Stalin and Harry Truman, had divided Europe. The United States was pulling its troops out of Western Europe, while Stalin was setting up puppet regimes in the east.

No matter. Some revisionists blamed Harry Truman for frightening Stalin; others went all the way back to Franklin Roosevelt. The United States should have been more accommodating. FDR should have made clear to Stalin that he could do whatever he wanted. Even the dropping of the atomic bomb, wrote the cold war revisionist Gar Alperovitz, was carried out not to end the war against Japan but as a move to intimidate Russia with America's nuclear monopoly. It was the precursor of the "blame America first" movement led by George McGovern, which exhorted America to "come home" from its foreign misadventures.

At the same time, Israel seemed to provide an example of martial valor, for which it suddenly came under vicious attack by the very forces that Podhoretz had been clamorously supporting. As the New Left began increasingly to denounce and demonize the Jewish state, Podhoretz began his move to the right.

Podhoretz has mythologized his turn to the right as the result of a purely intellectual process, but there were other, more personal reasons. A series of blows from the left and from people he considered his friends drove him out of the New Left, and finally out of polite intellectual circles altogether. With the publication of *Making It*, a brutally honest exposé of his own ambition, vanity, and careerism, he embarrassed his acquaintances, friends, and mentors—including Trilling, who had advised him not to publish it. Roger Straus, publisher of Farrar, Straus and Giroux, which had paid Podhoretz an advance of twenty-five thousand dollars, refused to print it. When it appeared in 1967 under the Random House imprint, the autobiography was too revealing for the establishment. It was trashed by Norman Mailer and by the *New York Review of Books* and other publications as vulgar, grasping, and undignified.

All of which was true, but sort of beside the point. It was like criticizing Lenny Bruce for using bad words. There was a raw, febrile energy to Podhoretz's book, which has since become a classic. In many ways it was the precursor of the confessional autobiography that has become a staple of modern culture. Podhoretz had produced a true Bildungsroman, except that it wasn't fiction. This latter-day Julien Sorel ventilated his social anxieties, his desperation to enter the New York intellectual "family," his pushiness, his contempt for his snobby classmates—including, of course, those "prissily bred middle-class Jews"—and his zeal for success. What was wrong with that? Podhoretz never published anything as good again, even though he essentially rewrote *Making It* in multiple successor autobiographies. *Making It* unmade and made him. He was history with the Family, but the Family itself was also becoming history. Liberated from it, Podhoretz was now free to put another finger to the wind and tack rightward.

Like many in his generation, Podhoretz was also driven rightward by the response of the left to Israel's problems in the Middle East. Until the 1960s many Jewish intellectuals viewed Israel as something of an anachronism, a relic of Europe's nationalistic past. Zionism was about the furthest thing that Hannah Arendt, for example, wanted to be associated with in any shape or form. She thought of herself as a cosmopolitan intellectual who was free from the atavistic tribal claims of the past. Trilling, too, had an ambiguous relationship with what would today be called his Jewish identity—his generation's concern, he said, "with Jewishness was about what is now called authenticity."[12]

But after the Jewish state's lightning victory in 1967, many Jewish intellectuals embraced Israel, while at the same time Israel suddenly became suspect in the eyes of the left. Formerly looked upon as a shining socialist experiment, it was now considered impolite to defend the "oppressor" and "occupier" of the Palestinian Arabs. For Podhoretz, who credits his awakening to Jewish issues to the Eichmann trial in 1961, the sudden antipathy of leading intellectuals to Israel was key. It was also a pivotal moment in the emergence of the neoconservative movement. As Podhoretz put it, "I think that Jews must once again begin to look at proposals and policies from the point of view of Jewish interest, and must once again begin to ask what the consequences, if any, of any proposal or policy are likely to be as far as the Jewish issue is concerned."[13]

The 1967 War and the Neoconservative Movement

While Harry Truman had audaciously taken the first step toward creating ties between Israel and the United States, his immediate successors tended to be more cautious than him. In retrospect, Truman's decision may be seen as one of the most important moments in the onset of the cold war. Truman's advisers were fervently opposed to recognizing Israel—and Truman, in the end, ignored them.

The neoconservative hatred of the foreign policy establishment is fueled partly by the memory of its opposition. Truman himself was as suspicious of the State Department as George W. Bush and the neoconservatives would be decades later. After the State Department allowed the American delegation to the UN to reverse its support for partitioning Palestine and to support a trusteeship, Truman wrote in March 1948: "The State Dept. pulled the rug from under me today . . . The first I know about it is what I see in the papers! Isn't that hell? . . .

There are people on the third and fourth level of the State Dept. who have always wanted to cut my throat." Truman overrode the State Department realists and boldly acknowledged the new state of Israel.

Still, today's close ties between Israel and the United States took decades to develop. With Dwight Eisenhower, relations, such as they were, had a distinctly frosty edge. Eisenhower undercut Britain, France, and Israel in 1956, turning their confrontation with Egypt over its nationalization of the Suez Canal into an international crisis. A good case can be made that toppling the Egyptian president, Gamal Abdel Nasser, from power at this time would have set the Middle East on a more democratic path. But it never happened. Eisenhower was enraged by what he saw as another instance of British imperialism. Perhaps it was also connected to the battles he had with the British during World War II over military strategy, when Eisenhower refused to race for Berlin or take any other measures to forestall Soviet gains after World War II.

What's more, Eisenhower had no patience for sentimental ideas about the importance of the Jewish state. He took the traditional realist view of Israel as an impediment to smooth relations with the Arab nations. "I gave strict orders to the State Department," he said, "that they should inform Israel that we would handle our affairs exactly as though we didn't have a Jew in America." The admonition to the State Department was, of course, superfluous.

John F. Kennedy was not initially captivated by the idea of closer relations with Israel. It was Nasser he wanted to appease, to keep him out of the arms of the Soviets. Kennedy wooed Nasser, but for naught. Nasser's 1962 invasion of Yemen threatened America's interest in Saudi stability, and the use of chemical weaponry and attacks on Saudi outposts by Nasser's forces did not go down well at the White House. In 1962 Kennedy began to supply Israel with HAWK missiles, which no non-NATO country had yet received. It was the beginning of what would evolve into one of America's closest alliances, involving diplomatic support and trillions of dollars in loans and military aid, to the fury of the Arab states, which saw Israel as an illegitimate, occupying force.

Whereas Kennedy supported Israel because he perceived close ties to be in America's strategic interest, Johnson followed more in the romantic Woodrow Wilson mold. After the Six-Day War in 1967, the Soviet premier, Alexei Kosygin, asked why the United States had sided with Israel rather than the Arab states. "Because it's right," Johnson reportedly replied.[14] Nevertheless, the foreign policy establishment loathed the idea of Israel and felt free to express it, whether it was George W. Ball fulminating about Jewish influence in Congress or George F. Kennan worrying about so-called ethnic lobbies. In 1967 Lyndon Johnson's hard-line adviser John P. Roche stated in a memo to the president:

> Reading the State Department's Staff Summary today, I was appalled to realize that there is real underground sentiment for kissing some Arab backsides ... The net consequence of trying to "sweet-talk" the Arabs is that they have contempt for us ... Which brings us back to the question once (perhaps erroneously) attributed to you: "Whose State Department is it?"[15]

It was a question the neocons would ask many times over the years, as they accused the State Department again and again—with considerable justice—of truckling to the worst despots in the Middle East. This is a deeply ingrained attitude among neoconservatives, surfacing once more in the wake of the Iraq war.

The war against the "WASP patriciate," as Norman Podhoretz liked to call it, really took off after the Six-Day War. The shock, and the heady flush of victory, that the war engendered among American Jews can hardly be exaggerated. It also gave the first real impetus to the birth of the modern neoconservative movement.

In May 1967 Egypt began massing forces in the Sinai desert and cut off Israel's access to the Suez Canal. Jordan had already placed its army under Egyptian command in 1966. On June 5, 1967, Israel launched a preemptive strike on Egypt and captured the Sinai and the Gaza Strip. Though Israel appealed to Jordan to remain neutral, Jordan quickly attacked; in a devastating counterattack, Israel took control of the West Bank and the eastern sector of Jerusalem. Israel also went on to capture the Golan Heights from Syria. The war ended on June 10. On September 24, Prime Minister Levi Eshkol announced plans for defensive settlements on the West Bank.

It was the beginning of a new relationship not only with Israel's Middle East adversaries but also with the United States—partly a result of renewed Jewish self-confidence: twenty-seven national Jewish organizations signed a statement declaring, "We vow that the victories won on the battlefield shall not be lost at the table of diplomacy." Yet criticism of Israel now came from the left—mainly from black radicals, whom Jewish liberals had tried to befriend. Podhoretz had published articles by James Baldwin and in 1963 had written a searing essay in *Commentary* ("My Negro Problem—and Ours") that laid bare white fear of blacks. Now Podhoretz's confession, which caused a furor at the time, came to seem mild.

The New Left and the black radicals were on the same page. In August 1967, for example, the Student Nonviolent Coordinating Committee charged that Zionism was racism. In its bimonthly bulletin, the SNCC came down on the side of the Arab states. It was "the Zionists" who had conquered Arab homes and land through force, terror, and massacres to create a bogus state called Israel. The editorial went on to say that the "famous European Jews, the Rothschilds, who have long controlled the wealth of many European nations, were involved in the original conspiracy with the British to create the 'state of Israel' and are still among Israel's chief supporters." H. Rap Brown, the national chairman of the SNCC, who was arrested in New York for carrying a semiautomatic carbine on an airplane flight from New York to New Orleans, stated, "We just don't think Zionist leaders in Israel have a right to that land."[16]

This kind of talk, implicitly equating Israel with the Nazis, horrified the Jewish intellectuals. It also fed their private view that the black radicals were mentally unstable. It was Saul Bellow, a kind of fellow traveler of the neoconservative movement, who would capture the anxieties of many Jews in his novel *Mr. Sammler's Planet*, in which an elderly Jewish survivor of the Holocaust now living in decaying 1960s New York is humiliated by a hulking, elegantly dressed black pickpocket who slowly unzips his pants and flashes his enormous member at a cowering Mr. Sammler. The message is clear: Sammler may have survived the Holocaust in Poland, but he has become even more vulnerable to the hostility of blacks in New York.

In 1968 Jewish-black relations suffered another blow during the New York teachers' strike. The Ford Foundation, under the leadership of McGeorge Bundy, wanted to carry out an experiment in local control over schools in the Brooklyn district of Ocean Hill–Brownsville. The result was that black radicals attacked Jewish teachers, calling them "Middle East murderers of colored people," and tried to kick them out of the schools. Just as Bundy had messed up in Vietnam, so this arch liberal helped bring about the neoconservative backlash domestically as well. Bundy, a Boston Brahmin, had been an aide to Secretary of War Henry Stimson, a dean of Harvard, even though he never earned a Ph.D., and national security adviser to John F. Kennedy. He had championed the Vietnam War, only to turn on it once Lyndon B. Johnson elected not to run again for president. Bundy became a prominent dove, arguing that the United States needed to reach arms-control agreements with the Soviets and pressure Israel to reach a peace agreement with the Palestinians. Together with his brother William, Bundy, famed for his arrogance and Brahmin accent, epitomized everything that the neoconservatives despised. The neocons concluded that it was their job to maintain the anticommunist crusade that the pallid establishment had jettisoned in order to curry favor with fashionable opinion on the left.

The crumbling of the establishment and the breakup of the civil rights alliance unnerved the Jewish intellectuals. For the neoconservatives, it was the origin of the themes that would dominate the culture war of the 1980s and 1990s—merit, the canon, affirmative action, black separatism, and the rejection of Western culture as inherently racist, corrupt, and imperialist. It was in the defense of the Western tradition that the neocons became true conservatives. It wouldn't necessarily have been their preference to play this role. But the WASP patriciate, led by such worthies as Kingman Brewster, a close friend of McGeorge Bundy's and a descendant of Elder William Brewster, the spiritual head of the *Mayflower*, at institutions such as Yale had collapsed in the face of the student radicals. The once manly establishment had become unmanned.

Brewster, like many in the liberal establishment, was actually a liberal Republican rather than a Democrat. But under the intense pressure of the Students for a Democratic Society and other radicals, he had flipped on Vietnam. Indeed, Richard Nixon, meeting with the shah of Iran in the early 1970s, would commiserate with him about the follies of student demonstrators and specifically condemn Brewster as a sign of how the liberal establishment had turned tail on Vietnam: "What can we expect of students," Nixon said, "if a person in that position and of that stature engages in such acts?" Henry Kissinger suggested that if the United States would benefit from the assassination of any public figure, it would be Brewster.[17] As usual, Nixon and Kissinger were venting.

But the deeper issue looming behind the culture wars was the fate of liberalism itself. America had defeated Nazism and was the only bulwark against Soviet totalitarianism. If American liberalism collapsed in a Weimar-style conflagration, what would become of the Jews?

The Assault on the Universities

On April 20, 1969, eighty members of the Afro-American Society (AAS) marched out of Cornell University's Willard Straight Hall with their fists raised in Black Power salutes. The students held up rifles, while the AAS minister of defense wore a bandolier of bullets across his chest. As the day wore on, the AAS, the Students for a Democratic Society, and several radical faculty members declared that they would seize other buildings.

Cornell had gone to great lengths to recruit black students from inner cities, but black nationalism, not integration, was what many of them espoused. Cornell had experienced numerous disruptions in the past year, including the beatings of three white students on campus—one of whom, suffering brain damage, almost died—and the roughing up by black students of President James Perkins at a conference on South Africa.

The Cornell faculty initially vetoed making any concessions to the Afro-American Society. As the standoff continued, the faculty split into two factions. One, led by President Perkins, wanted to reach an agreement with the students. The other, filled mostly with members of the creed that would come to be known, or reviled, as Straussianism, did not. For the professors Allan Bloom, Walter Berns, and Werner J. Dannhauser and their students, the idea of treating with the protesting students was tantamount to appeasement. They wanted to face down the rebellious students. Ultimately, they had a heroic conception of history with themselves in a Churchillian role.

Donald Kagan, a professor of classics at Cornell who vehemently disagreed with the Straussians about the nature of political science, nonetheless saw eye to eye with Bloom on the issue of radicalism. He later told me that during the events at Cornell, he understood for the first time how the Nazis could have come to power through mob violence. Bloom himself declared that the Cornell student uprising was nothing less than a repetition of the ominous events that took place in Weimar Germany, when the liberals had yielded to the threats and intimidation of the Nazis. In his words, it was "an entirely new thing in American universities, a complete capitulation under threat of firearms to a group of students who have a program for transformation of the university." Indeed, "the resemblance on all levels to the first stages of a totalitarian take-over are almost unbelievable."[18]

This wasn't really a totalitarian takeover, much as Bloom might have wished it were, so much as a short-lived (and dangerous) ebullition of hatred from black radicals. The bandolier-wearing leader of the Cornell rebellion, Thomas Jones, would end up as a prosperous Wall Street pension fund manager. The neoconservatives, by contrast, never left the claustrophobic mental world that they began to inhabit in the 1960s.

The importance of the radical attack on the universities for the neoconservatives cannot be exaggerated. For striving Jewish immigrants, the universities had represented an oasis. Kristol, Podhoretz, and the new Straussian camp were enraged by the New Left's antics at Columbia, Cornell, Berkeley, Harvard, and elsewhere. So were traditional social democrats like Daniel Bell. The demands of black radicals for race-based affirmative action came as a particular shock. The Jews had experienced a Jewish quota; were the blacks now, perversely, to insist on a special quota for themselves? Was merit to be supplanted by skin color?

As Jews, they felt personally menaced by these developments, which therefore served to unify them despite their differences. Nathan Glazer attacked the Berkeley Free Speech Movement, which would be the source of the student uprisings in coming years. Students at Berkeley, a number of whom had participated in the civil rights marches in the South, protested new restrictions on political activism on campus. In December 1964 they took over the administration building, and several hundred were arrested. It was the beginning of a protest against American society itself for its conformism and banality. Glazer denounced the New Left, declaring, "Anti-Semitism is only a part of this whole syndrome, for if the members of the middle class do not deserve to hold on to their property, their positions, or even their lives, then certainly the Jews, the most middle-class of all, are going to be placed at the head of the column marked for liquidation."[19] This is an extraordinary passage, invoking, as it does, the fear of Jews being stripped of their possessions, herded into ghettos, and shipped off to concentration camps.

Of course, the Jews were never in such danger. More to the point, perhaps, the old leftists felt insulted by the rebuff they received from their juniors. (This was particularly true of Irving Howe, who felt that the young radicals should have adhered to the socialist faith he tried to uphold.) But it was precisely the fear of a new liberal Weimar that was invoked most fervently by the Straussians. They were led by Allan Bloom, the political theorist from Cornell who would achieve fame with his best seller, *The Closing of the American Mind*, which mainstreamed Straussian warnings about the dangers of popular culture and relativism. Bloom would be affectionately depicted after his death by Saul Bellow in the novella *Ravelstein*, which came closest to capturing the wacky and endearing combination of frivolity and intellectual intensity, hedonism and earnestness that characterized Bloom. It was Bellow who had pushed him to write *The Closing of the American Mind*, signed him up with his literary agent, and wrote the foreword. One witty reviewer even surmised that Bloom was a fictional creation of Bellow's altogether. But Bloom was an American original, very much the author of his own larger-than-life personality.

Bloom was a precociously intellectual Midwestern Jewish kid who entered the University of Chicago at age fifteen, studied with Strauss, and earned his Ph.D. at the Committee on Social Thought in 1955. In 1961 he traipsed into Cornell with several acolytes from Yale, where he had been teaching. Bloom was a mesmerizing figure for the students at Telluride House, where he served as tutor. He seemed, to impressionable young minds, to be a Socrates come to life. Bloom lived beyond his means, buying expensive furniture and clothes. All his life he loved extravagant gestures, which he could afford only toward the end of it. One of his students purchased his rare silverware to keep him afloat, a transaction that appears in *Ravelstein.*

Bloom himself was an acolyte of Strauss, the man he and many others regarded as the virtual reincarnation of Socrates. Like Trotsky, Strauss was a Jew, a polymath, and a refugee. After a rigorous training in philosophy, including a period of study with Martin Heidegger, Strauss fled Nazi Germany for England, then immigrated in 1938 to the United States, where he taught political philosophy, first at the New School, then at the University of Chicago. Also like Trotsky, he gathered around him a fiercely protective circle of protégés. Many of these went on to become, or profoundly influence, several generations of neoconservatives.

Any mention of Strauss's name today in connection with neoconservatism often brings agonized howls from neoconservatives. There are two reasons for this. The first is that some of his disciples are apolitical and are genuinely puzzled that he would be linked to an overtly political movement. (The philosopher Stanley Rosen, one of Strauss's most distinguished students, dedicates a recent book to "the genuine Leo Strauss." Moreover, several books, including Catherine and Michael Zuckert's *The Truth About Leo Strauss*, seek to dispel the notion that Strauss was a progenitor of neoconservatism and, by extension, responsible for the Iraq war.[20]) The second reason is that a good deal of nonsense has appeared about him, beginning with a pamphlet distributed by the cult leader Lyndon LaRouche called "Children of Satan," portraying Strauss as an evil mastermind. Strauss's disciples conveniently seize upon these outré claims to argue that invoking his name is a sign of paranoia and latent anti-Semitism. This is clearly not the case. While Strauss has been wrongly used to tar the neoconservative movement as deceptive and dishonest, his influence on the movement is clear.

Strauss had nothing but disdain for most members of the political science department at the University of Chicago. He would mock them in his lectures. He loathed the abstract social science they practiced, which was devoid of values and morality, relying instead on polling data and behavioral studies. Strauss offered something different. Hired at the University of Chicago on the basis of a single interview with Robert Maynard Hutchins, who shared his passion for the classics, Strauss wanted his students to return to the great books. Strauss's students were supposed to shun commentaries. They weren't supposed to read the original works; they were adjured to decipher them—to read them, word by word, line by line, as the rabbinic sages had studied the Talmud. For some, this hermeneutical approach was liberating; others were permanently crippled by it.

Strauss was not an imposing presence physically, but he was a captivating lecturer. His American students had never seen anything like it. This Germanic sage would enter the classroom with only the primary texts in the original language—Greek, Latin, French, German. He would talk as long as he wanted to—some lectures went on for four hours—pausing only to take a drag on a cigarette. He needed no notes. But many of his lectures were taped, transcribed, and then passed around in binders that only the initiated were permitted to read.

Strauss believed that he had rediscovered the ancient art of esoteric writing and that the classic texts by the greatest philosophers did not really say what they seemed to be saying. To unlock their true teachings, one had to possess the secret key. Strauss believed, for example, that the numbers in Machiavelli's work had an esoteric significance. Some of Strauss's students believed the same of him. They believed that he, too, had a secret teaching. Some of them counted the number of paragraphs in his books to see if that might not reveal a secret.

Strauss himself intimated to his students that he had discovered the key to the highest form of knowledge and that as his disciples they would become part of an elect that included the greatest minds in human history. He made his students feel important, separate from and superior to their coevals. He told them, "It is not self-forgetting and pain-loving antiquarianism nor self-forgetting and intoxicating romanticism which induces us to turn with passionate interest, with unqualified willingness to learn, toward the political thought of classical antiquity. We are impelled to do so by the crisis of our time, the crisis of the West."[21]

Strauss (intentionally or otherwise) propagated the idea of an elite that could guide the vulgar multitude; he apparently regarded religion as a delusion, but a healthy one that had to be outwardly respected, lest society dissolve into relativism and anarchy; and he seems to have doubted that liberalism, and liberals, had sufficient resolve and will to stand up to totalitarian forces.

For both Irving Kristol and Gertrude Himmelfarb, who had already been bashing away at liberals during their Trotskyist phase, Strauss was a major influence. The pair had listened to his lectures at the New School in New York and been deeply impressed. As early as 1951, Himmelfarb wrote in *Commentary* that Strauss was "perhaps the wisest and most penetrating among contemporary political philosophers." Milton Himmelfarb agreed. Decades later, writing in *Commentary*, he declared that Strauss "may even regard himself as not altogether inferior to Socrates—Socrates!—the founder of classical teachings." Strauss played an even bigger role for the next generation. As William Kristol, who studied with the Straussian Harvey C. Mansfield at Harvard, has written, "Strauss, chiefly by way of his students, is in large part responsible for making the thought and principles of America's founders a source of political knowledge and appeal, and for making political excellence more broadly a subject of appreciation and appeal."[22] A legion of other students and admirers, ranging from Paul Wolfowitz to Francis Fukuyama, have picked up and amplified the master's teachings.

Now, it can be argued, as Mark Lilla has done in a perceptive essay in the *New York Review of Books*, that Strauss himself was not a Straussian and that his students drew lessons from him that he never meant to instill. Nor is every neoconservative a Straussian (though it seems safe to say that most Straussians are neoconservatives). But whether he intended it or not, Strauss had a huge impact on the neoconservative movement. His most basic achievement was to prompt many of his followers to take a second look at the United States. It's not necessary to call Strauss a fascist to see that his outlook was deeply conservative, even premodern, which is why his thought has appealed to conservative Catholics. When I met William F. Buckley Jr. for lunch at the New York Yacht Club, he was startled and flattered to learn that the only magazine Strauss subscribed to had been *National Review.* (But was he a "clubbable" person? Buckley wondered.)

The affinity was not accidental, and it presaged the later rapprochement between neocons and traditional conservatives. Just as *National Review* tried to stand athwart history, as Buckley's famous phrase had it, so did Strauss. It wasn't an easy task. In the postwar era, liberal America was exuberant, boisterous, confident of its new prowess to set wrongs aright at home and abroad. Strauss was wary of the claims of modern, American-style liberalism to have ushered in a new age of Enlightenment. His aim was nothing less than to revive the study of classical philosophy to rally the West against the threat posed by totalitarianism. Strauss was, he once boasted, training "princes." In reality, he was helping to midwife the neoconservative movement.

Writing in the *New York Review of Books* in May 1985, the British scholar Miles Burnyeat alluded to the political implications of Strauss "anti-idealist" thought, particularly for the Reagan administration. Several Straussians, including Allan Bloom, responded rather hysterically in a series of letters; according to Bloom, "Burnyeat's attempt to wake a sleeping America to the political threat posed to it by the late Leo Strauss is McCarthyite in the precise sense of the term."

Despite the overheated accusations that Strauss was some kind of crypto-fascist coming from less-sober quarters, aired at length by a Canadian academic named Shadia Drury and then ventilated by the *New York Times*'s Brent Staples in a 1994 op-ed piece, he was nothing of the kind. Instead, he was a German mandarin. German professors enjoyed, and continue to enjoy, a status that would be unthinkable for their American counterparts. The title "Herr Professor Doktor" continues to carry great weight in a society where professors are reverentially treated. It was also the case that in the nineteenth century, Germany experienced a craze for the classical world. The art historian Johann Joachim Winckelmann was a prominent promoter of philhellenism, which set out Greek art as the acme of Western civilization. The German *Gymnasium* sought to re-create the philhellene ethos; German art, poetry, and plays all looked back to the ancient world as a model and source of inspiration. This mania for all things Greek was satirized by the German composer Albert Lortzing in his popular opera *Der Wildschütz,* whose bluestocking countess is a fervent admirer of ancient Greek drama and constantly recites Greek quotations.

Strauss, who was born on September 20, 1899, in a small rural town in Germany called Kirchhain, attended a *Gymnasium*, where he learned Greek and Latin as a little boy. As a university student, he was a follower of the right-wing Zionist Vladimir Jabotinsky, who argued that Theodor Herzl's vision of a peaceful Israel with Jews and Arabs working side by side was a pipe dream. It was a stance Strauss would never jettison. In 1957, for example, he remonstrated with the editors of *National Review* for their antagonistic stand toward the Jewish state. It was "incomprehensible," he wrote, that the editors did not recognize that Israel was an outpost of the West surrounded by mortal enemies. What's more, Israel was fundamentally a conservative project—"heroic austerity supported by the nearness of biblical antiquity." It would be hard to think of a more succinct summation of the neoconservative view of Israel.

As a refugee from Germany, Strauss was acutely aware of the role that Israel played for the Jews as a haven and inspiration. But the rise of the Nazis also instilled in him a deep suspicion of nominal liberals. Strauss's experiences in Weimar Germany bred in him an antipathy toward what he viewed as weak-kneed liberals. Strauss may have preached that thinkers were timeless, but he himself was deeply shaped by his own era. In the 1920s, Strauss had not been immune to the idea of German spiritual rebirth espoused by the thinkers of the so-called German conservative revolution. These thinkers were not Nazis, but conservative nationalists who believed in charismatic leadership. According to Eugene R. Sheppard, "notable circles around Stefan George and Martin Heidegger, as well as the Jewish examples of Alfred Nobel, Martin Buber, and Franz Rosenzweig—all rejected liberal models of education in favor of the pedagogical principle of the charismatic leader . . . These circles represent the models under which Strauss' conservative elitism developed and that he would reestablish in the United States."[23] Strauss thus had a tortured relationship with liberalism. He wasn't opposed to it; he wanted to save it; but he didn't trust it. It wasn't just the rise of Nazism, two world wars, the Holocaust, Stalin's terror, and the refusal of the democracies to stand up to Hitler. The betrayal of liberalism was also very personal: Strauss, a onetime admirer of Heidegger, was stunned by his infamous rector's address at the University of Freiburg in 1933, which was delivered on German Armistice Day. Heidegger essentially hailed Hitler and the rise of Nazism as the fruition of his own philosophical ideas. This was (among other things) wrong, ahistorical, and an act of incredible vanity. Strauss was shocked. In the 1960s Strauss's students, most notably Allan Bloom, would feel that a second *Rektoratsrede* had taken place at Cornell.

Strauss's dubiety about liberal democracy was rooted in his distrust of modern intellectuals. Like many conservatives, from Burke to Buckley, he was contemptuous of rationalist "projectors" who would upend society to achieve their insane dreams. Intellectuals were utopians, and Strauss reinterpreted Plato as their enemy. Strauss reversed traditional interpretations of Plato. He said that the dialogues were dramas and opened the field to subversive understandings that only a philosophical elite, guided by Strauss, could comprehend. His students would understand Plato, and other philosophers, as they had understood themselves.

For this, Strauss and his students were shunned by their profession and denounced in the popular press as elitist and antidemocratic. The first charge is quite true, but the second needs a more careful interpretation. Strauss's own political opinions are notoriously hard to discern, and were perhaps deliberately obscured; but if he was not a democrat in the modern sense, he certainly understood that democratic regimes were the best hope for the revival of classical philosophy he hoped to bring about. Yet he was skeptical of the ability of the majority of citizens to rise above the intellectual idols of their time and commune with the greatest philosophers.

The Straussians had a sense of persecution. Hadn't Strauss said that the ancient philosophers had written in a kind of secret code because of the dangerous character of their teachings? Hadn't Socrates been condemned to drink hemlock by the democratic mob of ancient Athens? The neoconservatives took this lesson and ran with it. They, too, saw themselves as an elect. Once again, as in the Shachtman days, they were superior to the common herd. Most intellectuals were going one way, the Straussians, a small, defiant band, in another.

While the neoconservatives have been assailed as Trotskyist-Straussians, the gibe isn't quite right. The two clans, Straussian and neoconservative, overlap at many points but are not by any means identical. Allan Bloom was close to Irving Kristol, but not until he had become a millionaire. (When I visited Bloom at the University of Chicago shortly before his death, he said that his relationship with Kristol had become "easier" once he, like Kristol, was wealthy.) Like

Kristol, Bloom was a kind of impresario who oversaw the advance of the Straussian project. The first generation that studied under Strauss himself became academics. The second generation took a different route. Many of Bloom's own students went into politics: Paul Wolfowitz, Francis Fukuyama, Abram Shulsky, Charles Fairbanks, Alan Keyes, and Kenneth Weinstein, among others, all ended up in Washington. A Straussian reading group still meets in Washington.

Weinstein recalls that being a student of Bloom's was like "orbiting the sun." A mercurial personality, Bloom ran a kind of court in which students could be suddenly banished from favor. His students tried to model themselves on him, to the point of wearing Turnbull and Asser shirts and squeaky black leather shoes. Bloom cared a great deal about his students and went to extraordinary lengths to train and guide them. He found jobs for them, screened their friends, and, in some cases, played matchmaker. Like Abe Ravelstein, he "formed" and "indoctrinated" his students. As Bellow wrote:

> Abe's "people" in Washington kept his telephone line so busy that I said he must be masterminding a shadow government. He accepted this, smiling as though the oddity were not his but mine. He said, "All these students I've trained in the last thirty years still turn to me, and in a way the telephone makes possible an ongoing seminar in which the policy questions they deal with in day-to-day Washington are aligned with the Plato they studied two or three decades ago, or Locke, or Rousseau, or even Nietzsche."

Were they really thinking of Locke or Rousseau or Nietzsche? Perhaps. But another influence helped ground Wolfowitz and others in the day-to-day struggles over policy questions that staring into the Nietzschean abyss might not answer. That influence was exercised by a leading strategic thinker who was also a raconteur, gourmand, and dancer: Albert Wohlstetter.

Albert Wohlstetter and the Cold War

Albert Wohlstetter was the progenitor of what came to be called the defense intellectual. He was also—without really meaning to be—one of the intellectual founders of the neoconservative movement.

Though they taught for many years at the same university, Wohlstetter probably had only a vague notion of Strauss and an even vaguer one of neoconservatism. Indeed, it is one of the movement's many ironies that it is a misnomer to call several of its founding fathers neoconservatives. But Wohlstetter knew many neoconservatives, such as Norman Podhoretz and Midge Decter. He was a friend of Meyer Schapiro and Sidney Hook, beginning in the 1930s. He seemed to know almost everybody who was anyone, whether it was the jazz artist Billy Strayhorn or Henry Kissinger. He was a mentor of Richard Perle's and a close adviser to Senator Henry M. Jackson. And he, too, was an outsize, prophetic personality. Together with his wife, Roberta, a noted historian who won the Bancroft Prize for her study of American unpreparedness at Pearl Harbor, he played a big part in the cold war debates over American defense policy. Both highlighted the importance of assessing vulnerability to military threats. Their critics—anticipating later attacks on the neoconservatives— would accuse them of engaging in threat inflation.

Unlike many neocons, Wohlstetter was relentlessly upbeat. He was no brooding émigré from Germany who scented the decline of the West around every corner and viewed democracy itself with apprehension. Instead, he was a bon vivant-cum-nuclear strategist who believed almost as fervently in finding a great restaurant as he did in establishing U.S. tactical superiority. While Strauss's political beliefs can be difficult to pin down, as befits his rather evasive philosophical nature, the same can hardly be said of Wohlstetter. With him, there were no hidden depths. On the contrary, he radiated self-confidence, opinions, obiter dicta, sweeping away any and all objections almost before they had been voiced.

Wohlstetter, who was a kind of brilliant dilettante, too erratic and willful and self-indulgent to subordinate himself to a superior official, never occupied a government position, but his protégés, who include Paul Wolfowitz, Richard Perle, Ahmed Chalabi, and Zalmay Khalilzad, did. The cold war was fought on Wohlstetter's turf, which is to say that he almost single-handedly pushed for a ballistic missile defense system in the 1960s and savaged liberal illusions about Soviet military policies in the early 1970s. His influence on his acolytes cannot be exaggerated: Perle aped his mentor to the extent of becoming a gourmand himself.

Wohlstetter, who was born on December 19, 1913, grew up in New York. His father was a German immigrant, a lawyer, and, finally, a manufacturer of records and gramophones who went bankrupt because of hostility to Germans during World War I—a fact that would always predispose Albert toward defending embattled minorities, whether it was Japanese-Americans during World War II or Bosnians in the 1990s. His family retained its Central European roots: "We dined very late and the meals were very elaborate, and very Viennese." He had both an artistic and a scientific bent. As a teenager, Wohlstetter was always thinking in terms of numbers: "I would ... approach a girl on the theory that I would be turned down most of the time but, statistically ... the absolute numbers might be all right."[24]

During the Great Depression, Wohlstetter studied mathematics at the City College of New York. He also assisted Meyer Schapiro and worked as a reporter for the Park Row News Service as well as tutoring wealthy children headed to Hotchkiss. Wohlstetter met his wife, Roberta, in the mid-1930s, during a yearlong fellowship at Columbia Law School. They would become an academic power couple—one of their first joint publications was a linguistic analysis in the *Harvard Advocate* of T. S. Eliot's *Prufrock.* Wohlstetter focused on mathematics and philosophy, studying with Ernest Nagel and, at Harvard, with Willard Van Orman Quine. He and Roberta led a somewhat bohemian lifestyle, with Albert taking up modern dance: without marriage, re-called Wohlstetter, he might have remained "a permanent student."

At Harvard, Wohlstetter read Sidney Hook's *Towards the Under-standing of Karl Marx* and became increasingly interested in politics and economics. Like Kristol, he was a youthful Trotskyist, embroiled in the ideological struggles in New York during the 1930s. "If you want to find a Trotskyist," Daniel Bell told me, "then look at Albert Wohlstetter." Wohlstetter had been a member of the League for a Revolutionary Workers Party, which was led by one B. J. Field, who or-ganized the 1934 New York hotel strike. The party—known as the Fieldites—had all of eight members. But Wohlstetter's real interest was in economics and what would come to be called systems analysis. He landed a Social Science Research Fellowship and worked at the National Bureau of Economic Research during World War II. He ended up earning a Ph.D. in mathematical logic at Columbia University.

Immediately after Pearl Harbor, the Wohlstetters went to their fa-vorite Japanese restaurant for dinner—to show that they bore no hos-tility. During the war Wohlstetter assisted an electronics firm called Atlas, where he was in charge of a quality control department. In an oral history interview with several students that covered much of his life, Wohlstetter recalled that he had argued vociferously with the de-signers about what they were producing: "This was very much part of the sort of thing that made it possible for me to work with the en-gineers and physicists and so forth at RAND."[25] After the war he joined a company building prefabricated housing in California, but it failed.

Roberta had been working at the RAND research center as a part-time book reviewer. She would participate in a RAND study of Pearl Harbor and go on to write the Bancroft Prize-winning *Pearl Harbor: Warning and Decision*, which was published in 1962, the year of the Cuban missile crisis. Her study debunked Republican claims that Franklin D. Roosevelt had willfully ignored impending signs of Japanese aggression in order to ensure that the United States became ensnared in World War II. Instead, she carefully analyzed the intelligence data to show that organizational incompetence rather than conspiracy had resulted in U.S. vulnerability to attack. An excess of information had overwhelmed the military analysts, who became paralyzed with indecision about Japanese intentions.

Roberta—always the more scholarly of the two—inherited her academic bent from her father, Edmund Morgan, a Harvard law professor who had modernized the Uniform Code of Military Justice and helped defend the anarchists Sacco and Vanzetti. Unlike Albert, she was a patient researcher who collected and synthesized information; in this regard the Wohlstetters were rather like the Kristols. In the 1970s she wrote studies of terrorism. Her book on Pearl Harbor held up so well that it was recommended by former defense secretary Donald Rumsfeld to his associates after 9/11. Roberta's work also left a deep impression on Vice President Dick Cheney, who regards her essay "The Pleasures of Self-Deception" as something of a touchstone. In it, Wohlstetter argued against complacently accepting small changes that cumulatively add up to a disaster.

Both Wohlstetters spent much of their professional lives at RAND, where Albert became a consultant in 1951. RAND was perhaps the most important think tank of the cold war. It started in 1945, a product of General H. H. "Hap" Arnold of the U.S. Army Air Force, who wanted to keep the scientific experts who worked for him during World War II. Arnold was already alert to the implications of nuclear strategy, writing an essay called "Air Power in the Atomic Age" that appeared in 1946 and made the case for nuclear deterrence. "The anticipated cheapness of destruction with atomic explosives, coupled with the fact that their use with air-power weapons such as rockets prevents adequate defense," he wrote, "means that in the future the aggressor who destroys his enemy's cities may expect his own destroyed in turn. Neither side may care to fire the first atomic shot and thus bring destruction to its own cities."[26]

Bernard Brodie, an influential strategist at the National War

College, made the same point in his famous book, *The Absolute Weapon*: "Thus far the chief purpose of our military establishment has been to win war. From now on its chief purpose must be to avert them. It can have almost no other useful purpose." The question, of course, was how best to maintain and ensure that the Soviet Union never felt tempted to launch a nuclear strike.

RAND's primary mission was to devise nuclear doctrine, and no one was better equipped to do it than Wohlstetter. In the rarefied world of nuclear doctrine, he became chief theologian.

Wohlstetter argued that the United States was doing too little to maintain a credible deterrent. His first breakthrough was to revise American nuclear doctrine in the early 1950s, when he advised the air force that leaving bombers on the ground left them vulnerable to attack. The belief was widespread among American and European leaders that the Strategic Air Command (SAC) force was combat ready not only in the United States but also on hundreds of bases in Europe. The reality was different: bombers stationed in the United States itself had little or no warning against a surprise attack below five thousand feet. Wohlstetter showed that U.S. overseas air bases were even riper for a Soviet first strike because of their proximity to communist forces. In his view, the Soviets could destroy much of SAC's forces with a first strike. During seven months he briefed the air force ninety-two times about these weaknesses; his study was finally accepted in October 1953. Wohlstetter told the air force brass to have planes continuously in the air. He later recalled, in a lengthy letter to the British historian Michael Howard:

> The vulnerability of SAC had nothing to do with Air Force stupidity, or folly, or anything of the sort. Nuclear weapons were new, their implications were little understood; and the strategic force planners tended to examine the meaning of nuclear weapons to see how they affected the answer to the

questions of strategic bombing as these questions had been understood previously.[27]

(Howard later noted in his sparkling memoir, *Captain Professor*, that Wohlstetter "conducted his controversies with a ferocity strangely at odds with his debonair personality—a ferocity that, alas, his [neoconservative] pupils have imitated. There was always, it was once said, a distinct odor of burning when Albert was around.")

If dealing with the air force was tough going, Wohlstetter found the process of educating the National Security Council and its advisers even more difficult. In 1953 he had learned of fellow RAND researcher Bruno Augenstein's conclusion that large-yield warheads in ICBMs could compensate for initial inaccuracies. It was time for a new study about ICBMs and the air command. Wohlstetter was in his element: he "wanted this new project . . . to be grand and comprehensive. More than twenty RAND technicians and consultants ended up working on specialized studies within the project—on early warning lines, on infrared detection of missiles, on fallout estimates, on the practicality of bomb-alarm systems, on the hardening of aircraft shelters, on possible anti-missile defenses."[28]

By the end of the decade Wohlstetter believed the massive brute-force technologies had reached their apogee. The tremendous increase in destructive energy released by a single weapon and its fallout made them impractical as actual instruments of warfare. Wohlstetter was anticipating the key developments that would take place in the 1960s—the huge increase in the Soviet missile force and the eventual shift to MIRVs, or multiple warheads, based on a single missile.

The idea of an atomic stalemate, Wohlstetter believed, was overblown. He took aim at the advocates of a kind of minimum deterrence like George F. Kennan, who claimed that the United States required only a small missile force to deter the Soviet Union from launching a devastating first strike. Wohlstetter's 1958 article in

Foreign Affairs, "The Delicate Balance of Terror," made public his apprehensions about the deficiencies of the U.S. nuclear force, and it caused quite a stir.[29] At a meeting of the American Association for the Advancement of Science, Roger Hilsman declared that the Soviets might be able to wipe out the Strategic Air Command "in one blow," while the Harvard professor William Yandell Elliott, who was Henry Kissinger's mentor, complained that the United States did not have a limited war capability and decried the idea of a test ban on underground nuclear explosions.[30]

Wohlstetter noted that American nuclear capability in the 1960s would have to deter China as well as the Soviet Union. He was skeptical about Kremlinology and secret intelligence—anticipating the skepticism about the reliability of CIA estimates on Iraq that Wolfowitz and other Wohlstetter protégés would share decades later.

What he relied on was overwhelming his opponents through a wealth of detail and quantitative information. According to one critic, "This methodology exploited to the hilt the iron law of margin of error that was the asymptotic ideal for nuclear strategy. Even a small probable vulnerability, or a potential future vulnerability, could be presented as a virtual state of national emergency."[31]

He was, in many ways, the father of the idea of a missile gap. "Western journalists," he wrote, "have greatly overestimated the difficulties of a Soviet surprise attack with thermonuclear weapons and vastly underestimated the complexity of the Western problem of retaliation." The Soviet Union, he indicated, was not necessarily averse to a nuclear war. Wohlstetter reasoned as follows:

> Russian casualties in World War II were more than 20,000,000. Yet Russia recovered extremely well ... the risks of not striking might at some juncture appear very great to the Soviets, involving, for example, disastrous defeat in peripheral war, loss of key satellites with danger of revolt spreading—possibly to Russia itself—or fear of an at-

tack by ourselves. Then, striking first, by surprise, would be the sensible choice for them.

———

The cold language Wohlstetter employed—"sensible choice"—drove arms-control proponents crazy in the 1970s and 1980s, but he was onto something, even if they didn't want to admit it. Wohlstetter did not believe that the United States needed to mindlessly match the Soviets missile for missile. Rather, he was searching for the most effective way to deter an act of aggression. He pointed out that reliance on overseas bases had left the country vulnerable to Soviet attack since it was hard to defend them adequately. The United States needed to beef up its land and air missile capacity. What bothered Wohlstetter was what he saw as the "implicit abandonment of the basis for the U.S. to deter nuclear or other attack on an ally in the assumption that we wanted to be deterred from using nuclear weapons unless we ourselves had been attacked."[32] His article became a manifesto for foes of arms control who saw the United States as falling dangerously behind the Soviets.

Wohlstetter was not opposed to arms-control agreements per se. He believed that "useful agreements are possible because not all our interests conflict with those of our opponents. But our mutual interests are limited, and any realistic agreement is likely to be a limited one and to contain safeguards against violation."[33] He served as the American deputy chief science adviser at the ten-nation Surprise Attack Conference in Geneva. Dwight Eisenhower had proposed an "open sky" serial inspection system in 1955 to reduce the likelihood of an atomic Pearl Harbor. But the conference, as a *New York Times* editorial lamented, collapsed over "the determination of the Soviets to maintain the Iron Curtain and to prevent an effective inspection and control by any outside agency of their armed might."[34]

Still, there is no gainsaying the fact that Wohlstetter was a staunch hawk; as he saw it, the United States had become rather indolent about the outlays needed to protect itself militarily in the 1950s.

Wohlstetter's influence on the neoconservatives—and, by extension, the Bush Doctrine—was simple. He said that there was no real distinction between defense and offense. He set up the doctrinal basis for justifying preventive war. He even believed that protracted wars, rather than short ones, could be a good thing. Why? Because the West had superior economic resources and could outlast its foes. Andrew J. Bacevich has it right: Wohlstetter believed that safety was not to be found in a single-minded "focus on averting war; rather, safety lay in devising more effective ways of actually using force."[35] It was to this end that Wohlstetter focused on devising and promoting new weapons systems, ranging from missile defense to more accurate weaponry that would lower civilian casualties, in order to wage and win more wars.

Some of his ideas came to grief in both Vietnam and Iraq. All of these themes, however, would be pounded home by the neoconservatives, culminating in the Bush Doctrine. As we shall see, Wohlstetter had a profound influence on Senator Henry M. Jackson and would become a foe of Henry Kissinger's détente. His protégés, including Wolfowitz and Zalmay Khalilzad, as well as his close friend Robert Bartley, editor of the *Wall Street Journal* editorial page, would act as a kind of advance guard for his strategic ideas.

The Younger Generation

More than anyone, Paul Wolfowitz, a student of both Bloom and Wohlstetter, pushed their concerns, but without the skeptical detachment that characterized the older generation. The original neoconservatives had gone from being prophetic Jews to being rabbinic ones. The younger generation, traumatized in their own way by the 1960s, became the mirror image of their left-wing foe. Some of them became tenured radicals. Others went into government. But collectively they formed what Kristol père had always denounced: a new class. In the halls of academia, in think tanks, and ultimately in the corridors of power in Washington, they updated the Jewish prophetic tradition.

Like Bloom, Wolfowitz was transfixed by the threat of totalitarianism, a disposition he inherited from his father. The senior Wolfowitz, a mathematician at Cornell, had emigrated from Poland to the United States in 1920 and lost numerous relatives in the Holocaust. "His office in White Hall was filled with volume after volume on war and genocide, and the mathematician talked for hours on his family's fate," wrote David Dudley in the July/August 2004 *Cornell Alumni Magazine.* Paul grew up reading about Nazism and Hiroshima. For him it was both a political and a moral imperative to oppose totalitarianism.

By the time he entered Cornell in 1961, he was wholly susceptible to Bloom's influence. Bloom himself later said that "there was at that moment a spiritual yearning, a powerful tension of the soul which made the university atmosphere electric." Wolfowitz was captivated. Though his father wanted him to study the sciences and saw Bloom as a subversive influence, Paul was attracted to political philosophy. Those inclinations were strengthened when he and Fred Baumann, who would become a Straussian scholar, traveled with Ithaca church groups to hear Martin Luther King Jr.'s "I Have a Dream" speech in Washington, D.C., in August 1963. Wolfowitz would go on to study at the University of Chicago and missed the great upheaval that would take place several years later at his beloved alma mater.

The case of Wolfowitz was hardly an isolated one. If the rise of the left horrified Kristol, Podhoretz, Bloom, and a host of other intellectuals, it also left a deep mark on their progeny.

One of the most remarkable features of the neoconservative movement is the filial piety that pervades it. The sons and daughters of the neoconservatives as well as their students soaked up not only their parents' teachings but also their animosities. This was true of a wide range of what might be called the second generation of neoconservatives, which includes such figures as William and Elizabeth Kristol, Francis Fukuyama, Paul Wolfowitz, Douglas Feith, Daniel Pipes, Elliott and Rachel Abrams, John Podhoretz, Robert and Frederick Kagan, Seth Cropsey, Gary Schmitt, and Abram Shulsky. Far from rebelling against their elders, the younger neoconservatives entered the lists on their behalf. Their own university experiences would cement their political attitudes and stances.

Both Cornell and Harvard played a big part, but there were always distinctions among these younger neoconservatives. There were, in fact, always two strands to the neoconservative movement—one might be called the Kristol wing, which was sympathetic to Strauss, and the other the Podhoretz wing, which was not. Podhoretz told me he had little interest in Strauss—although he published many Straussians over the years. Others of the older generation inclined to the realist persuasion, like Jeane Kirkpatrick, were even more dismissive of the Straussian enterprise. Kirkpatrick was a believer in social science. That is one reason why it is inaccurate simply to equate neoconservatism with Straussianism.

In the second generation, the leading exemplar of the Podhoretz wing was Elliott Abrams. Abrams had no interest in Straussianism. He was interested in power and, initially, in reforming the Democratic Party. He later married Podhoretz's stepdaughter and would earn national attention at the center of the Iran-Contra scandal.

Abrams, who was born in 1948, grew up in New York. His father was an immigration lawyer. "The nature of the beast, the nature of that profession," he says, "is to deal with people whose greatest wish in life is to be American. It's hard not to pick up the sense that this is a very great country because of what it offers." Abrams had the classic neocon background. He attended Elisabeth Irwin, a communist-leaning high school. "They were genuinely communists," says Abrams. "They had connections with the party, socialist realism in art, and believed in the Marxist interpretation of history." He then went on to Harvard, where he was deeply impressed by the head of the history department, Samuel Beer. Abrams says he "was stunned to learn that what I had been taught as history was in fact the Marxist interpretation of the French Revolution."[36]

He joined the Americans for Democratic Action (ADA) in 1965, then a bastion of cold war liberalism. He also stirred up the campus radicals by joining up with Daniel Pipes (son of the distinguished Russian historian Richard Pipes) and Arthur Waldron, a neoconservative scholar of China. According to Abrams, "In dining room debates we three were often the ones who opposed SDS garbage. Before we had spoken, we were hissed." In 1968 Abrams was not reelected chairman of the ADA, because he supported Hubert Humphrey for president while the ADA backed Eugene McCarthy. The ADA was moving left, in tune with the times. Abrams, however, was unbowed. He, Pipes, and Waldron formed an ad hoc committee opposing the 1969 student strike that shut down Harvard. In effect, they were rebelling against the rebellion.

Harvard was also where Francis Fukuyama would complete his induction into the movement as a graduate student. Fukuyama had begun his undergraduate studies at Cornell in 1970. The campus was still recovering from the shock of the uprising the previous year. The government department had been badly split. Fukuyama, who already had conservative leanings, came under the spell of Allan Bloom, who together with fellow Straussian Walter Berns would end up decamping for the University of Toronto. Fukuyama later recalled:

> They [the black protesters] were on the cover of Time magazine, wearing bandoliers of ammunition. It was a horrible spectacle because basically the whole university administration capitulated to them. They admitted it was a racist institution, and that academic freedom didn't exist. Bloom was part of a group of professors who were outraged by the whole thing and left Cornell, but he owed one more semester, which I took.[37]

Born into a family of academics in 1952, Fukuyama was always interested in ideas. His maternal grandfather, who founded the economics department at Kyoto University, traveled, like many in his generation, to Germany to study before the outbreak of World War I. After the Japanese attack on Pearl Harbor, his paternal grandfather was interned in a detention camp in Colorado. His father's University of Nebraska scholarship narrowly allowed him to avoid the same fate. His parents met at the University of Chicago and soon moved to Manhattan, where his father worked as a Presbyterian minister.

After earning his undergraduate degree in classics at Cornell in 1974, Fukuyama briefly studied with the deconstructionist thinkers Roland Barthes and Jacques Derrida in Paris, but grew weary of such abstract thought. He left semiotics behind for topics like arms control, Middle East politics, and communism—these were the heady, concrete issues that he wanted to tackle. Fukuyama, who was Wolfowitz' protégé, spent a stint as an intern at the Arms Control and Disarmament Agency before heading to Harvard, where he studied with the Straussian thinker Harvey Mansfield and met a number of other young neoconservatives, including William Kristol, who would turn out to be the most influential political operator of his generation. Kristol would create a seamless web for the neoconservative movement. If Irving Kristol was the movement's godfather, William was its heir apparent.

Kristol, who was born in 1952, the year his father defended Senator Joseph McCarthy, absorbed his political and social views from his parents. When William was in high school, his father visited one of his classes and administered a tongue-lashing to the impertinent students for their radical-chic views. William cut his political teeth at the tender age of twelve, volunteering for Daniel Patrick Moynihan's campaign for New York City Council president.

In 1970 he entered Harvard, where one of his roommates was Alan Keyes, a young black Straussian who had fled Cornell to study with Harvard's Harvey Mansfield. (Keyes, who went on to become a deputy to Jeane Kirkpatrick at the United Nations, later became a flamboyantly outrageous public figure who ran unsuccessfully three times for Senate and twice for president. In 1988 Kristol ran his unsuccessful Senate campaign against Paul Sarbanes. Keyes later publicly disowned his daughter because of her lesbianism.)

Mansfield, an exponent of "manliness" and other classical virtues, inducted Kristol and other members of his generation into Straussian thought. Though Mansfield never studied with Strauss himself, which, in a philosophical movement riven with factional splits, has made him something of an object of suspicion, he nonetheless venerates him as one of the wisest men who ever lived. Strauss's picture hangs prominently in his office. (He told the younger Straussian scholar Peter Berkowitz, "There is a picture of the wisest man I have known.")

For the young Kristol, the government department was an oasis of sound thinking and a refuge from the radicalism that had rocked Harvard during the 1960s. Its members at the time were a roll call of prominent neoconservative thinkers, including Seymour Martin Lipset, Edward Banfield, Daniel Patrick Moynihan, and James Q. Wilson. Banfield, like Moynihan, earned fame as a critic of the welfare state. So did Lipset and Wilson. In a sense, the Harvard government department was the first academic neoconservative cabal.

Kristol fils stirred up controversy from the outset. He would wear a Spiro Agnew T-shirt or praise the B-52 raids on Haiphong harbor. Nothing was more certain to get a rise out of his fellow students. But he was no mere campus gadfly; there was more to it than simply earning the ire of the politically correct. He also immersed himself in Straussianism. Mark Blitz, a student of Mansfield's who taught Kristol at the time, told me, "Bill and his friends may have had a sense of embattlement. It wasn't the level of embattlement that conservatives feel now, but in retrospect it was the beginning of that." It was the feeling of being ostracized, on the margins of acceptable opinion as their parents had been during the 1930s, that gave the younger neoconservatives their raw confrontational edge.

The first book Kristol and his companions read under Blitz's tutelage was Strauss's *Natural Right and History*, his most impressive and accessible book. In it, Strauss delineates the progressive falling away from the wisdom of the ancients that took place over the centuries, and affirms the need to understand the great thinkers as they understood themselves. According to Blitz, the young neocons' attraction to Straussian thinking "had something to do with the notion of nature, that at some level you could say some things which were true, or more true than false about human happiness. That remains fundamental, not just for Straussians, but for Strauss himself." Part of the attraction was also the sense of belonging to a gnostic elite that viewed itself as somehow above the common ruck of humanity. As the author Nina Easton has shown, Kristol wrote in his senior thesis that the "natural inclination of a democracy, if left unattended, is to degenerate at least into a society whose members vainly try to satisfy vulgar passions, at worst into a despotism." The somewhat arch phrasing "if left unattended" suggests a role for an enlightened legislator to meddle in public affairs.

For the Straussians, Churchill remained the exemplar of the modern leader. Kristol himself fondly recalls carrying a pig back from Copley Square to Cambridge to roast it, in imperial style, on the hundredth anniversary of the great man's birth. He remained at Harvard, earning a Ph.D. (which decried judicial activism) under Mansfield.

As the writer Nina Easton has shown, Strauss supplied a mental framework that Kristol and his cohort employed to denounce the left in lofty terms of morality and virtue. It was a striking and refreshing contrast to the arid language of social science with its jargon-ridden vocabulary, based on game theory and behavioralism and realpolitik. The younger neoconservatives didn't simply want to analyze human behavior; they wanted to redeem it.

Kristol and company were themselves creatures of the late 1960s. They and their parents had seen the Democratic Party that once championed anticommunism captured by the liberal McGovern wing. McGovern himself had in 1969 become the chairman of a commission on party structure and delegate selection. He used it to outmaneuver the old Humphrey liberals and to establish quotas for blacks, women, and youth who would be loyal to him. As a result, the party fell captive to a narrow, sectarian interest group. Moving left, the party was quickly reverting, as the neoconservatives saw it, to the politics of the 1930s in modern dress.

If there was one Democrat whom the neoconservatives despised, it was McGovern. It was he who babbled about making the United Nations the arbiter of the Israeli-Palestinian conflict. It was he who wanted to retreat from Vietnam. It was he who epitomized the postures of defeatism and withdrawal from the world. He seemed to be a new Henry Wallace come to life.

But the neocons did not immediately leave the Democrats. Indeed, their first impulse was to battle for the party's soul from within. Only later and with great reluctance would they abandon the Democratic Party—home to American Jews since FDR—and make the painful passage across the political wilderness to the GOP.

The Jackson Ascendancy

Without a political vehicle, the first- and second-generation neoconservatives would simply have been spinning their wheels, writing academic treatises on Plato and Machiavelli and producing new translations of Tocqueville. How could they reclaim the Democratic Party? One step they took was to invent an organization called the

Coalition for a Democratic Majority, which was intended to counteract the malign influence of the McGovernites.

The neoconservatives announced the creation of the Coalition for a Democratic Majority in a December 7, 1972, advertisement in the *New York Times*, shortly after McGovern's ignominious defeat in the 1972 presidential campaign against Richard Nixon. The idea had been cooked up in Norman Podhoretz's Upper West Side apartment. Its organizing committee included Midge Decter and Jeane Kirkpatrick, and its sponsors were Richard Pipes, Eugene Rostow, and Daniel Bell. The ad was called "Come Home, Democrats"—a play on McGovern's campaign slogan, "Come Home America"—and it declared with a rhetorical flourish that McGovern's defeat was a "clear signal to the Democratic Party to return to the great tradition through which it had come to represent the wishes and hopes of a majority of the American people—the tradition of Franklin D. Roosevelt, Harry S Truman, Adlai Stevenson, John F. Kennedy, Lyndon B. Johnson, and Hubert H. Humphrey."

This was the first of what would become perennial calls to exhume the great tradition of cold war liberalism. Such calls have since come to seem stale and pointless, whether in the mouths of neoconservatives or of liberal hawks like Peter Beinart, formerly the editor of the *New Republic.* But in the early 1970s, especially given the shock of Nixon's election, the call seemed fresh and exciting. Moreover, it had attracted the sponsorship of one of the most influential members of the U.S. Senate.

————

In April 1945, Henry M. "Scoop" Jackson, then a young congressman from Washington State, traveled with six other House members to Germany. General Eisenhower had invited the group of lawmakers to visit Buchenwald, liberated a few days earlier by George Patton's Third Army. Jackson was stunned. He later recalled that he saw "evil written on the sky" at the death camp. He emerged "completely convinced that the Nazis were engaged in the systematic destruction of peoples who opposed their form of government and all peoples who they believed belonged to so-called inferior races. I also thought of how easily it could have happened to us if their program of world conquest had reached our shores."[38] It was a lesson he would never forget, leading to a fierce opposition to the Soviet Union and an equal devotion to the state of Israel.

Honors would be showered upon Jackson. In 1974 the Judaic Heritage Society named him "Man of the Year" and struck silver medallions with his image. The Jewish Institute for National Security Affairs, which includes the neocons R. James Woolsey, Joshua Muravchik, and (until her death in December 2006) Jeane Kirkpatrick on its board, hands out an annual award in Jackson's name; Paul Wolfowitz received it in 2002. Jackson's hard-line stance also prompted President Reagan to call him "one of our century's greatest lawmakers" and posthumously award him the Medal of Freedom in 1984.

In short, Jackson had become the neoconservative par excellence; yet it was unclear whether he would ever have used the term himself. As William F. Buckley Jr. observed, "I always thought the enthusiasm [for Jackson] was a little self-fabricated. The neos wanted a Democrat to enshrine. They found someone who was pretty much a welfarist but was anti-Soviet."

Still, Jackson was effectively the first prominent neoconservative politician, the man who promoted Richard Perle, Douglas Feith, Elliott Abrams, and a host of other young neocons while creating his own brain trust consisting of leading intellectuals such as Albert Wohlstetter, Richard Pipes, Bernard Lewis, and Robert Conquest. While Daniel Patrick Moynihan may have garnered headlines with his searing denunciations of the Third World, it was Jackson who had the more profound effect in reshaping American foreign policy.

Not everyone was pleased with his role in the Senate. "Who," asked the Saudi Arabian ambassador to the United Nations, Jamil Baroody, in the early 1970s, "is this Senator Jackson, who hails from a distance of 6,000 miles away from the Middle East to be the arbiter of the people of Palestine, when he gives the impression that he is more Zionist than the Zionists, more Jewish than the Jews?" (George H. W. Bush called Baroody "an unguided missile."[39])

Jackson's career shows that it's never been necessary to be Jewish to be a neoconservative, but that neoconservatism is nonetheless intimately linked with the memory of the Holocaust and the Allies' failure to save the Jews during the war. His career also shows how the issues of Israel and détente with the Soviet Union allowed neoconservatism to go from an intellectual movement to exercising real political influence—a heady experience that only inflamed the neocons' dreams of exercising power in their own right. Jackson delineated the course that neoconservatism would follow down to the present day. The debates over Soviet aggression and détente are not musty relics of yesteryear but simply a different version of the ones being waged over confronting terrorism today.

Born on May 31, 1912, in Everett, Washington, Jackson became interested in politics in high school. As the son of Scandinavian immigrants, he also inherited a firm belief in the Democratic Party. According to one of his associates, "From [his parents'] perspective, there was nothing whatever radical about the Roosevelt revolution which many Americans viewed with dismay. The economic and social legislation under the New Deal was much like the laws that had been written in Norway decades earlier."[40]

Jackson led anything but a privileged existence. In 1930, when he entered the University of Washington, the Great Depression hit Washington State hard. Jackson worked his way through law school, became an attorney, then ran for county prosecutor in 1938 as a reform candidate. Two years later he ran for, and won, a seat in Congress. He was twenty-eight.

Jackson had little influence on the course of World War II, but it left a lasting mark on him. According to his biographer,

> His core convictions about foreign policy and national security affairs derived largely from the lessons of World War II as Winston Churchill rendered them in his magisterial account of that war: the folly of isolationism and appeasement; the importance of democracies remaining militarily strong and standing firm against totalitarianism, and the need of the United States to accept and sustain its pivotal role as a world power.[41]

The German subjugation of Norway convinced him that the survival and independence of America had to be the priority of any president. "Of what avail to Norway's people was all its clean air and pure water," he would frequently ask, "once Hitler's troops had set foot on Norwegian soil?"[42] Jackson, who had entered Congress an isolationist, was now a full-fledged internationalist, championing Truman's interventionism and decrying Henry Wallace's 1948 presidential campaign. He backed Truman to the hilt, supporting aid to Greece and Turkey and the Marshall Plan, and welcomed his recognition of Israel. Jackson himself would subsequently champion the rights of the refuseniks (Soviet Jews denied permission to emigrate) and lambaste arms-control agreements with the Kremlin.

If Jackson was suspicious of Soviet motives after World War II, the Soviet detonation of an atomic bomb in July 1949 was decisive in turning him into a cold warrior. The CIA had bungled the prediction, claiming that the U.S.S.R. would, at the earliest, be able to explode a bomb in 1951. The head of the American atomic program had predicted that the Soviet Union might never be able to build a bomb. This failure of intelligence instilled in Jackson a deep suspicion of government assessments of Soviet weapons programs—a suspicion that has lingered in neoconservative circles.

As a new member, in January 1949, of the Joint Committee on Atomic Energy, Jackson, like other government officials, was stunned by the speed of Soviet technological development, which we now know was substantially assisted by spies at Los Alamos. The result of the Soviet breakthrough was a debate, at the highest levels of government, about whether the United States should pursue a hydrogen bomb. The physicist Robert Oppenheimer and the majority of members of the Atomic Energy Commission said no. Jackson disagreed. In the end, Truman gave the go-ahead for the H-bomb, convinced that the Soviets would build one whether or not the United States did.

The H-bomb debate foreshadowed all controversies during the cold war over nuclear weapons and arms control. Since the bomb was tested in 1952, "members of the scientific and arms control community have repeatedly argued that a crucial chance was missed to arrive at a new understanding with the Soviet Union and to gain important control over the arms race at this early stage."[43] Drawing on Bernard Brodie's *The Absolute Weapon*, advocates of a kind of "minimum deterrence" such as George F. Kennan said that it wasn't necessary for the United States to go all out on the nuclear weapons front. In 1950 Kennan argued that the United States should not only abandon the idea of an H-bomb but avoid reliance on atomic bombs and declare a "no first use" policy. Kennan's arguments may have been original, but according to Walter Isaacson and Evan Thomas, "his paper had no discernible impact on policy making . . . it was a tangent; the issue before Acheson was more narrowly whether or not to build the Super, not international control or 'no first use.' "[44]

Paul H. Nitze, the head of the State Department's Policy Planning Staff, disagreed. "The two most difficult points to meet," he wrote, "will be (1) what do we substitute for the present presumed deterrent effect of our atomic bomb policy to Soviet military aggression, and (2) in the event of Soviet military aggression, what do we substitute for our present net atomic strategic advantage." Nitze, who had scraped through Harvard on a "gentleman's C," went into government during World War II and became in the course of a long career one of the "wise men" who crafted America's national security strategy. Originally a White House protégé of James Forrestal's, he served at the State Department in the Truman administration and was appointed secretary of the navy by Kennedy. An unreconstructed hawk, Nitze would always charge, like Wohlstetter, that the United States wasn't doing enough to counter the Soviets. This ended up making him a close, if sometimes ambivalent, ally of the neoconservatives, beginning in the late 1960s. The relationship was symbiotic: Nitze provided legitimacy; the neoconservatives, intellectual firepower.

Back in the early 1950s, however, Truman, Nitze, and Jackson were just beginning to fight the cold war, arguing forcefully that there was no chance to avert an arms race. They were right. Stalin already had scientists working on his own H-bomb project. The result of Truman's insistence on confronting the Soviet Union was the famous national security directive known as NSC-68, drafted by Nitze, which recommended enhancing atomic capabilities and a massive buildup of conventional forces. The document emphasized that the Soviets were aggressively expansionist, not just in Europe, but around the globe. Later generations would seize upon its chiliastic language—"The grim oligarchy of the Kremlin . . . is seeking to demonstrate to the Free World that force and the will to use it are on the side of the Kremlin"—to attempt to discredit the Truman administration and the cold war. But it was the Soviet-backed North Korean invasion that convinced Congress to support the spending demanded by NSC-68.

Throughout the 1950s Jackson pressed for an aggressive nuclear weapons policy. In a top-secret memorandum he pushed the Eisenhower White House to develop ground-launched ballistic missiles. Anticipating John F. Kennedy's claims of a missile gap in 1960, he repeatedly warned that the United States was penny-pinching on defense and falling behind the Soviet Union. One of his closest advisers was Wohlstetter, who sounded precisely the same theme in his multifarious writings. Incredible as it may seem in the context of today's Democratic Party, the main complaint of Senate Democrats, including the majority leader, Lyndon B. Johnson, and the Missouri senator Stuart Symington, was that the Eisenhower administration was spending far too *little* on the military.

When the next big debate about military technology erupted, Jackson was once again at the forefront. In the 1960s Kennedy and Johnson, for all their former bellicosity, pursued arms-control agreements with the Kremlin. The arms race had started to heat up in earnest after the Cuban missile crisis, when the Soviet leadership vowed never again to be in a position of nuclear inferiority to the United States. Secretary of Defense Robert McNamara—another product of the WASP establishment—was determined to nip any spiraling arms competition in the bud through a series of agreements. He drew the lesson from the missile crisis that parity—or mutually assured destruction—not superiority, should be the aim of U.S. strategy. In his view, the much greater American missile force had been of negligible importance in the crisis since the United States had not seriously considered a first strike.

"At the root of McNamara's approach to the arms competition," writes Patrick Glynn, "was a principle that could be traced back to the thinking of British liberals before World War I—'moderation breeds moderation,' or goodwill breeds goodwill."[45] (Glynn himself is a classic neoconservative: a Harvard Ph.D. in English literature who ended up serving in the Reagan administration as an assistant to Kenneth Adelman, the head of the U.S. Arms Control and Disarmament Agency under Reagan—and himself a Shakespeare scholar.) Needless to say, it was a principle that would forever be associated with appeasement in the minds of neoconservatives who blamed the British prime minister Neville Chamberlain for making World War II inevitable.

On January 10, 1967, Johnson stated that he hoped to achieve a moratorium on antiballistic missile systems with the Soviet Union. But the Soviets were not responding to American overtures. To prod them to the negotiating table, Johnson announced in September 1967 that he was going to deploy a limited ABM system against China. In January 1968 he asked Congress for $1.2 billion for a missile system called Sentinel and $269 million for research.

Jackson was appalled. He wanted the United States to keep arming and to create a ballistic missile defense. In 1966 he and fellow Democrat John Stennis and GOP Senator John Tower began campaigning for such a defense. In a speech at the Hoover Institution in 1967, Jackson had already denounced McNamara for remaining oblivious to the imperatives of power. He drew the opposite lesson from the Cuban missile crisis as McNamara: American superiority had forced the Soviets to cave and withdraw their missiles. An ABM system would strengthen deterrence by preventing the Soviets from destroying America's land-based missile force in a surprise attack, and might offer the hope of a leakproof system in the future.

The war over foreign policy was twofold: it was waged inside the Democratic Party itself and against the détente espoused by Henry Kissinger and Richard Nixon. It really began in May 1969 when Senator Jackson, Richard Perle, Paul Wolfowitz, and Albert Wohlstetter attended a conference in Washington, D.C., about antiballistic missile defense. Concerned that the antimissile views of Democratic doves like J. William Fulbright, Edward Kennedy, and George McGovern were coming to dominate the party, Jackson, Nitze, and Wohlstetter founded an organization called the Committee to Maintain a Prudent Defense Policy. The committee, supposed to create what Nitze called a "balanced debate," was a direct counterpart to an organization called Citizens Concerned About the ABM, headed by the former UN ambassador Arthur J. Goldberg and Roswell Gilpatric, and to the ABM Information Center, which was run by the United Methodist Church's Division of World Peace.[46] Another anti-ABM group made up of scientists disgruntled with the

Vietnam War was organized by the patrician Cass Canfield, a backer of Adlai Stevenson who had helped found the journal *Foreign Affairs* and was editor in chief of Harper and Row. The bone of contention was an ABM system called Safeguard. By June the *Washington Post* could report that "regardless of what happens to it in Congress, the Safeguard anti-ballistic missile system already has caused a sharp and well-financed escalation in partisan activity throughout the country . . . Many thousands of dollars are being pumped into public relations, speaking engagements, direct-mail appeals and congressional pamphlets."[47]

The Committee to Maintain a Prudent Defense Policy was headed by the former secretary of state Dean Acheson and Paul Nitze and set up offices near Dupont Circle. It had a budget of fifteen thousand dollars, half of which Nitze kicked in. Perle was the chief researcher. Peter Wilson, Paul Wolfowitz, and Edward Luttwak all joined. An elated Acheson dubbed them "our four musketeers." Watching Acheson conduct meetings, Perle was amazed by the seventy-five-year-old's persuasive powers.

Acheson's committee wasn't the only pro-ABM group; a New York lawyer named William J. Casey, who would later become Ronald Reagan's campaign manager and CIA director, headed the Citizens Committee for Peace and Security, which operated out of New York's Plaza Hotel. But Acheson's was the most effective: by the end of the summer, the four musketeers had provided Congress with numerous position papers and analyses of the need for missile defense as well as responses to press inquiries. "The papers they helped us produce," Nitze fondly recalled, "ran rings around the misinformed and illogical papers produced by Cass's polemical and pompous scientists."[48] Under Jackson's guidance, the Safeguard system was approved by the Senate in 1969.

The successful campaign became a model for Perle and other budding neoconservatives. A small guerrilla organization could run rings around the establishment experts. Jackson turned his own

Senate staff into such an insurgency. It became known as "the bunker."

The central figure on Jackson's staff, building up his network of assistants and outside experts, was Dorothy Fosdick. Unlike her father, Harry Emerson Fosdick, a famous clergyman for whom John D. Rockefeller built Riverside Church in New York, Dorothy was no pacifist. Her guiding star was the tough-minded realism of Reinhold Niebuhr. After earning a Ph.D. at Columbia University, Fosdick taught at Smith College, then entered the State Department in 1942, where, among other things, she worked for George F. Kennan and Paul Nitze on the Policy Planning Staff.

When Jackson met Fosdick in 1954 at a dinner party, they clicked. Both shared a flinty liberalism rooted in Protestant Christianity. Showing an open-mindedness unusual for the age, Jackson made her his foreign policy adviser. It paid off. Fosdick created a network of prominent academic advisers, including the historians Bernard Lewis, Richard Pipes, and Robert Conquest, who would play a key role in bolstering Jackson's hawkish views on Israel and the Soviet Union. Lewis was one of the few scholars of the Arab world willing to warn about its innate deficiencies rather than assailing the West for them. Pipes, an expert on Russia, traced the Soviet Union's totalitarianism back to czarist times, embroiling him in debates with Aleksandr Solzhenitsyn, who saw such a view as bordering on racism. Conquest had written an article for *Foreign Affairs* in 1967 called "The Limits of Détente." His seminal book, *The Great Terror*, offered a reminder of the barbarism of Stalin's Soviet Union.

Fosdick also played a role in shaping Richard Perle's views. She and Jackson, in the words of Jackson's biographer Robert Kaufman, "lectured him incessantly about the imperative of maintaining a strong Israel and the greatness of the Jewish tradition. Thus Perle became an intrepid champion of Israel by the work of these two Niebuhrian Protestant missionaries in the Russell Building of the United States Senate."[49] (According to the former national security adviser Brent Scowcroft, Fosdick and Perle "were a nightmare. They were there all the time just like glue. As soon as Perle left, I had a great relationship with Jackson.")

Perle, who grew up in Los Angeles, had met Albert Wohlstetter as a teenager; he was brushing up for a debate on nuclear arms and impressed Wohlstetter with his grasp of his *Foreign Affairs* article, "The Delicate Balance of Terror." Perle, who admired Wohlstetter's epicurean tastes, yearned for more than the academic life. After earning a graduate degree at the London School of Economics, he entered a Ph.D. program at Princeton, but abandoned it to work for Jackson. He couldn't have been more welcome. Jackson took a paternal interest in Perle and gave him free rein.

If Jackson saw foreign policy in military terms, he viewed his work on the home front in much the same way. What Jackson was assembling in this unconventional staff amounted to a guerrilla organization within the Democratic Party. His aides saw themselves as a minority force whose real enemy wasn't right-wing Republicans but left-wing Democrats intent on subverting the Republic. As the author Jay Winik put it, "In their eyes, the inhabitants of the Bunker were a beleaguered few, fighting the lonely way against the left-wing forces of darkness, always on the precipice, about to be overwhelmed. Perle constantly talked about the lonely battles, the isolation, the attacks on himself and his colleagues."[50]

This description doesn't serve only for Jackson's aides, but can be applied to the neoconservative movement, down to the present. It is this sense of embattlement and loneliness, of foes and enemies everywhere, that helps to account for the stridency and militancy of the neoconservatives. There was, and remains, a good dose of self-pity among neoconservatives. They know that they will never be accepted by the establishment. Indeed, they revel in the knowledge that they are outsiders. But beneath the veneer of confidence is a seething rage at the government bureaucracy and social elites. Though Jackson himself was a modest man who did not suffer from these impulses, his followers did. They were tormented by their own version of the anxiety of influence—or the lack of it.

Henry Kissinger and the Betrayal of the Jews

Whatever abuse they may have received, no one was better at doling it out than Jackson and his staff. Indeed, it was Jackson and his aides who took on and toppled Washington's foreign policy czar, Henry Kissinger.

At first glance, Kissinger might seem like he would have made an appealing ally to Jackson and other neoconservatives: A young Jewish émigré from Nazi Germany makes good in the United States. He enters the U.S. Army in World War II, earns a Ph.D. from Harvard, uses the nuclear issue as a springboard to enter politics, warns about Soviet nuclear intentions, and serves in the Kennedy administration as a part-time consultant in addition to teaching at Harvard.

But in the hothouse world of the Jewish intellectuals, Kissinger was seen as a *Hofjude*, or court Jew, of the WASP foreign policy establishment. For one thing, he made his name at the Council on Foreign Relations, where he wrote his first big book on nuclear strategy (savaged by Paul Nitze in the *Reporter* magazine for its numerous errors). Kissinger had worked his way into the good graces of Nelson Rockefeller, then secretly met with Richard Nixon to become his national security adviser in 1969. Where the Scoop Jackson types advocated a tough stand against totalitarianism, Kissinger espoused accommodation. As he later recounted, "To my astonishment, I found myself in confrontation with a former ally in what became an increasingly tense relationship. What made the conflict both strange and painful was that I felt more comfortable with Jackson on most issues than with many newfound allies."[51]

Kissinger may well have been astonished, but he quickly became Exhibit A for neoconservative hawks ranging from Jackson to Daniel

Patrick Moynihan to Norman Podhoretz for what was wrong with American foreign policy. And to a large extent, they were right. Nixon and Kissinger pursued an essentially amoral foreign policy by prolonging the Vietnam War for political gain, by seeking to accommodate the Soviet Union and ignore the issue of human rights, and by conceding Eastern Europe to the Soviet sphere of influence. Perhaps Kissinger's most disgraceful move was advising Gerald Ford not to receive the Soviet dissident and novelist Aleksandr Solzhenitsyn at the White House.

As Kissinger portrayed it, the Vietnam War, in destroying the postwar bipartisan consensus on containment, required the United States to move toward a more cautious realpolitik. In his Harvard dissertation, published to wide acclaim in 1957 as *A World Restored: Metternich, Castlereagh, and the Problems of Peace, 1812-22*, Kissinger lauded the Austrian statesman Klemens von Metternich's emphasis on creating a balance of power that would allow the autocratic European empires to resist both reform and revolution. As he approvingly noted, "If Metternich considered the quest for formal constitutions chimerical, he saw in revolutions a physical disaster. In a universe characterized by a balance between the forces of conservation and those of destruction, revolution was due to a disturbance of the equilibrium in favor of the latter."[52]

What makes this passage so interesting is that Kissinger believed realism was the ticket for American foreign policy long before Vietnam and the collapse of the establishment. Kissinger was obsessed with stability rather than revolution. When Vietnam and the attendant student protests erupted, he saw himself as a modern-day Metternich, holding back revolutionary forces that threatened chaos at home and abroad. Wrongly, as it turns out, he saw the United States as essentially in decline and believed that it had to reach an accommodation with the Soviet Union. By creating a web of economic and military agreements with the Kremlin, Kissinger believed, the United States could help to transform the Soviet Union into a status quo power that would not seek geopolitical advantage against America. The balance of power would be preserved.

Jackson and his followers disagreed. "Stability" and "balance of power" and "equilibrium" were terms of abuse in the neoconservative lexicon. After the Soviets imposed a costly "education tax" on emigrants—that is, Jews leaving for Israel and the United States—in August 1972 (it was supposed to serve as a refund for state schooling), Jackson went into overdrive to undermine détente. The emigration issue became the first big effort by American Jews to lobby Congress. It resonated with them, and for good reason. As the *New York Times* perceptively observed, "The treatment of Russian Jews has weighed heavily on American Jews for generations. Today there are many who feel anger, even guilt, because they believe that their fathers and grandfathers did not do enough about the plight of the Jews in Russia and the slaughter of the Jews by the Nazis."[53]

On August 30, 1972, the Republican senator Jacob K. Javits spoke at a small rally in New York and raised the prospect of linking any trade agreement with the plight of Soviet Jews. At a meeting of 120 Jewish leaders held by the National Conference on Soviet Jewry on September 26, 1972, Jackson made a heartfelt appeal. "The time has come to place our highest human values ahead of the trade dollar," he said. "You know what you can do? I'll give you some marching orders. Get behind my amendment. And stay firm!" To Kissinger's fury, Jackson began a systematic campaign to stymie his attempts to reach an accommodation with the Soviets.

It was Perle who laid the groundwork for Jackson to link freedom of emigration for Jews with most-favored-nation status for the Soviet Union. A steering committee called the Washington Group led the campaign. It was an informal group that included congressional staffers like Perle and pro-Israeli lobbyists: I. L. "Si" Kenen, who founded the American Israel Public Affairs Committee (AIPAC) in

1954; June Silver Rogul, who worked for the National Conference on Soviet Jewry; and Morris J. Amitay, a legislative staffer for Senator Abraham Ribicoff and later executive director of AIPAC. The idea they came up with was their own form of "linkage"—attaching an amendment called Jackson-Vanik to any most-favored-nation status to the lifting of restrictions on Jewish emigration.

Nixon and Kissinger figured that the amendment would die, but they underestimated Jackson's tenacity. The AFL-CIO president, George Meany, a staunch cold warrior, backed Jackson-Vanik. So did conservatives. The Soviet dissident Andrei Sakharov urged Congress to pass it and called Jackson "our champion." Guilt over having failed to help Jews escape the Holocaust loomed large. Amitay declared at the time:

> There are now a lot of guys at the working level up here who happen to be Jewish, who are willing to make a little bit of extra effort and to look at certain issues in terms of their Jewishness, and this is what has made this thing go very effectively in the last couple of years. These are all guys who are in a position to make the decisions in these areas for these Senators . . . you can get an awful lot done at the staff level.[54]

The proposal might have died, but White House aide Peter M. Flanigan made a crucial mistake by putting most-favored-nation status with Russia into an omnibus trade bill. Jackson and the Ohio congressman Charles Vanik, whose grandparents emigrated from Czechoslovakia, reintroduced the amendment. George Meany, a lifelong anticommunist who had turned against free trade and saw détente as "appeasement to dictators," put labor behind the amendment.

Kissinger was livid. He called Perle "a little bastard" and "a son of Mensheviks who thinks all Bolsheviks are evil." An infuriated Nixon declared, "A storm will hit American Jews if they are intransigent." But Jackson prevailed. The House passed the Jackson-Vanik Amendment on December 13, 1973. In 1975, after lengthy negotiations with the Ford White House following Nixon's resignation, Jackson reached a compromise in which the Russians agreed to allow at least sixty thousand Jews to emigrate each year without restrictions: "It was unmistakable when the documents were released that Jackson and his allies were the victors . . . this was probably the first diplomatic agreement in American history to be memographed for distribution on a Senator's memograph machine. It was passed out in the White House press room by Perle and Amitay, two members of the Washington group."[55]

The Chimera of Arms Control

If Jackson obstructed Kissinger on human rights, he dealt him an even more severe blow on the arms-control front. In 1969 Nixon had asked Jackson to serve as his secretary of defense, but Jackson, hoping to preserve his own presidential prospects, declined. Jackson had taken the side of the administration in fighting for the Safeguard ABM system. When Nixon turned around and signed an ABM treaty with the Soviet Union that limited each country to two, not four, ABM sites, Jackson was enraged. According to Peter Ognibene, "He had invested his personal prestige and political capital to win Senate approval of four ABM sites of several hundred launchers each and felt betrayed because only one site with a hundred launchers could now be built to defend Minutemen [intercontinental ballistic missiles]."[56]

Jackson knew that he would be unable to stop approval of SALT I. But he pushed through an amendment, approved by a 56-to-35 vote, which insisted that any future negotiations not limit "the United States to levels of intercontinental strategic forces inferior to" the Soviet Union and that they be based on "the principle of equality." But Jackson did not really want the amendment to be passed by the House as well; he was using it as leverage with the Nixon White House. What Jackson wanted—his second move—was to purge the Arms Control and Disarmament Agency (ACDA) and the SALT delegation.

In 1973, after SALT I was signed, Nixon and Jackson stepped into the Rose Garden for a forty-minute chat. At Jackson's urging, Nixon agreed to a new SALT delegation and the overhaul of ACDA. Nixon, always ill disposed to the professional striped-pants set, had no compunctions about purging ACDA. Nor did Kissinger, who shared his boss's loathing for the State Department diplomats. According to one of the purged, Raymond Garthoff, "Senator Jackson and the hard-liners knew what they were doing. The long-run effect was to weaken the arms control constituency and make it harder—and ultimately impossible—for Kissinger to maneuver between hard-line and soft-line alternatives."[57]

Peter Rodman, a member of Kissinger's national security team who became an assistant secretary of defense in the George W. Bush administration, recalls that in the early 1970s, "Kissinger asked me to find out what was in *Commentary.* I found Norman to the right of us on arms control. We were fighting against the right on arms control!"[58] Kissinger himself recounted in his memoirs that "Nixon, great tactician that he was, never conceived that he, the renowned Cold Warrior, would in the end be attacked from his old base on the right wing of the Republican party."[59] Nixon and Kissinger's support of the Helsinki Accords, which essentially recognized the post–World War II borders of Europe, was seen as nothing less than a new Yalta.

But even as Nixon and Kissinger made concessions to Jackson, they never imagined that an all-out assault on détente was only beginning. What's more, the ferocity of the neoconservative attack did not diminish with Nixon's resignation. Gerald Ford was widely seen as Kissinger's cat's-paw in foreign policy. Podhoretz argued in an April 1976 *Commentary* essay called "Making the World Safe for Communism" that liberals had always led the fight against communism and been bolder in advocating the use of force than conservatives. Haunted by Vietnam, however, both the left and the right were losing their nerve and becoming isolationists. The danger, as he saw it, was that the United States might abandon Israel as it had abandoned Vietnam. In Podhoretz's summation:

> If it should turn out that the new isolationism has indeed triumphed among the people as completely as it has among the elites, then the United States will celebrate its two-hundredth birthday by betraying the heritage of liberty . . . and by helping to make [the] world safe for the most determined and ferocious and barbarous enemies of liberty ever to have appeared on the earth.

Indeed, once Nixon resigned, the attack against détente would also come from within the Ford administration itself, led by Secretary of Defense Donald Rumsfeld and Albert Wohlstetter, who was based at Pan-Heuristics in California. Rumsfeld, who wanted to curry favor with the right, forged an alliance with the neoconservatives in the mid-1970s that he would continue in the 1980s by joining and financially supporting an organization run by Midge Decter called the Committee for the Free World. In 1975 he was determined to displace Kissinger. State Department cables were routed through the Defense Department at that time, and Rumsfeld made sure to be apprised by his technicians of any important messages emanating from Kissinger. Thus Rumsfeld was the first to get hold of the remark by Kissinger's aide Helmut Sonnenfeldt that an "organic union" should take place between the Soviet Union and its Eastern European satrapies. This infamous declaration, which became known as the Sonnenfeldt Doctrine, helped kneecap Ford's chance for reelection. Rumsfeld saw to it that Richard Perle received a copy and leaked it to the newspaper columnists Rowland Evans and Robert Novak.[60]

The Republican Party was moving steadily to the right. "Under Kissinger and Ford," declared presidential candidate Ronald Reagan, "this nation has become number two in a world where it is dangerous—if not fatal—to be second best." In 1975, when Rumsfeld became defense secretary, one of the first things he did was to invite Wohlstetter down for lunch. They spoke for two and a half hours. According to Kenneth Adelman, who then worked for Rumsfeld as an assistant, he would often find him huddled with Wohlstetter, plotting how to counter Kissinger and undo détente. According to a former official in the Ford administration, Rumsfeld exercised a profoundly destructive influence: "I would be developing a policy, get all the things in place, sit down at the meeting, and Rumsfeld would toss in the monkey wrench. Not 'I think we ought to do this instead.' He was not constructive. He behaved the same way in the Bush administration." Rumsfeld, he believes, cost Ford his chance for reelection in 1976. After Rumsfeld took over the Defense Department, he would "call small groups of congressmen, not to the Pentagon, but to the Roosevelt Room in the White House and brief them on the Soviet threat. He stopped arms control. When it came to the campaign against Carter, Ford had no accomplishments ... Rumsfeld prevented it."[61]

The Israel Connection

In March 1974 the *New York Times* ran a story deep in its front section with the headline "Harvard Lecturer Buys New Republic for $380,000."[62] The buyer was the thirty-five-year-old Harvard assistant professor Martin Peretz. Peretz, as noted earlier, had dabbled in radical politics during the 1960s. With his wife, Anne Farnsworth, he had supported the presidential campaigns of Senators Eugene McCarthy in 1968 and George McGovern in 1972. He donated twenty-five thousand dollars to McGovern, explaining to the *New York Times* that he believed McGovern would end the Vietnam War and "turn the country toward social justice."[63] Now he was embarking on a new path.

In a joint statement, Peretz and Gilbert A. Harrison, *TNR*'s editor in chief and owner for twenty years, announced that they planned no significant changes in the magazine's staff, which over the years had included everyone from Walter Lippmann to Edmund Wilson to Theodore H. White. Two years later the *Washington Post* announced that most of the staff had resigned, including Stanley Karnow and Walter Pincus, who quickly became a star reporter at the *Washington Post* on national security issues. In the June 9 issue of *Time* magazine, Pincus declared that Peretz "is a guy on an ego trip, but he doesn't know where to go." Doris Grumbach, the literary editor, complained that Peretz's "interests are limited to books by friends, books that friends could review, Harvard-Cambridge books and books about Jews and Israel." She had a point. It wasn't that Peretz's friends were uninteresting—a kind of entrepreneur of ideas like Irving Kristol, he made a point of cultivating rising stars as well as established eminences in academia. But Peretz disagreed with Grumbach: "It simply isn't true that I can't think about anything without seeing it through the Jewish sifter." He continued, "In my moral perspective, [the Israel question] is just as important as Vietnam and there's no reason just because I'm Jewish why the *New Republic* shouldn't reflect that."[64] The complaints could be chalked up as a case of sour grapes by former staffers, but it was a charge that would dog Peretz for years. Again and again, the left would accuse him of traducing the magazine's liberal traditions and turning it into an echo chamber for the Israeli right.

The editorial shift at the magazine may have seemed inconsequential at the time. For a decade, it had been in the doldrums as far as its influence and circulation were concerned. Its decline mirrored that of liberalism itself. But the turnover was a significant development in the rise of neoconservatism. Prominent American Jews had begun to realize that they couldn't support Israel and not back a strong, interventionist America. Edward Luttwak, writing in *Commentary* in 1975, put it bluntly:

> As the military men see, while the Pentagon delivered [during the October 1973 war], the liberal supporters of Israel, and the Jewish liberals in particular, have not: instead of showing greater understanding of the importance of adequate defenses, they are still pressing for cuts in the military budget. Yet the truth is that such cuts could seriously damage America's capacity to deter Russian activism in the world at large, including the Middle East: they could even undermine America's ability to supply Israel with the weapons, ammunition, and high technology it needs for its survival.[65]

Norman Podhoretz, writing in the *New York Times Magazine*, declared that American Jews had been converted to Zionism en masse by the repeated Arab assaults on Israel. In his view, they had come to realize that

> if for the second time in this century, the world were to stand by while a major Jewish community was being destroyed, it would be hard to evade the suspicion that an irresistible will was at work to wipe every last Jew off the face of the earth, to make this planet entirely Judenrein—a will which . . . would not rest until . . . it found an equally effective instrument for disposing of the last remaining community of Jews, the one in the United States.[66]

Peretz held many of the foreign policy views associated with the neo-conservative movement, foremost among them his passionate advocacy of a crusading U.S. foreign policy that would protect small and beleaguered nations, beginning—but not ending—with Israel, and a strong American defense budget. Peretz, you could say, was an avatar of what would become known as neoconservative foreign policy by the late 1970s. His role, in its way, was almost as important as Podhoretz's and Kristol's. Where they made neoconservatism acceptable for the Republican Party, Peretz gave it a patina of legitimacy by endorsing its main tenets from outside the GOP. In short, he sought to transform liberalism from the inside.

To his detractors, and they were legion among liberal Democrats, Peretz was turning the *New Republic* into a vehicle for neoconservatism. By 1979 the *New York Times* could write, "Long regarded as an apostle of liberalism, the *New Republic* has in the last four years under a new editor made some pronounced shifts, mostly—in the views of many of its readers—to the right."[67] Mainly, it took a firm stand against communism and in defense of Israel. These stances had, partly because of the shift in the Democratic Party, suddenly become "conservative" or "neoconservative." The *Times* continued:

> In some ways, the magazine's change of direction reflects the assaults on liberalism from within and without. It may also reflect Mr. Peretz's progression of views, which have in the past embraced such groups as the Students for a Democratic Society but which now seem more allied with such Democratic Senators as Daniel Patrick Moynihan of New York and Henry M. Jackson of Washington.

The genteel "seem" was supererogatory. In the coming decades, until the aftermath of the Iraq war, the magazine would, by and large, espouse a neoconservative foreign policy. In fact, the further neoconservatism moved to the right, the more the magazine would tag along.

Indeed, in the Spring 1985 issue of *Policy Review*, Dinesh D'Souza would grudgingly welcome the *New Republic* to conservative causes, noting that the Reagan White House picked up twenty copies a week from its offices. "It is not clear why ideas long believed by conservatives and articulated in scores of books and articles should be surprising and indispensable," commented D'Souza, "when they resurface in the *New Republic*." But that filtering effect, of course, was Irving Kristol's goal all along.

Even as the *New Republic* drifted rightward, the last year of the Ford administration was sending the true neoconservatives into conniptions. One issue was the CIA's estimate of Soviet nuclear capabilities. The neocons managed to get George H. W. Bush, who was then director of the CIA, to agree to a Team B of outside experts that would face off against the CIA's Team A. It was no contest. The CIA analysts were totally overmatched by the likes of Richard Pipes, Wohlstetter, and Wolfowitz. The bureaucratic CIA types were plainly unused to the ferocious attacks leveled against them by Pipes, who argued that they had radically failed to appreciate Soviet intentions and were engaging in mirror imaging—assuming that the Soviet Union would act exactly like the United States. To Pipes, it was clear that the Soviet Union believed it should prepare to fight and win a nuclear war—the title of an essay he later published with great fanfare in *Commentary*. Pipes, like Wohlstetter, had assaulted the cherished foundations of liberal mythology about the efficacy of arms control. In essence, he was saying that arms control was largely beside the point unless the nature of the Soviet system changed—the same position Ronald Reagan would adopt. Reagan, to great effect, would argue that arms control had become an end in itself, a permanent industry for Washington policy wonks—in short, a liberal fetish for achieving peace that avoided the central issue of whether the United States or the U.S.S.R. was going to triumph in the cold war.

For their critics, this persistent alarmism about the Soviet threat has become Exhibit A of how neoconservatives twist and distort intelligence and the intentions of foreign foes. But the neocons always believe what they are saying with the utmost intensity; it's in their nature as prophetic personalities. What's more, in this case (like the proverbial stopped watch) they were clearly onto something. The Soviet Union was overconfident in the 1970s, convinced that the "correlation of forces" was on its side and that the United States was headed for defeat. The Soviet leader Leonid Brezhnev assured the Politburo that by the mid-1980s the Soviet Union would be well on its way to surpassing the United States. In retrospect, the Soviet Union was the victim of what the Yale historian Paul Kennedy would call "imperial overstretch." But this wasn't all that obvious at the time. What was clear was that the Soviet Union, to an unprecedented extent, was aiding subversive forces in Africa and Central America. There were genuine causes for concern. The failure, even refusal, of America's liberal elites to take this campaign seriously was a big reason that Ronald Reagan ended up winning the presidency in 1980.

For the neoconservatives, it's always imperative to have, somewhere, somehow, an enemy—both at home and abroad. This suits their need to see themselves as lonely prophets standing in the breach between implacable foes on the one hand and weak-kneed liberals (and paper-pushing bureaucrats) on the other. In the Soviet Union, they had found an enemy that really was working to undermine the United States, while at the same time waning liberal enthusiasm and wishful thinking about the cold war threatened to weaken American resolve at a crucial historical juncture. As a result, the neoconservatives enjoyed in this brief period what may well be considered the peak of their significance and value as a movement. Never again would they so clearly occupy the moral and intellectual high ground. Unfortunately for them, their prescience in the cold war only tended to convince them of their rightness on all issues in the future. The one neoconservative from the 1970s who avoided this trap was Daniel Patrick Moynihan.

Moynihan bridged the divide between neoconservatives who were interested in domestic policy and those who were primarily concerned with foreign affairs. He was quite expert in both. Indeed, in many ways, he may have been the most impressive neoconservative of all. Did he have a penchant for overstatement? Sure. But he was never dogmatic and displayed great intellectual flexibility over the years. He responded to facts, not dogmas. Moynihan had first been promoted by Irving Kristol, who published his essays in the superb magazine the *Reporter*. In the 1960s Moynihan demonstrated his trenchancy when he earned notoriety for his report "The Negro Family: The Case for National Action." Moynihan, who was assistant secretary of labor in the Johnson administration, deplored the collapse of the black family and its dependence on welfare, arguing that the rise of single-mother families could be traced back to Jim Crow and slavery. Ghetto culture was a product not simply of a lack of jobs but of a deeper cultural problem that had its origins in slavery. Moynihan concluded, "A national effort towards the problems of Negro Americans must be directed towards the question of family structure." Lyndon B. Johnson gave a stirring commencement address at Howard University about the need to help the black family, then abandoned the issue as the Vietnam War devoured his presidency.

And Moynihan? Himself a product of Hell's Kitchen, he had worked his way up by way of the Fletcher School and the London School of Economics and was familiar with the pathology of the ghetto. But it was considered rude to talk about it when discussing African-Americans. Black leaders, by contrast, said that this was blaming the victim, which became the title of a 1971 book by the activist William Ryan, who also denounced Moynihan in the *Nation*.

There were other complaints: Moynihan was playing into the old stereotype of black men as promiscuous; whites were just as frisky, but had more access to birth control. The black population wasn't responsible for its plight; the government was. Anyway, his critics said, Moynihan was a racist. It was as simple as that.

Moynihan was embittered and scarred by the experience, but it did not diminish his zest for intellectual combat (in 1994 he even caused a new flap when he suggested that the persistence of black single-mother families might be resulting in what he called a Darwinian form of "speciation"—the emergence of a new, permanent, and undesirable, even pathological, form of human behavior). In the 1970s, after a stint as ambassador to India, he returned to the United States to become Gerald Ford's ambassador to the UN, an experience he chronicled in his superb account *A Dangerous Place.* Moynihan would be the first in a series of neoconservative UN ambassadors who gained fame by attacking the world body as a forum for anti-Americanism. Moynihan was fearless and articulate. Moreover, unlike Podhoretz or Kristol, he didn't just write about events. He participated in them. At the UN he was in his element, becoming a hero to the average American for standing up to Third World thugs and their paladins.

In the 1970s the United Nations, and particularly its treatment of Israel, became a highly visible theater of U.S.-Soviet competition. In 1975 the UN had approved a resolution declaring that Zionism was racism. The resolution not only attacked Israel for supposed crimes against the Palestinians but also denied that Israel itself was a legitimate state. Moynihan forcefully decried the resolution. Had he not done so, it might have been passed without any real opposition. It was Moynihan, drawing on the work of the historian Bernard Lewis, who led the fight against it.

Lewis had recently chronicled the history of the belief that Zionism was indistinguishable from Nazism in *Foreign Affairs.* According to Lewis, the Soviet Union began, after World War II, to use the term "racist" for any non-Slavic movements inside its borders that harbored nationalist aspirations. After the upsurge of sentiment among Soviet Jews, who had been given, in theory, a homeland in Birobidzhan, Soviet propaganda targeted the Jews in general and Zionism in particular as alien and racist. In February 1971 *Pravda* ran a two-part series in which Jewish leaders were, among other things, accused of collaborating with the Nazis.

On November 10, the day before the debate in the General Assembly, Moynihan worked late into the night in the library of his official residence on the top floor of the Waldorf Towers. With him were his old friend Norman Podhoretz and his special assistant, Suzanne Weaver, on leave from Yale. Writing in the *New York Times Magazine*, the reporter Tom Buckley observed, "When it came to the politics of the Middle East, an area in which he has never set foot, Moynihan was happy to take his direction from the State Department, he had told me, but when it came to Zionism, Jewish history, anti-Semitism and related topics, Podhoretz is Moynihan's maven."[68]

This was not surprising, insofar as Moynihan owed his UN appointment to *Commentary* in the first place. Writing critically about the UN in the March 1975 issue, Moynihan—still a professor in the Harvard government department—joined the neoconservative war against Kissinger, détente, and realpolitik with a ringing endorsement of moralism and idealism in American foreign policy: "It is time that the American spokesman came to be feared in international forums for the truths he might tell. It is past time we ceased to apologize for an imperfect democracy . . . The Third World must feed itself, for example, and this will not be done by suggesting that Americans eat too much." The article caught the attention of Secretary of State Henry Kissinger, who showed it to Gerald Ford. They offered Moynihan the post of UN ambassador. But he was to prove vastly more controversial than they had anticipated.

During debate in the General Assembly, he assailed the notion that Zionism was tantamount to racism. He later recalled that "Charles H. Fairbanks, a young political scientist at Yale, a Straussian, prepared a long memorandum to the effect that words and their meanings do matter: 'To call Zionism a form of racism makes a mockery of the struggle against racism as the emperor Caligula made a mockery of the Roman Senate when he appointed to it his horse.' "[69]

For a measure of the hatred that Moynihan aroused among the left, it's useful to recall a brilliantly provocative article by Frances FitzGerald that appeared in *Harper's* in May 1976. FitzGerald–a leading and eloquent critic of the Vietnam War who wrote the book *Fire in the Lake*–denounced what she saw as the rise of the warrior intellectuals. She complained that whether Moynihan "is interested in foreigners or not, what he has done is to re-create the McCarthyite attack . . . He and others are finally creating a right-wing backlash . . . He is not himself a McCarthy . . . but he has accused several groups in this country of something approaching treason."[70] FitzGerald saw Moynihan and other neoconservatives as promoting a new nationalism that demonized the left as un-American and trumpeted militarism toward the Third World. The cover of *Harper's* showed middle-aged intellectuals in caps and gowns obediently marching in a prison yard under the watchful gaze of a guard. It was the old Irving Howe criticism of domesticated intellectuals who had forfeited their independence to serve the state. They had become intellectual prisoners of power.

But Moynihan, who had already demonstrated a knack for political survival, had little to fear from the left (he is the only American to have served in cabinet or subcabinet positions through four successive administrations). He was now on a roll. Capitalizing on his notoriety as UN ambassador, which earned him strong Jewish support, he campaigned for and won the 1976 election for the Senate in New York. For the neoconservatives, it seemed like a dream come true. Moynihan would carry the neoconservative banner in the Senate; he might even be presidential timber.

Meanwhile, Gerald Ford had effectively scotched his chances for reelection with his bizarre remark in a presidential debate against Jimmy Carter that Poland was a free country and that there were no Soviet troops there. It took a week for Ford to issue a clarification, compounding the perception that he was too weak to deal with the Soviets. So much for the Harvard professor who had shunned morality in foreign affairs and oiled his way to the White House. His realism had proven unrealistic. It was the ignominious end of Kissingerian détente with the Soviet Union.

Or was it? Under Carter, the United States pursued both human rights and détente with the U.S.S.R.; but this divided approach doomed his presidency and ensured that the neoconservatives would turn to Ronald Reagan in 1980. Carter had won by the smallest margin of electoral college votes since 1916—297 to 240. This slender victory was a harbinger of the fragility of his presidency and, incidentally, his relations with the neoconservatives. The neocons had helped tarnish Ford and Kissinger. Now they would help to destroy another presidency. Carter was so inept that he almost made it too easy for them.

The Carter Years

In January 1976 a young lawyer named Peter Rosenblatt took a list of members of the Coalition for a Democratic Majority (CDM) to DNC headquarters. Jimmy Carter had just been inaugurated. Rosenblatt's acquaintance Anthony Lake, who would become head of the State Department's Policy Planning Staff (and later Bill Clinton's national security adviser), had suggested that he drop off such a list, ostensibly so that the administration could reach out to neoconservatives. The list was indeed put to use, but not as Rosenblatt intended.

Instead, each name on it was denied any appointment in the new Democratic administration. It was, in other words, an inadvertent hit list. Rosenblatt himself was the only one who received an appointment (as ambassador to Micronesia).

Rosenblatt, who was born in New York and attended Yale Law School in the 1950s, remains a Democrat (he advised Joseph Lieberman during his abortive presidential primary campaign in 2004). Intellectually he followed the classic neoconservative path, but without ever lurching to the far right, as did so many other neocons. He had worked for the Johnson administration together with Richard Holbrooke, coordinating State Department agencies in Vietnam. The office next to his was occupied by Ben Wattenberg, who would go on to work for Scoop Jackson and end up at the American Enterprise Institute, while Rosenblatt joined Senator Edmund Muskie's staff. Rosenblatt's task was outreach to the Jewish community. He and Wattenberg, Podhoretz, Decter, and Kirkpatrick helped organize the CDM. But to the Carter administration types, the CDM was anathema. The last thing the Carter crowd wanted was to go back to cold war liberalism. That was what had gotten the United States mired in Vietnam. Carter wanted to expiate America's sins in the Third World.

The fact that Rosenblatt was the only neocon to receive an appointment did not go unnoticed. It was an early signal that the Carter team, far from seeking to build bridges to the neoconservatives, was determined to snub them.

Instead, Carter created a two-tier foreign policy operation that relied on establishment liberals such as Secretary of State Cyrus Vance and Paul Warnke, supplemented by Vietnam War protesters like Anthony Lake, Richard Moose, and Leslie Gelb, who were dubbed the "Junior Varsity." They had a different view of the world from the original neocons, who had been shaped by World War II and the Holocaust. For the new Democrats, in contrast, Vietnam was the defining issue of their lives. To them, the war had amply demonstrated that the United States was, more often than not, the bad guy, even if its intentions were noble. Lake even conducted a self-lacerating debate about U.S. foreign policy with his wife, Antonia, in the pages of the *New York Times Magazine*; she had marched outside the White House gates to denounce the Vietnam War while he served on the National Security Council.

The new Democrats believed that a new world was emerging, one in which North-South relations were more important than the super-power rivalry; they believed that issues like population control and malnutrition would be at the forefront of the administration's foreign policy. They believed that interdependence, not confrontation, would be the order of the day, that resisting communist expansionism was an expression of bad taste. They also believed, as Lake would later write in a speech that Carter delivered in 1977 at Notre Dame, that the United States suffered from an "inordinate fear of communism" and that America, not the Soviet Union, had the primary responsibility to curb the arms race and refrain from bellicose actions that might intimidate other nations. Even hard-liners like Zbigniew Brzezinski, who was national security adviser, foresaw a "Technetronic Era," a multipolar world in which the U.S.S.R. and the United States would move toward convergence.

Rounding out the Carter team was the UN ambassador Andrew Young, a former aide to Martin Luther King Jr. elected to Congress in 1972, who declared that he wished to place the United States "on the right side of the moral issues of the world." This prominently included taking a pro-PLO stand that incensed the neocons. In 1979 Young, after his secret meeting with a representative of the PLO became public knowledge, resigned. Carter seemed to be doing his utmost to live by his words as a candidate, when he had stated that "foreign policy ought not to be based on military might nor political power nor economic pressure. It ought to be based on the fact that we are right and decent and honest and truthful and predictable and respectful." To the neocons, this wasn't a program for reviving America; it was crackpot moralism.

Carter, who had been elected on a platform of reversing the sordid machinations of Nixon and Kissinger by trumpeting human rights, quickly became the central figure in the neoconservative demonology. He told the Foreign Policy Association in early 1976, "Our people have now learned the folly of our trying to inject our power into the internal affairs of other nations." But by September 8, 1976, he was sounding a contradictory note: "We cannot look away when a government tortures people, or jails them for their beliefs, or denies minorities fair treatment or the right to emigrate." Nixon had been indifferent to such issues: the Soviet foreign minister Andrei Gromyko recalled, "I cannot remember an occasion when he launched into a digression on the differing social structures of our states. He always presented himself as a pragmatist . . . a man who preferred to keep discussions on a purely practical level." Carter elevated such "digressions" into one of the main tenets of American foreign policy.

Indeed, it might have seemed, in some respects, that this approach would appeal to neoconservatives. Wasn't Carter trying to lead a democratic crusade around the globe? Wasn't he, in some sense, the precursor of Ronald Reagan, who championed promoting democracy? The neocons surely approved of using human rights as a stick to beat up the Soviets in the court of global opinion. What was it about Carter that so enraged them, and why did he despise them in turn? Ironically, Carter's spurning of the neocons would prove a fateful move that helped to undermine his presidency and embolden Reagan and the GOP. Had Carter followed a different course, he might well have been reelected, and the GOP would never have benefited (if that is the right word) from the influx of neoconservative intellectuals.

The contretemps between Carter and the neocons began almost as soon as he was sworn into office. Moynihan proved a thorn in the side of the Democrats. Once elected to the Senate, he showed no signs of being inhibited by the chamber's courtly traditions. Just as he had gone to battle at the UN, so he now targeted the Carter administration. His lifelong habit was to remain in the opposition, no matter who was president. He loved to challenge the conventional wisdom, whether on the left or the right. Ultimately, however, he was better at rhetorical fireworks than at getting legislation passed. He was also one of several prominent neocons who would publicly defect from the movement. But in 1977 Moynihan was still firmly on the reservation, eager to take shots at Carter for his pusillanimity toward the Soviet Union. Just as Nixon and Kissinger had coddled the Soviets, Moynihan believed, Carter was on the verge of doing the same.

Moynihan was not alone. The neoconservatives were flourishing, and a kind of military-intellectual complex was coming into existence, bemoaned by liberals such as the *New York Times* columnist Anthony Lewis and championed by hawks like Paul Nitze, who was enraged that Carter had failed to give him an appointment in his administration. Lewis complained in a 1976 op-ed,

> There is a new element, an intellectual one. It includes strong supporters of Israel who since the Yom Kippur War have become a significant factor in the growing support for larger U.S. defense budgets. The magazine *Commentary* is at the heart of this element, along with such Senators as Henry Jackson and Daniel Patrick Moynihan. *The New Republic*, now a leading pro-Israel voice, made a sustained attack on Paul Warnke before the election.[71]

It was a fatal error on Carter's part not to have co-opted Nitze. Instead, he left him outside the tent, free to agitate for a bellicose policy toward the Kremlin under the umbrella of the Committee on the Present Danger, which served as the locus of the convergence of the traditional right and neoconservatives. Founded at the Metropolitan Club in Washington, D.C., on November 11, 1976, the committee's members included Donald Rumsfeld, Richard Perle, Max Kampelman, Lane Kirkland of the AFL-CIO, Norman Podhoretz, Saul Bellow, Richard Pipes, and other inveterate foes of communism. The argument of the present-danger members was as simple as it was alarming. In one of their first papers, they declared: "The Soviet military buildup of all its armed forces over the past quarter century is, in part, reminiscent of Nazi Germany's rearmament in the 1930s." And just as it had been futile to negotiate arms-control agreements with Hitler, so it was useless in the case of the Soviet Union: "The SALT 1 arms limitation agreements have had no visible effect on the Soviet buildup. Indeed, their principal effect so far has been to restrain the United States in the development of those weapons in which it enjoys an advantage."[72]

The committee's first target (as noted by Lewis) was an obvious choice: Paul Warnke, Carter's nominee to head the Arms Control and Disarmament Agency. Warnke, like Carter's secretary of state, Cyrus Vance, and earlier, McGeorge Bundy, was the kind of patrician that the neoconservatives loved to loathe. He was a charter member of the eastern establishment. Born in 1920 in Webster, Massachusetts, Warnke attended Yale and went on to work for Dean Acheson's law firm, Covington and Burling. He was assistant secretary for defense during Vietnam and grew into a vocal critic of the war.

Warnke became a lightning rod for the right in the early 1970s, when he served as an adviser to George McGovern. In a famous article in the Spring 1975 issue of *Foreign Policy* magazine, he offered what amounted to a compendium of liberal bromides about dealing with the Soviet Union. He likened both superpowers to "apes on a treadmill," blindly amassing more and more nuclear weapons. But he saw the United States as the real culprit: "As its only living superpower model, our words and actions are admirably calculated to inspire the Soviet Union to spend its substance on military manpower and weaponry." (Interestingly enough, this was the very strategy that the Reagan administration would later consciously—and successfully—pursue.) As Warnke saw it, the United States should unilaterally halt development of the Trident submarine and B-1 bomber in the hopes that the Soviet Union would demonstrate "reciprocal restraint." A furious exchange ensued in *Foreign Policy* with Albert Wohlstetter, who sought to demolish Warnke's argument by showing that the United States had, in fact, been slowing down its production of nuclear weapons and that the out-of-control arms race Warnke perceived did not exist. Wohlstetter argued that there was indeed an arms race—by the Soviet Union.

Warnke's Senate confirmation hearings in February 1976 were, in retrospect, a measure of the difficulties Carter would face in getting any arms-control treaties approved. Carter called his nominee "thoroughly and totally qualified." But Warnke ran into a lot of flack created by the Coalition for a Democratic Majority, whose cochairman Ben Wattenberg was then an adviser to Henry M. Jackson. A memorandum written by the young neoconservative Joshua Muravchik, a protégé of the former Trotskyist Max Shachtman who would later become a leading proponent of a democratic crusade around the globe, highlighted Warnke's history of dovish positions toward the Kremlin. Indeed, Warnke came under fire for a seemingly picayune matter—namely, whether or not he had used a comma before the word "which" when stating, before a Senate committee in 1972, that there was "no purpose in either side's achieving a numerical superiority, which is not translatable into" military or political advantage.

In the end, Warnke was confirmed, but it was a bruising battle for Moynihan, who had closed ranks with Jackson to oppose him. The episode would trigger Moynihan's shift to the center, as he concluded that there was little to gain politically by continuing to wage the battles of the neoconservatives. He wanted to get reelected in New York, not go down in flames with a quixotic stand on principle. In addition, he had concluded by the early 1980s that the Soviet empire was doomed—and that the neoconservatives were wildly exaggerating the Soviet threat. Moynihan was, of course, right. It was not the first such sensible defection from the movement—nor would it be the last.

For the neoconservatives, propagandizing about human rights and upping the nuclear ante were the keys to victory in the cold war. Albert Wohlstetter warned that Soviet "spending on research and development has led ours since SALT I. They have been investing twice as much in their technological base. If SALT II prevents our exploiting technical advantage, can we afford it?"[73] Some, like Irving Kristol, even argued that NATO was outdated because it tied the hands of the United States—an early version of the unilateralism that would pervade the second Bush administration. Others, like Walter Laqueur, raised a point that many neoconservatives fretted about—the idea that Western Europe was being "Finlandized." The fear was that the détente pursued by Germany and other countries with the Soviet Union would render them utterly dependent on it.

What's more, Podhoretz and his wife, Midge Decter, saw the same moral failings at home. They condemned a culture of relativism that had taken hold after Vietnam, in which spoiled elites lacked the backbone for the fight against communism. They likewise alleged that cultural changes like the rise of feminism and increased tolerance for homosexuality would sap the vitality of the United States and lead it to perdition, a key reason that the neoconservatives would later find common ground with Christian evangelicals. The seed of the culture war of the 1980s and 1990s was thus planted in the cold war during the 1970s and was essentially a by-product of the neoconservative concern with maintaining a strong foreign policy.

Carter, for all his pious talk about religion, seemed to exemplify many of the failings of the liberal elite. For one thing, he was intent on pursuing détente even more wholeheartedly than Ford and Kissinger. Carter attached great importance to the Strategic Arms Limitation Talks with the Kremlin, which were supposed to reduce the numbers of intercontinental ballistic missiles on both sides. His talk of an "inordinate fear of communism" left Zbigniew Brzezinski, Carter's hard-line national security adviser, fuming impotently on the sidelines. But even Brzezinski never really met with the approval of the neocons; despite his anticommunist bona fides, he was suspect because of his Polish heritage (the older Jewish intellectuals could not forget the history of Polish anti-Semitism) and his adamant insistence that Israel had to cede the West Bank to the Palestinians. To this day, Brzezinski hates the neocons as much as they despise him.

During this period the lines of battle were set down over Israel and the Middle East between the neocons and their erstwhile Democratic Party brethren. As Carter saw it, only a comprehensive peace, rather than a step-by-step approach, could end strife between Israel and its neighbors. Anwar Sadat's visit to Jerusalem in 1978 and the Camp David Accords redounded to Carter's benefit and seemed to vindicate his diplomacy. Still, he was viewed with apprehension by the neocons. Didn't Israel remain in as much peril as ever? Didn't the prospect of further accords mean that Israel would have to give up even more territory that it had occupied since the 1967 war?

These were somewhat inchoate fears at the time. The Likud world-view had hardly gained the kind of acceptance it enjoys today. But a young Washington lawyer named Douglas Feith, who was working at a law firm headed by the neoconservative (and longtime Democrat) Max Kampelman, ventilated the fears of the pro-Likud faction in the United States in the spring 1979 issue of *Policy Review*, which was published by the recently established Heritage Foundation. Feith's article denounced what he saw as the Carter administration's abandonment of a mediating role in the Arab-Israeli standoff in favor of insisting on Israeli withdrawal from Judea-Samaria (Feith went out of his way to use the biblical term for the West Bank, which was, and remains, in vogue with hard-line Likudniks). Settlements in the West

Bank, Feith declared, were not an impediment to peace. Instead, the problem was Arab intransigence. "If the Jews have a claim to Judea-Samaria at least as rightful as that of the Arabs and if the purpose of the Israeli settlements there is to stake this claim," wrote Feith, "then it may be that Israel's stand on the West Bank is not irrational after all."

While this kind of statement was on the fringes of the fringe of right-wing thought in the late 1970s, it eventually became an established dogma, at least among neoconservatives. The notion was that Israel should never have to cede any of the territory it had conquered in 1967; rather, the Arab states would have to deal with Jerusalem. To some extent, this did actually occur; but the neoconservatives failed to anticipate that some flexibility would also be necessary. Instead, they condemned out of hand any attempt to nudge the peace process forward as a dire sign of appeasement and therefore a threat to American national security, since in their eyes Israel figured as a bulwark against Soviet encroachments in the Middle East.

Indeed, the neoconservatives have fought tenaciously over every inch of intellectual ground that concerns Israel and the Palestinians. For example, *Commentary* declared a long war on Edward Said, the influential Columbia University professor-cum–Palestinian activist who had concocted the theory of "Orientalism" in a 1978 book of the same title. Said was a smooth, urbane purveyor of much nonsense about the Middle East, but the neocons' attacks on him descended to the level of an unhealthy obsession. (Thus a lengthy review article in *Commentary* went to great lengths to debunk Said's claims, in a memoir, that his family had been expelled from Jerusalem.) Similarly, neoconservatives such as Daniel Pipes and Martin Peretz greeted with hosannas a meretricious book published in 1984 by a writer named Joan Peters, *From Time Immemorial*, which purported to show that Palestinians had no historical presence in the land that would become the Jewish state. According to Peters, Palestine had been barren until the Jews arrived. Arabs had, in fact, been attracted to settle in Palestine only because of the prosperity that accompanied Jewish immigration to the area. As the scholar Yehoshua Porath observed in the *New York Review of Books* in 1986, "The unfortunate thing . . . is that from a position of apparently great learning and research, she attempts to refute the Arab myths merely by substituting the Jewish myths for them."

These intellectual battles were like catnip to the neoconservatives. But they didn't go completely overboard in the 1970s. As prominently as Israel figured in the neoconservative world, Carter himself was not yet seen as an anti-Semite, as he would later be vilified. Instead, the neoconservatives' biggest complaint was that Carter was too aggressive in pursuing human rights issues, at least against America's traditional friends. While Washington might decry abuses in Uganda or Cambodia, it did not display the same zeal toward the Soviet Union, Saudi Arabia, and China. Worse, the Carter administration railed against human rights violations in Nicaragua or Chile or Iran. But these were America's allies in the battle against communist encroachments in the Third World. What was the point of undermining them? As Arthur Schlesinger Jr. observed in *Foreign Affairs* in 1978, "In short order the human rights campaign was hauled before a high court of indignation of its own, and readily convicted of hypocrisy, double standards, undermining détente, undermining stalwart anti-communist allies, of cultural imperialism, racism, messianism and so on."[74]

The chief prosecutor turned out to be an unlikely figure—a Georgetown University professor and longtime associate of Hubert Humphrey's named Jeane Kirkpatrick. Obviously, neither Humphrey nor Kirkpatrick was Jewish, and both were Democrats who had (moreover) flirted with Marxism in their youth. Kirkpatrick's Democratic credentials later came to be invaluable for the Reagan White House when she was appointed ambassador to the United Nations. In fact, many Reagan neoconservative appointees were Democrats, like Richard Perle—a sign of ideological flexibility that the Democratic

Party has never really displayed. How many Republicans have been adopted by the Democrats?

Jeane Jordan was born in Duncan, Oklahoma, on November 19, 1926. She studied at Columbia University with the German émigré Franz Neumann, who wrote a classic study of Nazi totalitarianism. Kirkpatrick became a staunch admirer of Humphrey and viewed the GOP with suspicion. During the Carter years, however, she steadily moved to the right as the White House appeared to follow what she called (in a famous 1979 essay published in *Commentary*) a policy of "dictatorships and double-standards." Kirkpatrick was right: the Carter administration was indeed applying double standards; but then, so did most White Houses. What gave her essay special force was its contention that communist regimes, unlike authoritarian ones, were not susceptible to reform. As the rise of the Soviet reformist Mikhail Gorbachev later showed, this wasn't, to put it mildly, quite right. But Kirkpatrick's article served as a rallying cry for Carter's opponents. It gave them a coherent theory, a basis of attack, one that presidential hopeful Ronald Reagan, among others, quickly embraced.

Kirkpatrick identified U.S. policy as actively collaborating "in the replacement of moderate autocrats friendly to American interests with less friendly autocrats of extremist persuasion." The problem with her thesis, as many recognized at the time, was that by focusing solely on the communist threat, it provided a fig leaf of justification for the worst human rights abuses by repressive regimes such as those of Argentina, Nicaragua, Chile, and El Salvador. Still, given the progress that Central America did make in the 1980s and 1990s toward democracy, Kirkpatrick was not wholly off base.

At this point, Kirkpatrick, like most of the neocons, saw herself as an embattled liberal rather than a fledgling Republican. She and others like her held out a ray of hope for the Democratic Party. If liberals could regroup, they might be able to pursue a more enlightened policy that defended rather than subverted American interests:

"Liberal idealism need not be identical with masochism, and need not be incompatible with the defense of freedom and the national interest." So the neoconservatives still thought of themselves as liberals. Indeed, given the extent to which the Democrats' shift to the left in 1972 has been mythologized by the neoconservatives themselves, it is often overlooked that they remained (for the most part) in the Democratic Party until much later in the decade. The climactic event came at a White House meeting after the Soviet invasion of Kabul in December 1979.

The Soviets were on the march in the Third World; now they had occupied a new country on their road to a warm-water port in the Persian Gulf. The result, as we now know, was quite different from what they expected. The Soviets' invasion of Afghanistan turned out to be a major strategic blunder that would ultimately bring down their empire. But very few saw it that way at the time, including Carter himself. Plainly shocked by the invasion, he declared that he had learned more about the Soviets in the preceding twenty-four hours than in all of his previous life. Seeking to mend fences, Carter met with a group of neoconservatives in a private session arranged by Vice President Walter Mondale, who wanted to reach out to the more conservative wing of the Democratic Party. Neoconservative eminences in attendance included Norman Podhoretz, Elliott Abrams, and Jeane Kirkpatrick; but the summit was a fiasco. The neoconservatives concluded that Carter was hopeless, incapable of facing up to the evil represented by the Soviet Union. As Peter Rosenblatt says, "They gave up on him and the party. They were fed up and disgusted with him. The funny part of it was that Carter had come around a long way. He should have appointed a number of them. But he didn't." While Carter now called for upping the defense budget, it was too late to salvage his reputation as a foreign policy weakling.

The neocons left their meeting more firmly convinced than ever that Carter was beyond redemption. As a result, a phalanx of Democrats would cross the aisle to join the soon-to-be-elected

Reagan team. Paul Wolfowitz, who had been working for Carter's secretary of defense, Harold Brown, decided to leave the administration. Jeane Kirkpatrick met with Reagan himself after he read her *Commentary* article—as with Moynihan, an article in the neocons' flagship publication was enough to catapult her to stardom and political influence.

Meanwhile, the Coalition for a Democratic Majority, which had considered disbanding upon Carter's election, was still trying to push the Democrats to the right—in order, as Scoop Jackson put it, to "bring the Democratic party back from the edge of extremism to its historical role as the party of the progressive center." It was a goal that would be enunciated time and again, most recently by Senator Joseph Lieberman.

The point man in Reagan's outreach to the neocons was his future national security adviser Richard Allen, who had asked Kirkpatrick to meet several times with candidate Reagan. Kirkpatrick described the GOP's efforts to woo the erstwhile Democrats this way: "We are really treated quite badly by the Democratic Party and meanwhile we are bombarded with friendly messages from Republicans. After a certain time it begins to seem irresistible, especially if the person seems very likely to be the next president of the United States."

Kristol's Handiwork

This was the moment Irving Kristol had long been preparing for. He would lead the neocons out of the Democratic Party and into the GOP. For almost a decade, he had worked to establish a network of right-wing organizations. Essentially, he created a neoconservative employment service; if you had worked for him as a young editor in your twenties, a decade later he could now place you in the Reagan White House. As Kristol saw it, in an updated version of his old Trotskyist analysis, a "new class" of lawyers, government officials, professors, and journalists had moved to seize power and establish its dominance over American society and culture in the previous decades. So he set about constructing his own new class—the neo-conservative movement.

The stirrings were everywhere on the right. The Heritage Foundation had been created in February 1973 with the backing of the Colorado brewer Joseph Coors and the philanthropist Richard Scaife. The *New York Times* observed as early as 1977 that the "far right" (as it defined the Reagan movement) "has grown more effective on a wide range of issues." "The far right has adopted the tactics of the left," observed Gary Hart, who had run the 1972 McGovern campaign (today the left seeks to emulate the tactics of the right). The *Times* went on to note the emergence on the right of formerly liberal writers and academics:

> In such small but influential magazines as *Commentary*, edited by Mr. Podhoretz, and the *Public Interest*, edited by Mr. Kristol and Mr. Glazer, they argue that the solution to the nation's problems lies in the free market system. Affirmative action quotas are demons of the highest order to neo-conservatives. Many of them are Jews of modest origins who see a latent anti-Semitism in the organized assaults on the meritocracy in which they rose to prominence.[75]

Essential to the rise of the neoconservative movement was the largesse of the John M. Olin Foundation, whose president, William E. Simon, had been secretary of the Treasury under Presidents Nixon and Ford. Simon's best-selling memoir, *A Time for Truth*, promoted the supply-side gospel that tax cuts could pay for themselves. The book was completed thanks to some help from Kristol, who had recommended a member of Ayn Rand's inner circle named Edith Efron, also a believer in forming a counter-intelligentsia, to collaborate on it. At the time, Kristol was an unofficial adviser to Gerald Ford;

Simon had come under Kristol's influence, which was clear in his comments at the time. "Why," he asked, "should businessmen be financing left-wing intellectuals and institutions which espouse the exact opposite of what they believe?"[76]

Simon was a neighbor of Olin's in East Hampton, Long Island, where they both maintained summer homes. Olin not only supported the American Enterprise Institute but started a new foundation that was the brainchild of Kristol, the Institute for Educational Affairs. As the late Michael Joyce, who headed the Bradley Foundation, explained to me: "I knew that Simon was an avid sportsman, raised Derby-winning horses. The metaphor I would use with him was that it takes a good horse to beat a horse. If Henry Ford is correct that major institutes of society have a left-wing agenda, you can't just leave the field." Joyce continued, "We began our work directed toward influencing opinion. This is right out of Kristol's playbook. Ideas are formed at the top of a pyramid and filter down to a wide bottom over time. If you make your interventions at the bottom, you won't have much effect."

Joyce himself, who became a power broker in the neocon movement, was a Kristol find. He had been CEO of a regional foundation in Baltimore when he met Kristol, who was then an editor at Basic Books. Joyce wanted to come to New York. Simon and Kristol, he recalled, "handed me a check and I had to find an office. Irving never paid any attention to details, never micromanaged. I needed a staff, they recommended Fred Baumann, a Straussian at Harvard, [and] he and I put the thing into motion."

Olin provided grants to the public television station WGBH, partly to support Ben Wattenberg's *In Search of the Real America*, which offered a sunny picture of the country's future. In short order, Wattenberg would publish a book called *The Good News Is the Bad News Is Wrong*, charging that the media routinely offered an excessively pessimistic portrait of the United States. This would become the conservative credo—as long as conservatives were in power.

When they weren't, the country, of course, was going downhill rapidly, thanks to liberal fecklessness.

The importance of Kristol himself to the success of these efforts can scarcely be exaggerated. According to Joyce, "Kristol is . . . central to this story. He knew of people, opportunities, he would convene dinners." The keystone of his efforts was taking over the American Enterprise Institute. AEI, founded as an organ of conservative business interests, had been run into the ground by its director, William Baroody Jr. Baroody also got into hot water for holding seminars at which speakers critical of Israel had appeared. Chase Manhattan's CEO, Willard C. Butcher, fired Baroody; in 1986 Christopher De-Muth, a former staff assistant to Richard Nixon and member of the Office of Management and Budget in the Reagan administration, replaced him.

With AEI in crisis, the road was open for the neoconservatives. AEI had already attracted Kristol in 1976, and he in turn brought on other neoconservatives such as Robert H. Bork, a solicitor general under Nixon, and Ben Wattenberg. Jeane Kirkpatrick, Michael Novak, and Charles Murray soon followed. AEI was commandeered by the neocons. This redoubt of moderate Ripon Society Republicanism became the neocons' fortress. They hauled one another up, always extending a helping hand to the next scholar, debarred from some Ivy League university for proclaiming a Straussian heresy, to clamber over the ramparts.

After his son William started working in the Bush administration as Vice President Dan Quayle's chief of staff (after a stint at the Department of Education under William Bennett during Reagan's presidency), Kristol himself abandoned New York ("no longer the nation's intellectual center") for Washington. This development marks a real turning point in the fortunes of the neoconservative movement. At the time, it signaled a triumphant arrival of intellectuals in (or near) the corridors of power. In hindsight, it looks more like the beginning of the end. The neocons, working through their network of journals and committees and as advisers to sympathetic political figures like Jackson, had been very effective as gadflies and critics. Now they would increasingly try their hand at exercising power directly.

The shift to Washington also marks a change in their tortured relationship with liberalism. In the 1930s and 1940s the neocons had been fiercely opposed to liberalism. After the war they seem to have realized that a strong and healthy American liberalism was crucial to victory in the cold war and (not coincidentally) to the survival of Israel. So they allied themselves with the liberal hawks in the foreign policy establishment. During the 1960s and 1970s, however, as American liberalism moved leftward and became both more averse to confronting the Soviets and more hostile to Israel, they had shifted to trying to save it from its own left-leaning tendencies. Now, with the Reagan ascendancy, the old hostility resurfaced—along with the radical temperament. Increasingly, they concluded that liberalism could not be saved and would have to be destroyed root and branch. This partly explains why they took the lead in the culture war of the 1980s and 1990s. (Another reason was to hammer out a series of "values" issues that could unite secular and religious conservatives.)

But would the neoconservative movement ever boast the same kind of heavyweight intellectual credentials it had enjoyed during the 1970s? It was no accident, as the Marxists used to say, that its best minds periodically jumped ship. Daniel Bell had scented problems early and left *Public Interest.* In the early 1980s Daniel Patrick Moynihan would do the same. He turned on the Reagan administration, much to the dismay of his younger neoconservative acolytes. More such defections would follow.

There was a tension between power and intellectualism that the neoconservatives never resolved. They started out as intellectuals who were attracted to power. Soon enough, however, the prospect of access to the high and mighty became an end in itself. The neoconservatives became progressively more inventive in dreaming up strategies and rationales to justify some of the worst excesses of the GOP. They had some startling accomplishments in the 1970s. But the further they moved to the right, the less intellectual independence they displayed—and the more partisan they became. Irving Howe was dead wrong when he claimed that intellectuals had surrendered their intellects in the 1950s, but he was right about where it would end. The neocons became what has been called "counter-intellectuals."

Still, in a Republican Party largely bereft of ideas, the neoconservatives smoothly and quickly became the most prominent spokesmen for a militarized foreign policy that challenged the Soviet Union. But they lacked a popular base inside the party as well as the infighting skills that seasoned Republican operatives, businessmen, deal-making lawyers, and all-around pooh-bahs such as James Baker and George Shultz had honed over the decades. The neoconservatives tried to become the arbiters of the Reagan revolution, but the sacerdotal role that they enjoyed under George W. Bush had not yet fallen to them. Despite their admiration for Reagan, moreover, he would gravely disappoint them, leaving some of them facing jail sentences in an almost literal exile from the conservative movement. Given their prophetic temperament, the neoconservatives could not help but be disappointed by their chosen leader. Their response would be to refashion him in their own image after he left office, while searching for a true apostolic successor.

Redemption

Lenin understood that very clearly. What communists call theoretical organs always end up through a filtering process influencing a lot of people who don't even know they're being
influenced . . . We've had ideological politics for quite a while
now. In the end, ideas rule the world because even interests are
defined by ideas. The closer you get to the game of politics the
less likely you are to see that.

—Irving Kristol, 1985

When Ronald Reagan won the presidency in 1980, he created what
quickly became known as the Reagan revolution. A new alliance took

shape composed of northeastern business conservatives, western libertarian conservatives, and evangelicals, topped off with neoconservatives. It wasn't just that government officials walked around wearing maroon ties bearing a golden profile of Adam Smith. They genuinely tried to overturn the postwar liberal consensus that had prevailed, whether Dwight Eisenhower, Richard Nixon, or Jimmy Carter was president.

Reagan's unique ability to hold together this inherently unstable coalition, and his extraordinary success in the cold war, would set off disputes over his true legacy that have not been settled to this day. Each faction in the GOP foreign policy establishment—realist and neoconservative—tries to portray itself as Reagan's true heir. Whether or not Reagan himself was a neoconservative, as the neocons like to state, or a dyed-in-the-wool conservative, as the paleoconservatives claim, or even an Emersonian liberal, as his latest biographer, John Patrick Diggins (himself a liberal), asserts, he did open the door to them in government. Reagan was a former New Deal liberal, and he was, unlike some conservatives, pro-Israel. His sympathy for Israel had deeply personal roots: he never forgot that his father bypassed a hotel that didn't admit Jews. Reagan, aghast at the Holocaust, backed the creation of Israel and in his weekly radio broadcasts often decried anti-Semitism. He had other things in common with the neoconservatives. He himself had converted to conservatism, and it was natural that he would welcome new converts. It was a move that permanently reshaped the GOP and altered the course of American foreign policy.

There was always a link between neoconservative gloom about cultural decay at home and the need to fight communism abroad in order to ward off the decline of the West. Much of the decade would be filled with lamentations on this theme, penned by the neoconservatives themselves or by foreign Cassandras like Aleksandr Solzhenitsyn and the French thinker Jean-François Revel, who wrote *How Democracies Perish*, an indictment of Western intellectuals and governments for their illusions about communism. (There was also an intriguing, unresolved tension between the decline-of-the-West school, which neoconservatives like Kristol and William Bennett embraced, and the belief in the unstoppable power of capitalism and democracy, which other neoconservatives such as Michael Novak trumpeted.) Whittaker Chambers had declared in his 1952 autobiography, *Witness*, with a touch of artificial melancholy, that he was joining the losing side of history. This attitude was common on the right, before Reagan transformed the conservative movement. Even the usually ebullient William F. Buckley Jr. sounded a similar note of high-toned pessimism when he famously defined a conservative as someone who "stands athwart history, yelling 'Stop!' "

Reagan, optimistic and buoyant, wanted victory. He would script his own scenario for the cold war, one with a happy Hollywood ending. Little did the neoconservatives, or even traditional conservatives, realize that Reagan was not their handmaiden but the choreographer of his own presidency, from start to finish. Initially, he attacked the Soviets, declaring on January 29, 1981, that "the only morality they recognize is what will further their cause, meaning they reserve unto themselves the right to commit any crime, to lie, to cheat, in order to attain that." But Reagan would perform a volte-face by his second term. While the neoconservatives saw Mikhail Gorbachev as a dangerously sophisticated communist, Reagan ignored their warnings. He wasn't about to remain stuck on autopilot once he had a genuine interlocutor in the Kremlin with whom he could negotiate an end to the nuclear peril—a dream he harbored ever since atomic weapons were invented.

Reagan wanted to remain above the fray, though his presidency was almost wrecked by the machinations of the neoconservatives who interpreted his anticommunist mandate rather broadly. He had the ability, not uncommon to successful politicians, to detach himself from his minions. Midge Decter bitterly reflected, years later, that Reagan "must at the core have been a very cold man," observing that "when he left Washington, he blithely left behind him, clearly without giving it another moment's thought, a group of public servants who were in deep trouble for doing nothing worse than loyally carrying out his policy."[1] Decter was mistaken. Reagan was not a cold man. He was his own man.

But in the early 1980s, optimism prevailed. For Irving Kristol, the Reagan revolution was the culmination of a war against liberalism that he had been waging for decades, and it marked the first moment that the neoconservatives enjoyed a real entrée to power. Kristol had helped popularize the idea of supply-side (or trickle-down) economics, which maintained that the more government lowered taxes, the greater entrepreneurialism and investment it would trigger, thereby increasing general wealth (and government revenues). Later, Kristol acknowledged that he was uncertain about the economic merits of the idea, but quite sure of its political utility. He also championed the alliance brokered by Reagan between mainstream conservatives and the religious right, which he said was the staunchest friend of Israel. Secular, liberal Jews in the United States, Kristol believed, were the true threats to the perpetuation of both the Jewish faith and Israel.

Once again, however, the neocons were distinguished by their lack of a real constituency. As intellectuals—and Jews—they were unable to deliver any votes. Jews were reflexively liberal. Most wanted nothing to do with conservatism, neo or otherwise. They maintained the political faith of their fathers and grandfathers. The real Reagan Democrats were primarily Irish Catholics who had become disenchanted with the Democratic Party's support for abortion and school busing. Indeed, on the left the contention that the neocons had betrayed the Jewish faith appeared with increasing frequency. In an impassioned book called *Jews Without Mercy: A Lament*, Earl Shorris provided an early and extended denunciation of the neocons. Shorris said that because they had committed apostasy, the neocons were not Jews at all: "A new political movement has come to Judaism, a movement of self-interest, without mercy for the old or the poor, a movement that condemns oppression only when it serves the interests of the movement to do so."[2]

This is one reason why the Jewish neoconservatives felt rather insecure within the GOP establishment. Always regarded as interlopers (doubly so as Democrats and Jews), their influence rested on their intellectual abilities. Under the tutelage of Kristol and Norman Podhoretz, the neocons made a place for themselves at the GOP table by wielding their pens. It was their self-anointed role to serve as the court theologians of the right, contriving to hold together and invigorate the Reagan coalition by taking the lead in the culture war, hammering out the "values" themes that would unify its disparate elements despite their many differences. As Midge Decter put it, they saw their task as "making useful arguments." The key word here is "useful."

In particular, Kristol kowtowed to the religious right. Writing in the *New York Times*, Kristol suggested that Darwinism was simply a "theory," a "hypothesis," and far "from an established scientific fact." In his view, it was science teachers who were needlessly antagonizing the Christian right by insisting upon teaching unadulterated Darwinism: "As things now stand, the religious fundamentalists are not far off the mark when they assert that evolution, as generally taught, has an unwarranted antireligious edge to it." Evolution, he concluded, should be taught more cautiously.[3]

Decter herself, in another sign of the rise of the neoconservatives, became a trustee of the Heritage Foundation, which banged the drum on social issues such as abortion and affirmative action, helped staff the Reagan administration, and played a key role in advising Republican legislators such as Newt Gingrich, who created a guerrilla insurgency in the 1980s. After the Senate rejected Robert Bork's nomination for the Supreme Court in 1987, for example, Heritage held an emotional meeting in its Lehrman Auditorium, where hundreds of "movement" conservatives vented their spleen at the perfidious liberal elite for besmirching one of the greatest jurists of the century. It was this sense of rage and exclusion, felt most keenly by a younger generation that had formed its conservative views on hostile, liberal elite college campuses, that would further radicalize the conservative movement.

In January 1988 Heritage also hosted a talk by Henry Kissinger—a sign of both sides' eagerness to reach a rapprochement. In his introduction Heritage's president, Edwin Feulner, acknowledged that conservatives had been suspicious of Kissinger but said that they would like what they would hear that evening. Ironically, Kissinger warned about the dangers of dealing with the Soviet Union precisely at the moment that Reagan was able to achieve real accomplishments with Gorbachev. In later years he would move closer to the neocons, ultimately becoming a prominent supporter of the Iraq war—another sign of Kissinger's almost infallible ability to get it wrong.

Mark Lilla, who was an executive editor of *Public Interest*, recalls the early 1980s as a unique, heady moment when it really seemed as though intellectuals could have an impact on policy. The neocons were on a roll that defied the expectations of many political observers. Nicholas Lemann, then a reporter at the *Washington Post* (now dean of the Columbia School of Journalism), noted that the neoconservatives who were on board with Reagan "have one problem: most of them are registered Democrats."[4] This group included Jeane Kirkpatrick, Eugene Rostow, Paul Wolfowitz, Elliott Abrams, Douglas Feith, and dozens of other neoconservatives. Much of the board of the Committee on the Present Danger, which included Richard Allen, Kenneth Adelman, Midge Decter, Jeane Kirkpatrick, and Max Kampelman and which had steadily attacked the Carter administration, would serve in the Reagan administration. Meanwhile, the committee would continue to exhort the president to maintain the faith and treat arms-control negotiations and agreements with profound skepticism, if not hostility.

Membership in the Democratic Party turned out to be the ideal neoconservative entrée into the GOP. Their status as defectors meant that they were welcomed as though they were coming in from a political Siberia. Had the Democratic Party managed to retain the neoconservatives, it might never have suffered the devastating defeats it experienced in the 1980s, when it lost three successive presidential elections. At a minimum, it would have been more difficult to paint the Democrats as weak on foreign policy—a charge that has dogged the party.

In 1983 Walter Mondale, then preparing to challenge Reagan for the presidency, made a stab at wooing the neocons in the hopes of staving off this charge. He solicited their advice, prompting Daniel Patrick Moynihan to declare, "You can't hold Carter against him permanently. The labor connection is much more important."[5] But Mondale's overture went nowhere. The neocons were firmly embedded in the GOP. In addition, taking their cue from Kristol, they were cultivating the Christian right.

When Reagan entered office, the United States—so he and the neoconservatives argued—had experienced a decade of national humiliation. The arms race continued to roar ahead. Soviet encroachments in the Third World, most notably in Africa, continued. Afghanistan had been invaded. Cuba was meddling in Angola, Nicaragua, and El Salvador. The shah of Iran had been toppled and American diplomats taken hostage.

At the same time, both the realpolitik of Kissinger and the moralpolitik of Carter looked like colossal failures. Reagan promised to restore American greatness and to return to the cold war precepts that had safeguarded the United States during the late 1940s and the 1950s—the ones originally enunciated by Harry Truman and John F. Kennedy. As Kristol, Kirkpatrick, and other neocons saw it, the greatest danger was an erosion of liberal will, a collapse of bourgeois virtues that was sapping the ability of Western leaders to confront communism. Podhoretz declared, "The conflict between the United States and the Soviet Union is a clash between two civilizations. More accurately, it is a clash between civilization and barbarism." Kirkpatrick saw a "new class," as did Kristol, that was unmanning the West. The family, business, and schools were all under attack by the left. Somebody had to fight back.

The neoconservatives thought of themselves as Reagan's intellectual shock troops, a kind of guerrilla army staking out positions that he himself shared, especially in his first term. Three goals or issues in particular animated them: backing anticommunist movements in Central America; ramping up the arms race with the Soviet Union; and pursuing the Strategic Defense Initiative, an antiballistic missile system that was swiftly labeled Star Wars by its critics.

The longer the Reagan presidency went on, the more disgruntled the neoconservatives became. When Reagan entered office, the Soviet leader, Yuri Andropov, the former head of the KGB who had helped organize the suppression of the Hungarian revolution, was trying to overcome the Brezhnev-era "time of stagnation," as it was known in the Soviet Union, by cracking down internally on a lax work ethic and alcoholism. When Andropov died, Konstantin Chernenko assumed office, only to pass away thirteen months later. Throughout, the aging Soviet leadership seemed unstable and insecure and dangerous.

Mikhail Gorbachev, a dynamic young leader committed to reform, was intent on saving the Soviet system. Gorbachev's highly calculated charm offensive—aided by his wife, Raisa, who, unlike the previous roll call of Kremlin milkmaids, looked rather fetching in her Russian furs (to the consternation of Nancy Reagan)—made Western audiences swoon, and this drove the neocons into a frenzy of suspicion and anxiety. "We Surrender!" ran the cover of a *New Republic* issue after Gorbachev got out of his limousine to shake hands with onlookers in Washington, D.C., in December 1987. The truth, of course, was precisely the opposite. Gorbachev was surrendering. But the neoconservatives were horrified by Reagan's attempts to reach arms-control agreements with the man they called "Iron Mike." The duty of the West was to arm itself to the teeth and prepare for a nuclear showdown, not negotiate with an implacable adversary that resembled Nazi Germany.

When it came to domestic policy, the neocons were remarkably unified and could find common ground with most other conservatives. On foreign policy they were at odds with the other wings—too interventionist for the libertarians, the isolationists, and the business conservatives. These differences would widen into deep fissures during the second Bush administration, when they seemed altogether too Wilsonian for the comfort of their coalition partners.

Yet in the 1980s the neocons were themselves divided over the issue of human rights versus realpolitik. Even as individuals, their positions could seem contradictory. Irving Kristol despised utopianism and condemned the human rights lobby, but he himself would declare, "Realpolitik à la Disraeli is unthinkable in America." As Kristol saw it, the issue of human rights was a left-wing cause. Just as the American left was concocting rights for the underprivileged or disabled, so it was using the same tactic to create universal rights abroad. Nathan Glazer, meanwhile, criticized the self-righteous hubris of the United States. "We cannot and should not go around the world pinning medals on some countries, recording debits for others," he said. Podhoretz disagreed. He argued that to battle communism in the "world of ideas and ideologies is . . . in itself a necessary condition of fighting for human rights; anyone who fails to oppose Communism forfeits the intellectual and moral right to speak in the name of human rights." Podhoretz believed that only by starkly stating that threats existed could the public ever be aroused to back necessary military programs.

Throughout the Reagan years the neocons were the bad guys in the media—a mere taste of the obloquy they would receive under George W. Bush. Though they were not yet seen as embodying a dangerous conspiracy, they were routinely vilified as heretics by liberals and leftists: Jewish traitors to the liberal movement who had abandoned whatever vestiges of reason and decency they still clung to in the 1970s. As long as the Soviet Union existed and the Democratic Party remained stuck in McGovernism, however, the neoconservatives were united on the basic issue of preserving peace through strength. The ostracism, the exile from the Democratic Party, was so fresh, and still so wounding, that they suppressed any intellectual disagreements to continue to reach out to Reagan and the far right. But even so, they were riven by their own internal disputes. The battle between older neoconservatives such as Jeane Kirkpatrick and Irving Kristol, who shunned the notion of idealism and human rights, and a younger generation led by Elliott Abrams raged for several years. In the end, Abrams and the idea of a democratic crusade would prevail—and set the stage for the Bush presidency.

To understand this struggle, we need to look back at Kirkpatrick's unusual influence in the early years of the Reagan administration.

Jeane Kirkpatrick: Reagan's Democrat

On August 20, 1984, Jeane Kirkpatrick was the keynote speaker at the Republican National Convention in San Diego. Invoking Harry Truman in her first lines, she decried the "San Francisco Democrats" who "blame America first." She quoted the French neoconservative Jean-François Revel, author of the book *How Democracies Perish*, on the dangers of national self-denigration. Her talk was less about the greatness of Ronald Reagan than about the terrible mistake the Democrats had made in straying from the policies of Truman, Kennedy, and Johnson. Kirkpatrick's own astonishing ascent was confirmation of how far the neocons had come—and how far they still had to go.

Almost overnight, Kirkpatrick achieved stardom. Like Moynihan, she was an Irish Catholic and a former academic who reveled in intellectual disputes. As UN ambassador, she became a heroine for her denunciations of Third World kleptocracies and her ringing defense of the United States. She and Reagan adored each other. But to the intense disappointment of her admirers, Kirkpatrick was never offered the post of secretary of state or national security adviser in the second Reagan administration. Her nemesis George Shultz said he would resign if she was appointed national security adviser. Kirkpatrick had a tendency to shoot from the hip. Shultz did not. He took a more somber view of the cold war and did not regard negotiations with the Soviet Union as tantamount to appeasement. By the end of the Reagan presidency, he had outmaneuvered the neocons.

What Kirkpatrick offered the Reagan administration was intellectual legitimacy to cover its sympathy for right-wing regimes (including, at the time, apartheid South Africa) and its attempts to overthrow hostile ones in Central and South America. She never really cottoned to the idea of a democratic crusade. She was more of a realist than the modern-day variety of neocon. She did, however, support Joshua Muravchik, who would land at the American Enterprise Institute (AEI) in the late 1980s, after completing his Ph.D. study of the Carter administration and human rights at Georgetown University. Muravchik would become one of the key neoconservative theorists in providing the movement with a new cause after the cold war, shifting from anticommunism to democracy promotion. (Muravchik was a former chairman of the Young People's Socialist League and a protégé of Max Shachtman, and his dissertation was called "The Carter Administration and the Dilemmas of Human Rights Policy." Published in 1986 by AEI Press, and titled *The Uncertain Crusade: Jimmy Carter and the Dilemmas of Human*

Rights Policy, it pointed to the successful transformations of Germany and Japan by the United States into democracies as a template for the rest of the world.)

Kirkpatrick spent four years at the UN. She devoted herself in part to making speeches outlining what she thought U.S. foreign policy needed to achieve. This was not as naively professorial as it might sound. The speeches were well crafted, stocked with information, and delivered with panache and often humor. (Speaking to the National Urban League on July 20, 1981, about Africa, she began, "To persuade you of the virtues of the Reagan administration's foreign policy is probably impossible; so I propose instead a more modest goal: to convince you that our foreign policy is not as bad as you think it is."[6]) Like her great predecessor Moynihan, Kirkpatrick managed to arouse considerable sympathy for her defiance of the Third World and its stranglehold on the United Nations. In a 1981 speech titled "The Reagan Phenomenon and the Liberal Tradition," Kirkpatrick insisted that the United States should champion democratic freedoms allied to military might. In "The Reagan Reassertion of Western Values," she argued for a return to hard-nosed ideological precepts. But her speech contained an internal contradiction that the neoconservatives were reluctant to face up to: on the one hand, she argued that "the functional scope of Soviet expansion has enlarged alongside its expanding geographical focus"; on the other, she stated that "the Soviet empire is decaying at its center." Kirkpatrick wanted to portray the United States as strongly on the offensive under Reagan yet still menaced with total destruction. At what point would the country be secure? The neoconservatives could not say. They were locked into seeing a permanent and perpetual menace.

Kirkpatrick never stopped sounding these alarms and denouncing the American left and the Third World. The same confrontational style was later employed by John Bolton, another neoconservative favorite who enjoyed a brief, stormy tenure as UN ambassador under George W. Bush.

None of this went down well with liberal elites in Washington and New York, who portrayed her as a maniacal cold warrior. Kirkpatrick made it too easy for them. Overly taken with her own distinction between authoritarian and totalitarian regimes, she came down on the side of the Argentine generals during their takeover of the Falkland Islands in April 1982. This was probably Kirkpatrick's worst moment. A scholar of Latin America, she displayed an unseemly avidity for supporting the Argentine junta, to the extent of having dinner at the Argentine embassy on the eve of the Falklands War. Notwithstanding her talk about democratic values, she wasn't all that keen on pushing them onto friendly allies, no matter how reprehensible their domestic arrangements. The flip side of her belief in the slow reform of authoritarian regimes was that it could never happen under communism. Only after the cold war ended did she acknowledge that she had been too hasty in dismissing the possibility of change in the Soviet Union.

Indeed, if anything, the neocons in the Kristol-Kirkpatrick camp were terribly suspicious of democratization. They viewed it as a lingering vestige of the Carter administration rather than as a Reagan administration issue. Senseless blather about human rights had, for example, brought down America's longtime, loyal friend, the shah of Iran. So at this point the neocons were decidedly ambivalent about the idea of a global crusade for democracy. Kristol and Kirkpatrick were drawn more to Niebuhrian pessimism than to Reaganite optimism. Writing in the inaugural issue of the *National Interest*, Kristol took aim at the human rights lobby, even putting the term itself in quotation marks to underscore his contempt for it:

> This current of thought, now dominant (at least temporarily) in the Democratic Party, sets great store on American

preachments about "human rights," insists on American subordination to international organizations (most of them dominated by nations with left-wing regimes), and believes that the United States has no right to the independent use of American military power anywhere, including in Latin America.[7]

Ironically enough, Kristol's unilateralism would ultimately be linked by Reagan, and even more by the Bush administration, with human rights to forge a global democratic crusade.

Shultz and Abrams

The Kirkpatrick view was fiercely opposed by Secretary of State George Shultz and his assistant Elliott Abrams. A sharp-faced man with severe, bristling eyebrows that made him look like the quintessential hawk, Abrams achieved the distinction of becoming the most reviled neocon among liberals because of his support for the Nicaraguan contras. He was, in a sense, the Scooter Libby of the Reagan administration. He was pilloried by the liberal press—and he fired back in kind. Abrams could never resist returning the potshots his foes took at him. At one point, his house was the subject of a silent vigil by protesters of the Reagan administration's Central America policies.

Abrams, like most other neocons, was a lapsed liberal. He was a leading member of the new generation of younger neoconservatives and would prove to be one of the most effective.

Abrams's entrée into politics came through the Harvard professor Nathan Glazer; Abrams had lived in Glazer's attic as a law student; Glazer got him to write for *Public Interest* and introduced him to Podhoretz. He worked for Henry M. Jackson in the 1972 Massachusetts primary after Richard Perle, whom he had met at an

Americans for Democratic Action (ADA) convention, introduced him to the senator. On January 24, 1975, which was his birthday, Abrams decided it was time to bolt Breed, Abbott and Morgan, the high-powered New York law firm that he had been working for—"these people don't even read *Commentary*," he told a friend—and join Jackson as assistant counsel on the Permanent Subcommittee on Investigations. However, Abrams was never a member of the Jackson bunker; that honor was reserved for Jackson's closest aides—Fosdick, Perle, and Charles Horner.

In 1976 Abrams transferred to Moynihan's staff, serving first as special counsel, then as chief of staff. As a New Yorker, via the Harvard government department and law school, he was a logical pick for the newly elected senator from New York. The initial team included Abrams, Tim Russert (now an NBC news correspondent), Chester Finn (an education policy expert closely allied with the "honorary neoconservative" Diane Ravitch), and Penn Kemble—a heavy dose of neoconservatives. Moynihan, as we saw, devoted his maiden speech in the Senate to denouncing Paul Warnke's nomination as head of the Arms Control and Disarmament Agency. But Moynihan himself would soon shed his neoconservative views. As a senator, moreover, he would prove remarkably ineffective, apart from an exhortatory role. Indeed, an argument could be made that the Senate ruined one of the great public intellectuals of the latter half of the twentieth century.

In any case, by 1979 Abrams had become disillusioned with Moynihan, who was, in the best of circumstances, difficult to work for. Instead, he went to work for the law firm of the Democratic lobbyist (and former LBJ counsel) Harry McPherson—an experience Abrams recalls as "boring and horrible." After the excitement of Capitol Hill, how could it be otherwise? The famous neoconservative meeting with Carter in December 1979, in which Abrams participated, sealed his antipathy toward the Democratic Party. Family ties also played a role—in 1980 he married one of Podhoretz's stepdaughters and became linked to the neoconservative movement by marriage as well as ideological inclination. Abrams united the Washington (political) and New York (intellectual) worlds of neoconservatism. The other members of the Podhoretz family were all involved in neoconservatism: John Podhoretz was then executive editor of the Moonie-owned publication *Insight*; Midge Decter was executive director of the Committee for the Free World; and Norman, of course, was editor of *Commentary*. Decter's daughter Naomi contributed to the Committee for the Free World's publication *Contentions*, referred to by its detractors as *Conniptions*; her husband, Steven Munson, was the committee's deputy director.

If Moynihan could work for Richard Nixon and Gerald Ford, then Abrams could sign on with Reagan. William Casey, who would become CIA director, put him to work on the campaign. Then, during the transition, Abrams assisted Edwin Feulner, who was president of the Heritage Foundation.

It was Moynihan who pushed Abrams: they had lunch at the Green Hat, a Capitol Hill haunt, in January 1980, and Moynihan, when he heard that Abrams thought he could aim for a deputy assistant secretary of state post, responded incredulously, "Deputy? Deputy?" Abrams returned to Casey and told him that he wanted to be assistant secretary for international relations. Secretary of State Alexander Haig promptly called and offered Abrams the post.

Reagan was initially rather disdainful of human rights, which he showed unmistakably by nominating Ernest Lefever, a member of the Committee on the Present Danger as well as the Washington-based Ethics and Public Policy Center (which Abrams himself would head in the 1990s), to be assistant secretary of state for human rights and humanitarian affairs. Lefever had declared that human rights were irrelevant to U.S. foreign policy and, furthermore, that any legislation making foreign aid conditional on a nation's observance of human rights should be repealed. The Senate Foreign Relations Committee, which had a Republican majority, rejected his nomination. As Patricia Derian, a fire-breathing liberal in the Carter State Department, observed in the November 7, 1981, *Nation*:

> It is likely that even before Reagan's bid for the Presidency, some of his industrialist friends had complained to him of the losses American business had suffered because of human-rights restrictions. They may have convinced Reagan that those off-limits governments with which they wanted to do business had had just provocation for their repressive actions.

Abrams got the job that was supposed to have been Lefever's.

Abrams spent much of the early Reagan years defending El Salvador against charges of human rights violations. The American left wanted the United States to suspend its military aid to El Salvador, complaining that the armed forces there were little better than a criminal organization. While Abrams conceded that the situation could use improvement, which was putting it mildly, he was right to back the government. In 1982 El Salvador held free elections for a new constitution, and in 1984 José Napoleón Duarte, a staunch democrat, was elected president. The infamous death squad killings declined dramatically, the civil war came to an end, and El Salvador turned into a thriving democracy. Like Jeane Kirkpatrick, however, Abrams belittled human rights abuses that had taken place in El Salvador. It was emblematic of the neoconservative penchant for overselling a policy. The neoconservative desire to link up with the Christian right was also a factor in the administration's calculations. According to Sara Diamond, documents at Stanford University's Hoover Institution reveal that

> on a regular basis, more than 50 groups met secretly with White House personnel to coordinate media and lobbying activities on behalf of the Nicaraguan contras. The

Working Group included: Jerry Falwell's Moral Majority, Pat Robertson's Freedom Council, Maranatha Campus Ministries, the Heritage Foundation, Conservative Caucus, Accuracy in Media, Young Americans for Freedom, the neoconservative Institute on Religion and Democracy, the Ethics and Public Policy Center, the Jewish Institute for National Security Affairs, and the Anti-Defamation League of B'nai B'rith. The meetings were conducted by officials from the National Security Council, the CIA, the Defense and State Departments.[8]

Abrams hoped to do more than defend individual countries, however. He wanted to seize the opportunity to help create an overarching Reaganite ideology of human rights. Thus he declared that anticommunism was itself a human rights policy. But Reagan was divided on the issue, showing reluctance even to use the term "human rights." This schizophrenic attitude was evident from the outset. For example, on April 30, 1981, he remarked, "Even at the negotiating table, never shall it be forgotten for a moment that wherever it is taking place in the world, the persecution of people for whatever reason ... persecution of people for their religious belief ... that is a matter to be on that negotiating table or the United States does not belong at that table." But the *New York Times* reported on the same day that "after the speech, a White House spokesman said Mr. Reagan had not meant to alter his policy of playing down the rights issue in foreign relations." This was typical of the kind of ambiguous performance that frustrated the neoconservatives.

It was the self-immolation of Alexander Haig that opened the door for the democratizing neoconservatives. Haig, an old-school military man who had served under Henry Kissinger at the National Security Council, was no fan of the neoconservatives. He worshipped at Kissinger's altar of realpolitik. He wanted to be what he called the "vicar" of U.S. foreign policy, like his old boss at the NSC. But Haig flamed out when he declared, "I'm in charge," after an assassination attempt on Reagan. In June 1982 Reagan replaced Haig with George Shultz.

Shultz viewed the neoconservatives with some trepidation when it came to U.S.-Soviet relations. But as a skilled and tenacious bureaucrat, he knew that having Abrams as his right-hand man on Central America would propitiate the neoconservatives and neuter them on the larger task of dealing with the Kremlin.

The turning point for Shultz came in the Philippines. Ferdinand Marcos, who had ruled the island nation since 1965, was feted during a state visit to the United States in September 1982. Four years later he resigned from office in response to mass protests mobilized by Corazon Aquino following the assassination of her husband, a popular opposition figure, by Marcos's goons. This was a seismic event, showing that authoritarian dictatorships could be peacefully brought to an end, and it not only helped create the Reagan doctrine of promoting democracy but made it central to the neoconservative movement. It made the younger neoconservatives upbeat about the potential for democratic revolution, in contrast to old-line, Burkean conservatives who abhorred the notion of rapid, tumultuous change.

Another Shultz protégé who took part in the Philippine drama was Paul Wolfowitz, then a State Department official. It hadn't been a simple matter for Wolfowitz, as a Democrat and former Carter administration official, to join Reagan. But his conservative bona fides and ties to Fred Iklé (a RAND Corporation analyst, a member of the Committee on the Present Danger, a friend of Albert Wohlstetter's, and an expert on nuclear strategy) pulled him through. Iklé served as undersecretary of defense in the Reagan administration. Wolfowitz landed a job as State Department planning director. Once again, as in the Carter administration, he was supposed to come up with a new approach to geopolitical change. Wolfowitz tapped Scooter Libby,

Francis Fukuyama, and Zalmay Khalilzad, a former Wohlstetter student, to join his team. Like Abrams, he flourished under Shultz's tenure.

Shultz was an able mentor to his protégés. They, in turn, formed a bridge to the neoconservatives. Shultz, an economist and former secretary of the Treasury under Nixon, was an experienced bureaucratic warrior. But he had served as president and chairman of the Bechtel Corporation, which had extensive investments in the Arab world, and was viewed with intense suspicion by the neoconservatives. Initially, they suspected him of being pro-Arab. This was wrong. Shultz, in contrast to Defense Secretary Caspar Weinberger, was unflinching when it came to intervention in Lebanon in 1983. He viewed as nonsense the determination of Weinberger and his aide Colin Powell to set out extremely limited parameters for U.S. intervention abroad.

Shultz was pro-democracy, not pro–right wing regimes like Kirkpatrick. But the neoconservatives were right to see in him a pragmatist who, along with Nancy Reagan, would counsel the president to reach out to Gorbachev and, ultimately, wind down the cold war. This, too, was part of Shultz's embrace of spreading democracy around the globe. An unabashed proponent of technology and capitalism, he didn't think the Soviet Union could continue to exist as a repressive state given the inroads new information technologies were making. Reagan liked Shultz because he kept a steady hand on the foreign policy tiller. Unlike his noisy and ambitious predecessor, Haig, Shultz exuded competence. But his readiness to embrace pro-democracy movements abroad flew in the teeth of GOP orthodoxy, as represented by Henry Kissinger and, to some extent, Kirkpatrick, who were both antipathetic to the policy of toppling right-wing authoritarian regimes.

Part of the pro-democracy campaign also involved supporting guerrillas abroad. The Carter administration had, in some ways, anticipated this strategy. Carter's hawkish national security adviser,

Zbigniew Brzezinski, pushed hard for a more aggressive policy in Afghanistan; according to the former CIA director and current defense secretary Robert Gates, "Carter and Brzezinski saw the Soviets beginning to increase their role in Afghanistan almost a year before the invasion, initiated work on a covert response nine months before, and implemented a covert finding to help the insurgents resist the Soviets almost six months before the massive Soviet move."[9]

It was Nicaragua that ended up destroying Abrams's career in the Reagan administration. The melancholy story began in 1982, when Congress passed the Boland Amendment, forbidding intelligence agencies to provide appropriated funds to the Nicaraguan contras, thereby leaving a loophole, so administration officials would argue, for private sources of money. The contras were fighting the communist Sandinista regime, led by Daniel Ortega, which received support from Cuba and the Soviet Union. Reagan feared a communist beachhead. The National Security Council thus embarked upon the arms-for-hostages deal known as Iran-contra, which almost brought down Reagan.

The Democrats were wrong to try to restrict Reagan's foreign policy maneuvering room. They were trying to micromanage America's response to what really was a budding communist regime in Nicaragua. But the Reagan administration's actions were inept and illegal. Once a pro-Syrian newspaper revealed the scandal in 1986, the congressional Democrats sought to exploit it for political gain by holding hearings to expose the principal participants in the scheme. Colonel Oliver North, together with his boss, National Security Adviser John M. Poindexter, embarked upon a secret policy of selling weaponry to Iran and then diverting the funds to help pay for arms for the Nicaraguan contras. North admitted to Congress that he had previously lied to it about the Iran-contra scheme, which he said was a "neat idea." He became a public hero by depicting himself as a loyal soldier defending America's interests in defiance of Congress; but the damage to the neoconservatives and Reagan was severe. The

1987 Tower Commission report exonerated Reagan only by declaring that he had been passive and unaware of what his subordinates were concocting.

Abrams was, of course, one of those subordinates. In April 1985, Shultz had promoted him to assistant secretary for Latin American affairs—the youngest assistant secretary in the history of the State Department. A month later Congress, trying to have it both ways, modified the Boland Amendment by appropriating twenty-seven million dollars for the Nicaraguan Humanitarian Assistance Office, which was headed by Abrams. The idea was that the United States would provide so-called humanitarian assistance to the contras, but Oliver North wormed his way into this operation by merging its flights with his other weapons shipments. Soon enough, Shultz was using Abrams as his emissary to investigate what other actions North was taking. Shultz, according to his assistant Charles Hill's notes, instructed Abrams on September 4, 1985: "We don't want to be in the dark. You suppose to be mgr [manager] of overall C.A. [Central America] picture. Contras are integral part of it. So y[ou] need to know how they getting arms. So don't just say go see the WH [White House]. It's very risky for WH."

Abrams was not only the public champion of aid to the contras; he ran the weekly interagency meetings, which included Colonel North as well as officials from the CIA and Defense Department, on aiding the contras. Abrams also gave the number of North's secret Swiss bank account to agents of the sultan of Brunei, who deposited ten million dollars, which subsequently "disappeared," to assist the contras. As Eric Alterman noted in the *Washington Monthly* in 1987:

> Since taking responsibility for the contras, Abrams, a brilliant bureaucrat when it comes to turf protection, has professed a startling degree of ignorance before congressional committees, not only on North's activities and the Costa Rican operation but also of the constant resupply of the con-

tras by mercenaries using the Ilopango airbase in El Salvador, a base we practically own and operate.[10]

It's not hard to see why the Reagan administration took this course. In the summer of 1985, Democratic congressional intransigence meant that funding to the contras was being cut off. The Democrats were living in the past; just as they had cut off funds to aid the Angolan resistance in the aftermath of Vietnam, they now saw a new Vietnam looming in every conflict. Reagan's method was to rely on proxy forces, and on local populations who wanted to oppose dictatorships. In 1985, in his State of the Union speech, Reagan said that America had to help anticommunist fighters: "We must stand by all our democratic allies. And we must not break faith with those who are risking their lives—on every continent, from Afghanistan to Nicaragua—to defy Soviet-supported aggression and secure rights which have been ours from birth." This was the essence of what came to be known as the Reagan Doctrine—the polar opposite of what had been known as the Brezhnev Doctrine in the 1970s, when the Soviet Union was on the march. Now the United States was going on the offensive—a crusade that would be dusted off by George W. Bush at the beginning of the new century. Few areas were seen as more pivotal in Reagan's attempt to roll back communist advances than Central America, America's "backyard."

On October 10, 1986, Abrams testified to Congress that he did not know of Oliver North's illegal sale of arms to Iran and the diversion of funds to the contras. But this was not true. After a lengthy investigation by Special Counsel Lawrence Walsh, Abrams pleaded guilty to two misdemeanor charges of withholding information from Congress. According to the Walsh report on the Iran-contra affair, Abrams acknowledged that he had misled the Senate Foreign Relations Committee and the House Permanent Select Committee on Intelligence in October 1986.

But Abrams was fighting, as he saw it, not for authoritarianism but for democracy. His belief in democratization was why he supported elections in El Salvador, which ultimately brought about a peaceful transition to democracy, and it was why he supported the contras. He also argued, in opposition to Senator Jesse Helms, that it was imperative to maintain pressure on Chile's strongman, Augusto Pinochet, to continue with a transition to a constitutional democracy. Thus to dismiss Abrams as a retrograde right-winger, as many leftists have, is to do him an injustice.

The Iran-contra debacle, however, exemplified the lawlessness and contempt for rules that seemed to pervade the Reagan administration. The journalist Haynes Johnson observed, "In the Reagan White House, laws were something to be evaded rather than executed. Instead of trying to change a law by pointing out its inadequacies, the Reagan people chose either to disregard it or find a way to get around it." Sound familiar? Those same instincts would destroy the George W. Bush presidency. Interestingly, however, Abrams is the only neoconservative who seems to have learned the lesson that in order to perform effectively in government, you're often better advised to stay behind the scenes and keep out of the headlines. During the George W. Bush administration, as national security adviser on Middle East affairs, Abrams has done just that.

Prodigal Son: Richard Perle

If the Iran-contra affair represented Reaganism run amok, it did help push Reagan to reach out to the Soviet Union. Reagan needed a big success to restore his tarnished image. He got it by jettisoning the neoconservatives who wanted to keep the cold war going. At the same time, there can be no doubt that the neoconservatives helped create the conditions for Reagan's ultimate victory.

Richard Perle played a major role during the Reagan administration. If any neoconservative exercised real power early in his career, it was Perle. Perle went from serving as an aide to Scoop Jackson to becoming assistant secretary of defense in the Reagan administration. There he battled his State Department counterpart, Richard R. Burt, over arms control with the Soviet Union. Burt, a former *New York Times* correspondent, was smooth and polished, a favorite of the Georgetown set. He wore well-tailored suits and spoke in sonorous establishment phrases; Perle, by contrast, was rumpled and unkempt, an intellectual who showed up for work late in the morning, but Caspar Weinberger didn't care. He knew that Perle was an unconventional thinker who didn't put much stock in what the foreign policy elite thought about the Soviet Union. Moreover, he consistently outmaneuvered the State Department types like Burt. It was, some joked, the war of the Richards.

Their battle was chronicled in a wretched novel written by Perle himself, after he resigned from the Pentagon in 1987, called *Hard Line*. (Consistent with his habitual mixing of business and personal interests, Perle signed a contract for $300,000 for the book while in office—a lucrative deal that prompted the Democratic Georgia senator Sam Nunn to rebuke him publicly.) Breathlessly written, the book features a tough-minded Pentagon official—guess who?—intent on saving the Republic from the machinations of a State Department official who is ready to sell out national security in order to win the plaudits of the liberal press. The story is recounted by Harvard professor Michael Waterman, who is dismayed by the claim "made by the liberals of the period that the Soviet Union never really threatened the Free World, that the Pentagon overstated Soviet military power to justify huge military budgets, that *liberal* policies (of *restraint*, no less) led to the Western victory in the Cold War and the subsequent breakup, first of the Warsaw Pact and then the Soviet Union itself" (emphasis in original).[11]

On paper, Perle's position was not particularly powerful, but he served as Weinberger's intellectual enforcer in insisting that the United States confront the Soviet Union whenever and wherever possible. Perle's bellicosity would also earn him a backhanded compliment as the "prince of darkness" from British defense minister Geoffrey Howe. The moniker stuck and has been associated with him ever since. Later, during the second Bush administration, Perle's numerous ties to defense contractors again led to public controversy, forcing him to resign from his position as chairman of the Pentagon's Defense Policy Board.

Perle also hired as his deputy assistant Stephen J. Bryen, a former Senate Foreign Relations staffer who got into hot water when the FBI launched an investigation into his handling of classified documents and meetings with Zvi Rafiah, an Israeli embassy staffer. Bryen resigned but, thanks to Perle, he was rehabilitated and became a behind-the-scenes player in the neoconservative world. But the episode foreshadowed the Larry Franklin affair, when a Pentagon official working for Douglas Feith was sentenced in 2005 to twelve years in prison for passing classified information to two pro-Israel lobbyists and an Israeli diplomat.

A vital part of Reagan's rearmament program was to install Pershing missiles in Europe to counter the Soviet buildup of intermediate-range nuclear missiles. In 1975 the Soviet Union had begun deploying a new missile that carried three warheads called the SS-20. German chancellor Helmut Schmidt, in an address in 1977 at London's International Institute for Strategic Studies, warned about the Soviet move. In November 1983 the German parliament voted to approve the stationing of Pershing missiles on West German territory. The Soviet Union launched a propaganda war against "German revanchism." Reagan was portrayed as a warmonger. The Reagan administration needed some kind of arms-control proposal to counter the Soviet peace offensive.

Perle provided it. He came up with what he thought was a neat idea: the so-called zero option, that is, the removal of all Soviet intermediate-range nuclear weapons from Europe and Asia in exchange for a U.S. promise not to deploy cruise and Pershing missiles.

Perle wasn't interested in phony negotiations, which is why he came up with a proposal that he believed the Soviets would find more difficult to reject than accept. In Alexander Haig's view, this idea was "not negotiable"; he predicted that it would "generate the suspicion that the United States was only interested in a frivolous propaganda exercise or, worse, that it was disingenuously engaging in arms negotiations simply as a cover for a desire to build up its nuclear arsenal." No matter. The administration ran with it.

What Perle did not realize was that Reagan wasn't just jockeying for tactical advantage. He was actually intent on mutual disarmament, something that the hawks found inconceivable. Reagan was a utopian. He wanted to banish nuclear weapons. The hawks didn't. Reagan was worried about the rise of the nuclear freeze movement and had always harbored dreams of eliminating nuclear weapons, which is why he embraced the Strategic Defense Initiative in an address to the nation on March 21, 1983. But he was also (again unlike the hawks) receptive to arms-control agreements. Perle and others were amazed when Reagan came close to concluding a deal with Gorbachev in Iceland in 1986 to abolish the U.S. nuclear missile force. To the relief of the neoconservatives, Reagan balked at giving up SDI in return. But the Soviet Union capitulated on a number of arms-control disputes. In essence, Reagan won the disarmament battle.

Obviously, Reagan did not share the outlook of many conservatives about America's supposed decline. The neoconservatives claimed that they wanted to reverse America's lapse into weakness under Jimmy Carter. But they were trapped in an apocalyptic view of the cold war. The more perceptive members of the movement, such as Daniel Patrick Moynihan and the historian Walter Laqueur, bailed out during the early 1980s. Moynihan never ended his friendships with Podhoretz and Kristol. But he went on the attack against Reagan over the issue of aiding the Nicaraguan contras. In part this was because he was a congenital contrarian. But it was also because

he no longer believed in the Red menace. Moynihan, who was fasci-
nated by the dynamics of nationalism, believed that the Soviet empire was doomed to succumb to its fissiparous tendencies. He simply
did not believe that the Kremlin would be able to contain peacefully
the various nationalities that Stalin had cobbled together. So he decried excessive military spending and generally denounced the cold
warriors. The Reagan II that emerged to befriend Mikhail Gorbachev
was much more to Moynihan's liking.

And why did Reagan II emerge? Gorbachev's nice-guy makeover at
the helm of the sinking Soviet ship appealed to Reagan's Hollywood
sense of a happy ending. Reagan now was no longer the cowboy strid-
ing into town to gun down the black hats but a kind of benign father
figure offering redemption and solace and a message of peace on
earth to his former antagonist, which was gratefully received. For
many of the neoconservatives, this was anathema. The imminent
Soviet collapse was like a Christmas present handed to a grumpy
child who was not in the mood to accept it.

Reagan's failure fully to embrace the neoconservative program
caused much consternation in the ranks. In 1981, for example,
Reagan lifted the grain embargo against the USSR and signed a five-
year agreement to sell it nine million tons of grain per year. In 1983
he pulled American troops out of Lebanon after a Shiite suicide
bomber struck a marine barracks. It was also the case that Reagan
was not reflexively pro-Israel. Contrary to later neoconservative
mythology, he took some tough stands toward Israel. For one thing,
in February 1981 he insisted on selling Saudi Arabia offensive missiles for its F-15 jet fighters, which the Carter administration had
refused Riyadh. Reagan also approved selling the Saudis AWACS
aerial surveillance aircraft, to the intense displeasure of Israel. After
Israel bombed the Iraqi nuclear reactor at Osirak, Reagan instituted
a temporary embargo on aircraft shipments. According to Wolf
Blitzer, "That readiness to impose military sanctions against Israel

was a departure from the policies of Jimmy Carter, who had taken office in 1977 promising never to impose any 'reassessment' of policy toward Israel along the lines of the Ford-Kissinger period."[12]

Nor was Reagan gung ho about sending U.S. troops into Central America. The neoconservatives expected more of the Gipper. In 1983 Norman Podhoretz declared in *Commentary* that the administration's policy amounted to "appeasement by any other name" and demanded that U.S. troops be sent "to stop and then to reverse the totalitarian drift in Central America." This was bad advice. Reagan shrewdly refused to mire U.S. troops in foreign combat and allowed proxies to carry on the battle. As a result, democracy, not communism, spread in Central America. But many neoconservatives were constitutionally unable to recognize this. One of the original neoconservatives who had a sober view of Soviet affairs was Richard Pipes. Pipes, who served on the Reagan national security council and was a professor of Russian history at Harvard, figured prominently in the liberal demonology of conservatives in the 1980s, partly because of his service on Team B during the flap over CIA estimates of Russian military strength. He was seen as a strident cold warrior. But Pipes was more than that. As his book *Survival Is Not Enough* shows, he was attuned to internal Soviet weaknesses. In it, he noted that "the Stalinist system now prevailing in the Soviet Union has outlived its usefulness and . . . the forces making for change are becoming well-nigh irresistible. The West can promote these forces by a combination of active resistance to Soviet expansion and political-military blackmail and the denial of economic and other forms of aid." While Pipes did not foresee the total collapse of the Soviet Union—who did?—he was one of the few neocons who did not commit the mistake of seeing it as an impervious force. And when it came to the Iraq war, Pipes, with his attentiveness to the importance of political culture, was dismissive of the notion that Iraq could be turned overnight into a democracy.[13]

Ironically, the neocons became only more despairing as Reagan's presidency went on. In July 1985 Midge Decter declared, "To say I'm extremely disappointed in the way the President is dealing with terrorism is wrong–I'm disgusted! It's worse to make thunderous speeches and do nothing, like Reagan, than to be quiet and do nothing. He is substituting words for deeds." Kristol complained that the State Department view of the world continued to dominate: "They're always thinking in terms of world opinion, how our allies will react, how the U.N. will react, what our obligations are under various treaties. They don't act in a vigorous way, which one anticipated Ronald Reagan would do."[14] So Kristol tried to reignite the ideological wars. After his move to Washington in 1983, he founded a new magazine–a foreign policy counterpart to *Public Interest.* Kristol, who had played a decisive part in promoting supply-side economics (through his role as intellectual tutor to Jack Kemp, through his sway with conservative foundations, and through his column in the *Wall Street Journal*), wanted to create an ideological foreign policy to supplement it. "If there's going to be a new Republican Party," he told the *Washington Post,* "then it will need a foreign policy to match . . . The function of the magazine is to come up with principles and ideas."

National Interest, which first appeared in 1985, enjoyed snazzy headquarters on Sixteenth Street only a few blocks from the White House, with a view, from the corner office of Owen Harries, the new editor, of the Washington Monument. " 'Present at the Creation . . . ,' read yesterday's half-page newspaper ad," the *Washington Post* observed. "Perhaps only in Washington would such a grandiloquent claim introduce not a new hotel or line of haute couture, but a journal of foreign policy."[15] At the magazine's coming-out party, much of official Washington showed up, including Secretary of State George Shultz. In retrospect, it is somewhat amazing how many of the names that would resurface in the George W. Bush administration were represented in the first issue–Douglas Feith, Michael Ledeen, Richard Perle–a testament, if nothing else, to the enduring, tribal ties of the neocons. As Owen Harries saw it, Reagan had become a captive of the "old foreign policy establishment"—the Carnegie Endowment for International Peace, the Council on Foreign Relations, the State Department—which was "still very powerful, entrenched, [and] has run out of ideas, doing it from memory." Reagan "hasn't armed himself with people to provide him countervailing advice . . . None of the neoconservatives has been ideally placed."[16]

What also irked the neoconservatives was that the one person they had expected to support their intellectual and political crusade had publicly abandoned it—Daniel Patrick Moynihan. Moynihan declared in an October 4, 1985, speech at the U.S. Military Academy at West Point that a "myth of invincible communism" had taken hold during Vietnam and that American officials "lost sight of the options and sank into the continuous low-level warfare imagined in Orwell's *1984*." He went on to drub the neoconservatives, complaining that the syndrome of using "ideologists to fight ideologists" had become "a vogue in Washington," particularly "for those whose early training was Marxist but anti-communist, or at least anti-Stalinist." He concluded that this "new elite disposition" was trying to create what Orwell called " 'a continuous frenzy' over the threats we face in all corners of the world" and that the United States had become "mesmerized by the presumptive strength of totalitarian symbols."[17] Moynihan, who suspected that the Soviet Union's nationality crisis might bring it down, was echoing what Orwell had said about James Burnham and his conviction that the West was doomed to lose the battle against communism unless it pursued a policy of rollback.

In the mid-1980s, then, the neoconservatives were in a state of shock. Moynihan had deserted them. So had Reagan. Indeed, the adamantine hero they had constructed proved far more flexible than they, or his critics on the left, had ever expected. When Reagan began to meet with Gorbachev, the neocons became apoplectic. The movement had begun to stiffen into rigidity when it came to the Soviet Union. It was stunned when Gorbachev in the spring of 1987 accepted Reagan's zero option for eliminating intermediate-range missiles in Europe. The United States had won, but the neoconservatives didn't want to admit it. They saw the deal as a way for the Soviet Union to detach Western Europe from the United States by eviscerating its military commitment to the continent. They also feared that illusions about Gorbachev were permeating the Reagan administration. In an article called "The Fantasy of Communist Collapse" in the *Washington Post*, Podhoretz declared, "The idea that communism is a spent force first began circulating a few years ago as a way of saying that we no longer have anything to fear from Soviet expansionism and that we can therefore safely cut back on defense spending. Now the same idea is also being used by a number of commentators (some of whom should know better, and once did)."[18]

This, too, was wrong. Communism was indeed a spent force. The signs were everywhere. At Reykjavík, Reagan came close to signing an agreement with Gorbachev banning all nuclear weapons. On February 8, 1988, Gorbachev announced he was withdrawing Soviet troops from Afghanistan. In May 1988 Reagan visited Moscow for another summit with Gorbachev and stated that the Soviet Union was no longer an evil empire: "No, I was talking about another time, another era."

Not the neoconservatives. Reagan was accused of selling out to the communists, of appeasement, of willful naïveté. Podhoretz, like James Burnham a generation earlier, was hypnotized by the communist threat. He could not recognize that America's long, vigilant policy of containment had succeeded, much as George F. Kennan had predicted it would. By damming up the Soviet Union at "every nook and cranny," as Kennan had proposed, the United States had caused the Soviet empire to crumble from within. Yet even as it came crashing down, Podhoretz and others maintained that the edifice remained impervious. They had invested too much emotionally in the Soviet Union to conceive that it might disappear. It was their mental balustrade, something they could lean on in their battles against the effete liberals at home. Deprived of it, they lost their footing.

Suddenly the neoconservative moment seemed to be over. As Jay Winik, the former executive director of the Coalition for a Democratic Majority, observed in *Foreign Policy* magazine, "With the warming of U.S.-Soviet relations and the ratification of the Treaty on Intermediate-Range Nuclear Forces, America is witnessing the end not just of the Reagan era, but perhaps of the neoconservative era as well."[19] It was the first of many obituaries to come. But all of them would turn out to be premature.

The neoconservatives got a few breaks, but they only served to underscore their overall weakness. William Kristol, for example, landed a job in the new Bush administration working as an adviser to Vice President Dan Quayle. The Tiananmen Square massacre permitted the neoconservatives to resume their role of moral scold, chastising Bush for coddling the butchers of Beijing. But the neoconservatives had really lost their way. The Soviet enemy was gone. Was there anything that could replace it? Or were the neoconservatives dinosaurs destined to go out with the cold war?

In late April 1990 the Committee for the Free World did what intellectuals always like to do when a big event has taken place. They held a conference. Or was it a wake? The conference took place at Washington's Omni Shoreham Hotel and asked, "Does the 'West' still exist?" Everyone was there, from *Encounter*'s Melvin Lasky to the *New Criterion*'s Hilton Kramer, from *Commentary*'s Norman Podhoretz to the *National Interest*'s Owen Harries.

It might have seemed like an auspicious moment to talk about the end of Soviet communism. In the *annus mirabilis* of 1989, Gorbachev had stood by while one Eastern European satrapy after another toppled and democratic movements took over. Romania, Hungary, Czechoslovakia, Poland, and East Germany were all free. The Berlin Wall was gone. Communism was vanquished. Reagan's successor in the Oval Office, George H. W. Bush, was doing yeoman's work managing the transition.

The neocons were bewildered by the sudden fulfillment of their dream of a liberated Europe. "Are we a gang of friends, a family?" Midge Decter asked the assembled anticommunists. "Or are we a long, sour marriage held together for the kids and now facing an empty nest?"[20] To all appearances, the neocons had worn out their welcome with the conservative movement. Livid with President Bush for failing to denounce Gorbachev for not letting the Baltic States go more quickly, they accused his administration of appeasement. The only person from the Bush administration to show up at the conference was William Kristol.

In the Reagan administration the neocons had soared to prominence—Elliott Abrams, Jeane Kirkpatrick, Kenneth Adelman, Eugene Rostow, Linda Chavez, and others. Now, in the Bush administration, it was good-bye to all that. The neocons thought their wilderness years had ended. They had plighted their troth to Reagan only to discover that with Bush's ascendancy, the realists were back in charge. Human rights and moral crusades were out. Hard-boiled cynicism about the limits of power was in.

The eastern establishment Republicans brought in by Bush, men like James Baker and Brent Scowcroft, represented everything the neocons despised. Suddenly it was back to the desert after an all-too-brief respite in the promised land. George H. W. Bush would later refer to the neocons in the Reagan administration as the "crazies in the basement" who had dreamed up the Iran-contra fiasco. The neoconservatives had almost turned Reagan's presidency into a catastrophe. Now these would-be prophets were sent packing to the wilderness where they belonged.

Reagan had left the neoconservatives behind, and Bush had never wanted anything to do with them. It would be up to a new generation, led by those like Francis Fukuyama, William Kristol, Robert Kagan, Paul Wolfowitz, and Douglas Feith, who had served in the second tier of the Reagan administration, to forge a new path back to power and influence for the neoconservative movement. They would take the highly ideological approach and maneuverings of Irving Kristol and meld them with their own new crusade for freedom and justice around the world.

The End of Neoconservatism?

If anyone can be said to have set forth the hubristic lineaments of what would become the neoconservative dogma of the younger generation, it was Francis Fukuyama. His essay "The End of History?" published in the summer 1989 *National Interest*, still serves as the credo of the neoconservative movement, even if Fukuyama himself has since largely disowned, or reinterpreted, it. Fukuyama's article—an abstruse meditation on Hegel's philosophy of history—declared that the Western idea had triumphed in the battle against communism, not just against the Soviet Union but against all other rivals. There was no competing ideology anywhere in the world that could hope to prevail against the Western idea. Liberal democracy was on the march.

This was the very opposite of the lugubrious decline-of-the-West prophecies that many neoconservatives had indulged in for decades. Fukuyama had devised a triumphalist, Reaganite message for the neoconservatives that would allow them to claim that their years battling in the trenches against communism had helped bring the cold war to a successful and peaceful conclusion. It also provided them with a new raison d'être for the coming decades. If liberalism was the wave of the future, then why not give it a little shove?

Fukuyama exemplified the hubris that would overtake the neoconservative movement. The younger neoconservatives could never quite shake their attachment to liberalism, or, to put it a little differently, the impulse to do good in the world. They inherited the

Manichaean worldview of their elders, but lacked their skepticism about actually altering the state of current affairs. The neoconservatives, flush with a sense of victory, ascribed excessive credit to themselves for the collapse of communism. This prompted them to overvalue their own wisdom later when it came to tackling the challenge of Islamic extremism.

Fukuyama's conceit could hardly have come at a more propitious moment for the neoconservatives. The fortunes of the movement were, in many ways, reflected in the plight of the *National Interest.* It had been founded as a cold war magazine, but the cold war was coming to an end, and the magazine was struggling. The Reagan revolution was winding up with overtures to Mikhail Gorbachev. Who really needed another magazine on the right—wasn't neoconservatism passé?

The magazine's editor, Owen Harries, and publisher, Irving Kristol, were, to put it mildly, apprehensive about its future. It hadn't scored the big article that would put it on the map. Fukuyama's "End of History?" was it. The essay had originally been delivered at an Olin Center seminar at the University of Chicago, sponsored by Fukuyama's old teacher Allan Bloom. As Fukuyama saw it, liberalism had triumphed on the world-historical stage. In an echo of Daniel Bell, he discerned an "end of ideology" in international relations. Indeed, drawing on the French philosopher Alexandre Kojève, Fukuyama argued that the death of Marxist ideology "means the growing 'Common Marketization' of international relations, and the diminution of the likelihood of large-scale conflicts between states." The new liberal era would be rather boring, he predicted, consisting of the solving of technical problems. There would be no great disputes about ideas. All of that was over.

This was bold stuff, and the piece seemed promising to Harries, who resorted to an old editor's trick to try to gain some attention for it. He solicited a symposium of contributors to respond to it, including Bloom, Kristol, Gertrude Himmelfarb, and Pierre Hassner.

Kristol, as usual, had the best crack: "I am delighted to welcome G. W. F. Hegel to Washington, D.C."

Embassies, governments, and journalists from all over the globe contacted the *National Interest*, desperate to obtain a faxed copy. The magazine had to order several more print runs to keep up with demand. Once again, it seemed, the neocons had proven that ideas did matter, and had consequences. The neoconservatives, like Trotsky, believed in the power and primacy of ideas. Politics, in their view, was less a pragmatic clash of interests than a question of contending philosophies. Now it appeared that classical liberalism was on the march—freedom was spreading around the globe—and that given the proper tools, they could direct its course.

James Atlas, writing in the *New York Times Magazine*, marveled at the way an article by a relatively obscure State Department official, which hadn't even been read by his superiors, could be such an intellectual firecracker, reaching the desk of Margaret Thatcher. In his article Atlas teased out all the odd connections: Fukuyama's apprenticeship under Bloom and the unusual ties that bound the neoconservative world. It was a highbrow precursor of the conspiracy theories that would torment the neocons a decade later, when some of them began to deny that there even was such a thing as a neoconservative movement.

Interestingly, Harries and Fukuyama both ended up as neoconservative heretics after the second war against Iraq. Harries, in fact, would become the chief antagonist of the new neoconservative ideology. A shrewd analyst of world politics and a graceful writer, Harries scored a number of telling points.

Harries, who featured many debates in the pages of the *National Interest* between realists and neoconservative idealists, was not an American. He belonged to the older mold of neoconservatives—the *Encounter* generation that seasoned its fighting spirit with a healthy skepticism about the limits of state power. Unlike many of the younger neoconservatives, Harries is interested in literature, art, and poetry. He is a true intellectual who has traveled extensively, as opposed to a Washington, D.C., neoconservative policy wonk. As editor of the *National Interest*, he had initially tried to ally realist precepts with neoconservative doctrine. He failed. But Harries turned out to be one of the most impressive figures in the neoconservative movement because he illuminated its flaws.

Harries, who was born in 1930, grew up in the Welsh village of Garnant. The Depression hit the coal-mining area hard. As a child, Harries listened to the impassioned party leader (and fellow Welshman) David Lloyd George denounce the privileged aristocracy. His father owned a drapery store, and Harries worked his way up, attending Oxford University. In 1955 he became associate professor of political science at the University of New South Wales.

Harries was a vocal backer of the Vietnam War, and it was his lonely status that turned him into a neoconservative. He joined, among other things, the Congress for Cultural Freedom, which published the Australian journal *Quadrant.* Harries himself was editor of *Highway*, published by the Workers' Educational Association. He began as a socialist, but in 1968, revolted by the rise of the counterculture, he met Irving Kristol in New York at a Congress for Cultural Freedom meeting, where Harries began to cultivate his ties with American neoconservatives. Harries continued to work his way up in Australian politics. His fervent defense of the Vietnam War made him a rare bird in Australia. The erstwhile socialist Harries became something of an academic celebrity in his new guise as cold warrior. In 1972 he started advising the Liberal Party. In the mid-1970s he went on to head the policy section in the Foreign Affairs Department before becoming an adviser and speechwriter for the conservative prime minister Malcolm Fraser.

In 1982 Fraser appointed Harries Australian ambassador to UNESCO in Paris. With his penchant for bespoke suits and his crisp British accent, Harries was a perfect fit. His eloquent denunciations, and a detailed study that he produced, of the organization's corruption, cronyism, and anti-Western policies, further endeared him to U.S. neoconservatives. He played a key role in prompting the Reagan and Thatcher administrations to withdraw from it. After himself departing UNESCO, Harries visited Norman Podhoretz and Irving Kristol to discuss working in the United States. He became the first John M. Olin fellow in 1984 at the Heritage Foundation, where he wrote numerous articles on foreign affairs and made a name for himself in Washington. He founded, together with Kristol, *National Interest*, which, as we have seen, became the first Washington-based neoconservative foreign policy vehicle. It was supposed to wage a war of ideology against the Soviet Union and the domestic liberal establishment.

Harries always felt some unease with neoconservative idealism, but he managed to reconcile it with his belief in realism. He felt realism could give neoconservatism a more sophisticated edge. Harries deeply believed in the evil of the Soviet system and the menace that it posed to the West. But after the cold war ended, he came into his own. He used his magazine to battle the neoconservatives and argue for a more restrained U.S. foreign policy. He felt that the United States was running amok without another superpower to check its worst impulses. It is precisely his belief in the perfidy of communism that prompts him to reject the analogy today between the fight against Islamic terrorism and the cold war: "I think it's to belittle the historical experiences of World War II, not to speak of the Cold War, to equate the terrorists of today and the damage they're capable of with the totalitarian regimes of the previous century."[21]

———

What changed between 1990 and 2002 to create such disdain for neoconservatism itself with some prominent neoconservatives? The answer lies in the fractured neoconservative response to the end of the cold war. Soviet Russia had been both a geopolitical enemy and an ideological rival. As a result, during the cold war the realists and moralists on the right were largely aligned, their positions almost indistinguishable. With the collapse of the communist enemy, the latent tension between the realist and the idealist tendencies on the right broadly, and within neoconservatism itself, came to the fore.

When communism suddenly collapsed, an intellectual fight broke out among the Washington foreign policy elite: Could the neoconservatives, having claimed that the cold war would never end, now demand credit for the victory? Michael Kinsley and Strobe Talbott, among others, said no. As Kinsley observed with his trademark acerbity, "Conservatives, having said the collapse of communism would not happen, now claim credit for it."

Harries offered the most persuasive response. Unlike many neoconservatives, he acknowledged that conservatives had indeed failed to realize the extent of Soviet decay, but he also declared that you didn't have to predict something in order to claim credit for it. Perhaps the neoconservatives had been alarmist about Soviet intentions. But theirs were errors of prudence, Harries argued, not a cause for condemnation. Fair enough. The liberal record during the 1970s and 1980s was nothing to brag about. The Democratic Party had engaged in hairsplitting about whether and how to support anticommunist movements in Central America, embraced arms control as a panacea, and resisted attempts to raise military spending.

For the neocons, however, it was a moment of uncharacteristic self-doubt. A few tried to combat the sense of malaise. In 1991 Paul Wolfowitz, working for Defense Secretary Dick Cheney, tried to come up with a new grand strategy guaranteeing continued American domination around the world; he drew it up with the help of his aide I. Lewis "Scooter" Libby, whom he had helped climb the Washington escalator of success since his days as a Yale professor. The goal, it stated, was to keep any rival power center from challenging the United States, whether it was Japan or Germany. (Many foreign policy experts believed that Germany and Japan were about to surpass the United States economically.) But a storm of criticism, led by the *New York Times* editorial page, erupted. The liberal critics lambasted it as a recklessly expensive and dangerous plan for American imperial expansion. In truth, the plan was less an exercise in cynical imperialism than an expression of Reaganite optimism. But in the withering barrage that ensued, Cheney (and Wolfowitz) publicly beat a retreat. The last thing George H. W. Bush wanted was a debate about American hegemony as he was preparing for reelection. Foreign affairs were supposed to be his strong suit. Anyway, Bush wasn't interested in any form of Reaganite crusading. It would be another decade before the neoconservatives could recycle their plan via the Project for the New American Century, which became a kind of blueprint for the foreign policy of the George W. Bush administration.

Some of this criticism came from the right. Jeane Kirkpatrick, among others, didn't want America to throw its weight around the world on a democratic crusade. In an intriguing collection of articles solicited by Harries, Kirkpatrick asserted that America's chief purpose after the end of the cold war was to mind its own business. What's more, she declared that there is no mystical American "mission" or purpose to be discovered outside of the U.S. Constitution. She continued, "There is no inherent or historical 'imperative' for the U.S. government to seek to achieve any other goal—however great—except as it is mandated by the Constitution and adopted by the people through elected governments."[22] Other neoconservatives such as Edward Luttwak claimed that America was on the ropes, doomed to be surpassed by the thriving Asian economies.

Irving Kristol, who had long believed that NATO was an intolerable encumbrance upon American foreign policy, believed, of course, that the United States should follow a more unilateralist course. He also believed that it should jettison what he saw as a touching faith in an international community. So much for international law. Once again, Kristol could not have been more hostile to liberal internationalism, which he saw as synonymous with the United Nations. The United States needed to pursue a unilateralist foreign policy that would protect its own interests.

But it was none other than William Kristol, influenced by his friend Robert Kagan, who would lead the way by resuscitating the principles of liberal internationalism in neoconservative garb. The Kristol-Kagan duo—both sons of proud neoconservative fathers—would triumph over the fears of the older generation about excessive intervention abroad. Part of the new approach was an attitude of open contempt for the old "realist" concern with maintaining stability. Like Joshua leading the Israelites into Canaan, Kristol descried a promised neoconservative land that could be settled by a younger generation.

The Invasion of Kuwait

Saddam Hussein's invasion of Kuwait on August 2, 1990, was a neoconservative dream come true. Here was a golden opportunity to take out a Middle East despot and upend the old order. The Arab world (since the end of the cold war, somewhat up for grabs) would realign itself with American interests, giving us new regional leverage. And as a happy by-product, Israel could consign the Palestinian problem to the sidelines. Joshua Muravchik declared,

> If—as seems all but certain—the war ends in Saddam Hussein's utter humiliation, the sobering effect should be enormous. With Mr. Hussein's Baath Party in tatters, Soviet influence a thing of the past, Islamic extremism losing its luster in Iran, and the myth of unity shattered as never before, the Arab world may be ready finally for realism and moderation.[23]

Here, in embryo, was the neoconservative vision that would emerge fully grown in the second Bush administration.

As was his wont, Patrick J. Buchanan went on the attack against the neoconservatives. Appearing on *The McLaughlin Group* on August 26, 1990, he charged that a pro-Israel "amen corner" of neo-conservative Jews was banging the drum for war. The *New York Times* columnist A. M. Rosenthal accused Buchanan of a "blood libel." William F. Buckley Jr. called him "insensitive." But Buchanan's charges lingered sulfurously in the air and were revived during the second Iraq war, when it became fashionable on the left to argue that the war had been prosecuted largely, if not exclusively, for the benefit of Israel and its neoconservative allies.

The neoconservatives were on the defensive in the early 1990s. They had no voice in the administration, apart from William Kristol. It was the realists such as James Baker and Brent Scowcroft who prevailed. Defense Secretary Dick Cheney had no interest in a crusade, either. Worst of all, George H. W. Bush was impatient with Israel. A Texas oilman, he felt closest to Saudi Arabia and created a grand coalition to check Saddam Hussein. Indeed, Bush prosecuted the Gulf War very differently than the neocons would have liked. His aim wasn't to create a better world but to restore the balance of power in the region. Bush's foreign policy adviser, Brent Scowcroft, was a pure product of Henry Kissinger and the Nixon White House. Accordingly, Bush, Baker, and Scowcroft patiently assembled an international coalition, which meant that going to Baghdad, as the neoconservatives demanded, was out of the question. The *Wall Street Journal*, for instance, editorialized that General Norman Schwarzkopf should have become viceroy of Baghdad. This was something that might sound good in theory but would have been a disaster in practice. It was another example of the delusions to which the neoconservative intellectuals were prey. Bush also kept Israel firmly on the sidelines, to the extent of supplying it with

Patriot antiballistic missile defenses; when Saddam lobbed Scuds at Jerusalem, Israel did not respond.

The neocons had been shut out of the Bush administration. They were experiencing the same ostracism that they had experienced during the Carter years, but from a Republican president. Ever since Bush's refusal to denounce the suppression of the student democracy movement in Tiananmen Square in 1989, they had attacked him as a scion of the WASP foreign policy establishment who was too cautious to criticize his Chinese friends. Bush was also too slow to recognize the independence of the Baltic States and the collapse of the Soviet Union. Still, the neocons volunteered their services in the buildup to the Gulf War, setting up another of their perennial committees. This one, called the Committee for Peace and Security in the Gulf, was cochaired by Richard Perle and the New York Democratic representative Stephen Solarz, chairman of the House Foreign Affairs Subcommittee on Asian and Pacific Affairs. The new pressure group would focus on mobilizing popular and congressional support for the war. Neocons and their allies, such as Perle, Frank Gaffney Jr., A. M. Rosenthal, William Safire, and the *Wall Street Journal*, emphasized that America's objective should be not simply to drive Iraq out of Kuwait but to destroy Iraq's military potential, especially its capacity to develop nuclear weapons. The latter result, of course, had been Israel's objective since its 1981 raid on the Iraqi nuclear installation at Osirak.

George H. W. Bush, however, would never concede that he should have gone to Baghdad. Bush put it bluntly in his memoirs: "We would have been forced to occupy Baghdad and, in effect, rule Iraq. The coalition would instantly have collapsed, the Arabs deserting it in anger ... Had we gone the invasion route, the United States could conceivably still be an occupying power in a bitterly hostile land."[24] But it was a decision that was never forgotten by the neocons, who brought it up ad nauseam. Bush I's decision to leave Saddam in power was derided as a cowardly act of misguided realism that would only defer the problem until later. In the neocons' eyes, Bush was nothing less than a traitor to the Reagan legacy. The betrayal of the Kurds and Shiites after the war—encouraged to rebel against Hussein, yet left to face him alone without American aid—was particularly galling to its neocon supporters. Rosenthal asked, "Were Americans sent into combat against Saddam Hussein so that Washington should now help him keep together the jigsaw country sawed out of the Middle East by the British after World War I?"[25] William Safire agreed. "Must history remember George Bush as the liberator of Kuwait and the man who saved Iraq for dictatorship?" Safire wrote. "U.S. troops will return home with a sense of shame at the bloodletting that followed our political sellout."[26]

Bush's response? Together with Secretary of State James Baker and National Security Adviser Brent Scowcroft, he attacked, not Iraq for murdering the Shiites and Kurds, but Israel. Bush, who was always friendly with the Saudi monarchy, was convinced, along with Scowcroft, that the only real solution to Middle East peace was reaching a settlement between the Israelis and the Palestinians. He opposed the expansion of settlements on the West Bank. Bush insisted that if the Jewish state wanted "10 billion in loan guarantees" for immigrants from the former Soviet Union, Israel would have to end the building of new settlements in the West Bank and Gaza Strip. Baker and Scowcroft saw eye to eye with Bush. Baker declared that there was no bigger obstacle to peace than Israel's continued construction of settlements. Meanwhile, Yitzhak Shamir's Likud-led government refused to back down on the settlements issue. In the United States the American Israel Public Affairs Committee (AIPAC) mobilized to defend Israel by lobbying Congress to oppose Bush. Finally, Bush backed down on the conditions for the loan guarantee. In a September 12, 1991, news conference, he stated that he was one "lonely little guy" trying to stand up to the Israel lobby.

The neoconservatives responded by establishing yet another one of their myriad organizations, called the Committee on U.S. Interests in the Middle East, and it included Richard Perle, Elliott Abrams, and Douglas Feith. As Feith explained, "We wanted to put together a group of people who have some grounding, experience, and credentials in helping determine what is in the U.S. national interest, and who will say, 'Mr. President, we don't agree that the current policy of antagonism toward Israel is in the U.S. national interest.' "[27]

On February 26, 1992, the new committee took out an advertisement in the *New York Times* that stated, "We advocate support for a US policy toward Israel that would—in contrast to current American policy—reflect the traditional, strong American support for the legitimacy, security and general well-being of the Jewish State: a proven, valuable, democratic friend and ally of the United States." This wasn't a cynical desire to manipulate American foreign policy, as the critics of the neoconservatives would allege, but a sincere belief that (Pat Buchanan to the contrary) there was a deep and abiding tie between Israel and the United States. The question came down to a definition of interests: Was any criticism of Israel, however mild, a betrayal of U.S. national interests—or did it reaffirm them?

In the early 1990s, with Bush acting like Jimmy Carter when it came to Israel, the neocons needed somewhere to turn, and there were no other options on the right. Bush was running for reelection in 1992, and his only real competitor in the primaries was . . . Patrick J. Buchanan.

Strange as it may seem today, some of the neoconservatives looked hopefully to Bill Clinton. During the 1992 campaign Clinton was hailed as a "New Democrat" who would pull the party back to the right, or at least to the center, in foreign policy and, incidentally, appoint neoconservatives to important positions. Certainly Clinton himself did little to discourage that belief. One unexpected sign of support for him from hawkish Democrats came in a *New York Times* advertisement that appeared on August 17, 1992, in which a number of neoconservatives announced their support for Clinton's candidacy, including R. James Woolsey, who would head the CIA; Richard Schifter, a former State Department Reagan administration official; Morris J. Amitay, a member of the Jewish Institute for National Security Affairs; Paul Nitze; and Penn Kemble, former head of Social Democrats, USA. In an obvious jab at Bush, they praised Clinton for his opposition to the "brutal and archaic communist dictatorship in Beijing, and to diplomatic and trade concessions that comfort it," and lauded his readiness to use "U.S. air and naval forces—in support of UN relief efforts in Bosnia-Herzegovina, and to prevent Serbia's national communist regime from doing violence to neighboring peoples."

Indeed, Schifter, assistant secretary of state for human rights under Reagan and Bush, had joined the Clinton campaign. Together with AIPAC's David Ifshin, he reached out to his neoconservative chums. Clinton's claim was that he would be tougher than Bush on China and the Serbian leader, Slobodan Milošević. Where Bush had temporized, Clinton would act. Where Bush had shamefully coddled the "butchers of Beijing," as Clinton termed them, he would whip them into line. Where Bush had passively acceded to the Serbian aggression against Bosnia, Clinton would stop it. At least this was the claim. In the short term, it was enough to draw more than a few neocons into the Clinton camp. As the *New York Times* reporter Michael Kelly put it, "In a city where every Democrat suddenly wants to be known as a 'friend of Bill,' Mr. Clinton is a man for all advisers."[28]

Or was he? Peter Rosenblatt, the head of the Coalition for a Democratic Majority, sent a blunt letter—notable among other things for its invocation of the exodus motif that keeps cropping up in neoconservative thought—to Samuel R. Berger, Clinton's chief foreign policy adviser:

> Kelly got it wrong. They [Democratic hawks] are not put
> off by the presence in the campaign of people who have been

on the other side of the party divide. It is, rather, that they do not see anyone featured in the foreign policy operation known to them to have been on their side during the bitter years of our exile ... You often speak of the "big tent." We are speaking of people who have been outside the smaller tent of the past quarter century. They want to believe us but suspicions have become ingrained and we must work hard to overcome them.[29]

The suspicions were justified. Back was Anthony Lake as national security adviser, he of the "inordinate fear of communism" speech at Notre Dame in 1977. Back, too, was Warren Christopher as secretary of state, he of the interminable Iran hostage negotiations. Both apparently saw the United States, not its enemies, as the main problem in the world. Both were squeamish about the exercise of U.S. military might.

To be sure, Clinton ordered the firing of twenty-three Tomahawk missiles into Baghdad on June 26, 1993, in retaliation for Saddam Hussein's attempted assassination of George H. W. Bush during a visit to Kuwait City. Clinton declared that the American people could "feel good" about the attack. At this point, however, it wasn't Iraq but the Balkans that was the center of the hawkish foreign policy world.

Even though they did not join the administration, neoconservatives such as Perle, Wolfowitz, and William Kristol sided with Clinton on the issue of stopping Serbian aggression against Bosnia. The neoconservative support of Clinton's Bosnian intervention suggests the new tilt of the younger neocons toward Reaganite democratic idealism coupled with the use of American power.

The Rise of the Younger Generation

As we have seen, the role of little magazines was central both in the formation of a changing neoconservative "identity" and in the rise of neocons to power and influence. In the first generation, Irving Kristol had played a leading role in the creation of propaganda outlets for the neocons, first at *Encounter*, then by founding *Public Interest* and, finally, *National Interest.* Kristol took the lead in attempting to define the direction of the neoconservative movement. In terms of foreign policy, he rejected isolationism as obviously retrograde and unacceptable for a great power, but he, too, voiced considerable skepticism about the notion that the United States had a missionary role. A sensible foreign policy, he stipulated, would "disburden itself of the incubus of liberal internationalism, with its utopian expectations and legalistic cast of mind."[30]

In 1993, in an essay called "My Cold War" in *National Interest*, Kristol set out the lineaments for the culture war of the 1990s. According to Kristol,

> There is no "after the Cold War" for me. So far from having ended, my cold war has increased in intensity, as sector after sector of American life has been ruthlessly corrupted by the liberal ethos. It is an ethos that aims simultaneously at political and social collectivism on the one hand, and moral anarchy on the other. It cannot win, but it can make us all losers . . . We are far less prepared for this cold war, far more vulnerable to our enemy, than was the case with our victorious war against a global communist threat. We are, I sometimes feel, starting from ground zero, and it is a conflict I shall be passing on to my children and grandchildren.[31]

At the time, *Dissent* magazine (loyal to the ideals of its founder and editor Irving Howe) mocked this essay, calling it "Mr. Kristol goes to war." Daniel Bell told me that he was stunned that Kristol would condemn liberalism outright rather than pointing to specific flaws. But Kristol had sketched out, in lofty terms influenced by his understanding of Leo Strauss, the new battleground for the entire GOP. It was yet another war of ideology that Kristol wanted to launch. He was simply making explicit what had been implicit in his thinking over recent decades.

Norman Podhoretz agreed about the need for a vigorous domestic culture war against liberalism. *Commentary* assiduously began to promote the Christian right by publishing essays with titles like "The Deniable Darwin." In addition, *Commentary* recharged its batteries by attacking gays, warning in one essay about the danger that the homosexual ethos posed to "waverers" who might be persuaded to adopt the gay lifestyle because of peer pressure. The poet and critic Bruce Bawer sundered his ties with Hilton Kramer's *New Criterion* after its movie critic, James Bowman, wrote a piece that Bawer viewed as ridiculing gays. The neoconservative movement continued to move as fast as possible toward an alliance with the Christian right, based on its support for Israel and traditional values in the United States. In August 1991 in *Commentary* Kristol argued that the greatest danger to the United States came not from Christian fundamentalism but from the secular humanism of the new class. "Americans Jews, alert to Christian anti-Semitism," he wrote, "are in danger of forgetting that it was the pagans—the Babylonians and the Romans—who destroyed the temples and twice imposed exile on the Jewish people." Podhoretz himself likened the "liberal culturati" to the "Stalinist of the '30s" and deplored the "bigotry with which the Christian Coalition itself is routinely discussed in liberal circles." Whether Kristol and Podhoretz really had anything in common with the followers of the Christian right is another matter. But there can be no question that they saw it as politically useful—another way of drawing average working stiffs away from the Democratic Party to the Republican Party.

It was on foreign policy that the neoconservatives were divided. Here they were confused, and their writings showed it. Podhoretz expressed reservations about the neorealist course that Kristol was staking out in foreign policy: "The same criticism can be made of those like Irving Kristol and Jeane J. Kirkpatrick who, trying to escape or transcend the interventionist-isolationist alternative, took refuge in the realist argument for a foreign policy based strictly on considerations of national interest." This was an important divide, one that would increasingly manifest itself in the neoconservative movement over the next decade.

It was Irving's son William who sought to create a new platform for the next generation. The younger Kristol had already made a name for himself in conservative circles as chief of staff to Bush's vice president, Dan Quayle. The VP was viewed as something of a dim bulb by the national press, which soon dubbed Kristol "Quayle's brain." Under Kristol's tutelage, Quayle regularly denounced the "cultural elite"—another word for the "new class" demonized by Kristol's father. According to William Kristol at the time, "He's used the term to refer to people who look down on middle-class bourgeois values. It's a shallow sophistication, not generic culture. It's bicoastal snobbery, and I think that's worth criticizing."[32]

Quayle, who wanted to run for president, was intent on cultivating the conservative base of the party. Quayle had already become close to the neoconservatives in the early 1980s, when he met with a monthly strategy group held by Kenneth Adelman, a friend of Richard Perle's and the director of the Arms Control and Disarmament Agency. In 1988 Quayle attacked the idea of trying to work with Mikhail Gorbachev: "Perestroika is nothing more than refined Stalinism.... It's not changing the system."[33] Kristol saw to it that Quayle's office got public credit for warning Bush about the perils of raising taxes and failing to take social conservatives seriously. In 1992 Quayle garnered headlines when he criticized the CBS comedy series *Murphy Brown* for celebrating the birth of a child out of wedlock and stated that the riots after the Rodney King beating in Los Angeles in 1992 were caused by a "poverty of values"—a classic neoconservative phrase. "It doesn't help matters," Quayle said, that Brown, "a character who supposedly epitomizes today's intelligent, highly paid professional woman," ends up mocking "the importance of fathers, by bearing a child alone, and calling it just another 'life-style choice.' " Quayle got good marks for this speech with *Time*, which declared, "If for nothing else, Dan Quayle deserves points for audacity. In modern America taking on a popular TV character, even a fictional one, is politically more precarious than taking a clear stand on a substantive campaign issue."[34]

After leaving the White House in 1991, Kristol solidified his reputation as a shrewd and tenacious operator by running a two-man shop with David Tell called the Project for the Republican Future. It blasted out faxes to congressional Republicans exhorting them not to compromise with Hillary Clinton on health care. The notion that there was a health-care crisis, Kristol claimed, was bogus. Business groups worshipped Kristol for his success at almost single-handedly stopping "HillaryCare" in its tracks.

Essentially, Kristol was marrying the Reagan anti–big government message with his parents' "Straussian" ideas about the importance of personal virtue in a democracy. In an article titled "The Future of Conservatism" in *American Enterprise* magazine, he stated that the "agenda of American conservatism today can be defined as the construction (or reconstruction) of a politics of liberty and a sociology of virtue." He wanted to work "tirelessly toward the diminution of the centralized, omnicompetent, and unitary state with its ever-soaring debt and deficit." According to the *Washington Post* columnist E. J. Dionne, "Please, Kristol was saying to the Christian right, join us in battling the liberal, bureaucratic enemy. Once that enemy is routed, the harder questions could be confronted in a new context that would see the forces of virtue and religion vastly stronger."[35]

Kristol's campaign was seen as instrumental in helping the Republicans (led by Newt Gingrich) to topple the Democrats in the 1994 midterm election. Now—like his father—he wanted his own magazine.

A younger neoconservative triumvirate—Kristol, John Podhoretz, and David Brooks—came up with the idea for what became the *Weekly Standard* in 1995 in a New York eatery aptly named Café Utopia. Kristol himself persuaded the Australian press mogul Rupert Murdoch to back the magazine as a way of earning influence in Washington, D.C. It soon proved an effective vehicle. With its *Mad* magazine-type covers, youthful contributors, and irreverence, it would surpass the *New Republic* in circulation figures.

To call the magazine combative is an understatement. "Early in the magazine's history," Kristol recalled, "I remember mentioning to a friend that I seemed to have made more enemies in one year at the *Weekly Standard* than I had during my previous ten years in government and politics combined." Along with the rest of the right, the magazine went overboard during the Clinton years in ridiculing the president's sexual peccadilloes and indulging in wild conspiracy theories about his nefariousness. One cover depicted him swinging Tarzan-like through the White House Rose Garden with Monica Lewinsky on his arm. But Kristol and company were deadly serious in their opposition to Clinton and led the Republican charge for his impeachment. In addition, all the "values" issues that were supposed to appeal to religious conservatives were trumpeted by Kristol. He made it a particular point to attack homosexuality, even participating in a conference at Georgetown University about "curing" gays of their supposed pathology. It is hard to imagine that Kristol himself harbors any real prejudice against gays. Politically, however, it remained a highly effective wedge issue—as would be demonstrated in the 2004 election—and in this respect the *Weekly Standard* was no different from other conservative outlets. Perhaps the best that could be said for Kristol in this regard is that he was adhering to the

Straussian belief that morality had to be nominally upheld so that the masses would not run wild. By 1997 William F. Buckley Jr. was fretting that the *Weekly Standard* was overtaking *National Review* and, in a meeting with George F. Will, started casting about for an editor to replace the British realist John O'Sullivan. O'Sullivan's successor, Rich Lowry, turned out to be much closer to the neoconservative position, embracing the Iraq war.

It was in foreign, not domestic, policy that Kristol helped battle the isolationist sentiments that were gaining sway in a Republican Party opposed to Clinton's use of force abroad in Bosnia and elsewhere. The neoconservatives were trying as hard as they could to keep the GOP on the straight and narrow. Norman Podhoretz, writing in *National Review*, marveled at how Clinton had, in essence, pursued a more hawkish foreign policy than that being espoused by many in the GOP. Both Douglas Feith and Richard Perle acted as consultants to the Bosnian government during the 1995 Dayton peace talks. To the consternation of many conservatives who hoped for a return to a more isolationist foreign policy, Kristol backed the Clinton administration's intervention in Bosnia and (along with David Brooks) called for a return to a program of "national greatness." In the cynical 1990s it seemed peculiar to call for great crusades. "What's missing from today's American conservatism is America,"[36] wrote Brooks and Kristol in the *Wall Street Journal* in 1997. In a way it was a precursor of the greatness that Bush would aspire to after 9/11, when conservatives rallied around the idea of an assertive foreign policy. But Kristol didn't really know much about foreign policy. He was a national interest hawk until he met Robert Kagan, who persuaded him that developing a "neo-Reaganite" foreign policy was the way to earn influence, if not friends, in the GOP.

No one did more to shape the foreign policy stance of Kristol's magazine than Kagan. Kagan like Kristol is a second-generation neoconservative. His father, Donald Kagan, was a distinguished classical historian at Yale; he was also a friend of Allan Bloom's who had taught at Cornell during the student uprisings. Kagan is a genial man, but he recalls that year at Cornell with a shudder: "For the first time I understood what happened in Nazi Germany." Neither Kagan nor his sons embraced Straussianism. Strauss believed that each thinker should be viewed on his own terms, minus the accretion of later interpretations. Kagan, by contrast, correctly believes that history is inescapable even for the greatest philosophers.

As an eight-year-old, Robert got to see his father square off against Bloom in the faculty lunchroom at the Statler Hotel. According to Kagan:

> I learned from my father that the problem with Straussians was that they were ahistorical. They were consumed with the great thinkers and believed the great thinkers were engaged in a dialogue with one another across time. This made Straussians slight the historical circumstances in which great thinkers did their thinking. Indeed, my father, the historian, taught me to mistrust not only Straussians but also political philosophy in general, and I have pretty much done so—though, again, I have to admit it's partly because I find it hard to understand.[37]

As an undergraduate at Yale, Robert threw himself into the study of politics and history, also editing a magazine called the *Yale Political Monthly* and playing marathon sessions of the board game Diplomacy.

Upon graduation from Yale, Kagan immediately entered the Kristol network, working for the *Public Interest* as an assistant editor in 1981. He had a nose for intellectual combat, writing up the controversy at Yale in which the Straussian political scientist Thomas Pangle was denied tenure in 1979 in a flagrantly unfair proceeding. (Pangle was another student of Bloom's who had received his Ph.D. from the University of Chicago in 1972.) One panelist reportedly declared, "Academic freedom is one thing, but there are two types who will never be permitted tenure at Yale: Leninists and Straussians." The decision was overturned by a judiciary panel led by the Yale historian Edmund S. Morgan—the brother, incidentally, of Roberta Wohlstetter—but Pangle decided to decamp for the University of Toronto, where Bloom had likewise repaired to lick his wounds after the Cornell debacle in the late 1960s. In the wake of this preposterous "scandal," young Kagan entered the lists with an article in the February 1982 issue of *Commentary* that bore the title "God and Man at Yale—Again." He attacked Yale's president, A. Bartlett Giamatti, for warning against the dangers of the far right embodied by the likes of Jerry Falwell and the moral majority: "The faction which Giamatti's speech served was that of the liberal intellectuals among whom he was raised and educated, and whose ideological dominance on the Yale campus has not abated for a moment since [William F.] Buckley complained about it thirty years ago in *God and Man at Yale*."

Kagan worked as a policy adviser to Congressman Jack Kemp, a friend of Irving Kristol's who was seen as a future presidential candidate and who pushed hard for supply-side economics. But Kagan's real love was always foreign policy. Kagan was, and remains, an idealist, a crusader. He worked for Elliott Abrams at the State Department and as a speechwriter for George Shultz, all before earning a Ph.D. in U.S. history at American University. Along the way, Kagan made a name for himself as a hard-liner, writing a series of pungent articles in *Commentary* that challenged the conventional wisdom in the GOP that realpolitik was the way to go in the post-cold war world. Kagan engaged in long disquisitions about the father of realism, Hans Morgenthau, in order to show that following the Kissingerian prescription of neutrality with regard to human rights would condemn the GOP to political impotence. The party needed a positive rallying cry based in Reaganite optimism, not the dour strictures of the Nixon era.

Kagan would end up winning the battle against realists close to the GOP, such as Fareed Zakaria, who counseled a more moderate path. Both Yale graduates, they would end up viciously feuding in the pages of the *New Republic*; Kagan claimed that Zakaria was contemptuous of the idea that democracy could be exported. Zakaria responded, "He tries to portray the work as a paean to tyranny and aristocracy—a mischaracterization so perverse that it can be sustained only through selective or manipulated quotations, ad hominem innuendo, and outright falsehoods. The signature element of Kagan's review is not intellectual disagreement, which I welcome. It is intellectual dishonesty."[38] This was a precursor of the intellectual spats that would emerge between the neoconservatives and the realists as the Iraq war went south.

In 1992 the Bradley Foundation asked William Kristol to study the future of conservatism. Kristol, who had little interest in foreign policy during the early 1990s and hewed, more or less, to the views of his father, took a cramped view of the national interest. Kagan changed that. His mission was to keep alive the 1992 Defense Planning Guidance that had called for the United States to build upon the successes of the cold war to create a permanent "benevolent domination"—in other words, world hegemony. The first President Bush may have repudiated the report, but Kagan wanted to make it a working reality with Kristol's help. According to one official in the George W. Bush administration who was close to both, "Kagan went to him and said, 'Look, Dole isn't going to have a foreign policy that sings in 1996. We need to give him some wind in his sails. Let's make a case for what a Reaganite foreign policy would look like—expanded defense, benevolent hegemony, and democracy promotion.' "

Their first step in extending American benevolence was to create the Project for the New American Century (PNAC), which was essentially a front organization to champion the democratic crusade and, specifically, the overthrow of Saddam Hussein. PNAC had only a few employees, but it sent out a steady stream of faxes warning about perils to the United States and helped create an echo chamber in which *Fox News*, the *Washington Times*, the *Wall Street Journal*, and the *New York Post* repeated its adjurations.

At the same time, the liberal hawks and neoconservatives held hands underneath the PNAC umbrella. In 1997 Paul Wolfowitz wrote a cover story in the *Weekly Standard* demanding that Clinton topple Hussein. What's more, a January 26, 1998, PNAC letter to Clinton from Kristol, Wolfowitz, Francis Fukuyama, John Bolton, and others stated: "American policy cannot continue to be crippled by a misguided insistence on unanimity in the UN Security Council." The *New Republic* would play a part in Kagan's and Kristol's calculations about forging an alliance with the liberal hawks.

Like Norman Podhoretz, *New Republic* literary editor Leon Wieseltier had been a student of Lionel Trilling's; he came of age in the 1970s. He studied with Isaiah Berlin at Oxford before becoming a member of the Harvard Society of Fellows. Wieseltier wrote several striking pieces for the *New York Review of Books* and became literary editor of the *New Republic* in 1983. Right from the outset, he attacked realists such as Ronald Steel for their "moist" failure to understand the dangers of Soviet aggression. Wieseltier's noisy moralism, which could easily shade into sanctimony, meant that he always occupied, or claimed to occupy, the high ground. He never shared the neoconservative loathing of the counterculture. He delighted in ridiculing the founding of the *New Criterion* in 1982 and had nothing but disdain for Podhoretz. To all appearances he remained a Democrat. But he shared the views of neoconservatives about the dangers of multiculturalism, lambasted American Jews for having an impoverished understanding of their own traditions, and, above all, agreed with many of their foreign policy stands. Still, his approach wasn't to defend every Israeli action but to concentrate on writing anti-anti-Israel essays.

Kagan became a contributing editor to *TNR* even as he pounded out editorials for the *Weekly Standard* blasting GOP isolationists and the Clinton administration. He was cultivated by Wieseltier, who blurbed his book *Of Paradise and Power* in rather extravagant terms: "Nothing like this has been written since the death of Raymond Aron." The historian Tony Judt scoffed at this in the *New York Review of Books*, a harbinger of his eventual feud with Wieseltier over U.S.-Israeli relations. Indeed, in an essay in the *London Review of Books*, Judt would number Wieseltier among the "useful idiots" who had helped sanitize neoconservatism and pave the way for the Iraq war.

But the right was more radical than the liberal hawks may have realized. For example, there was Laurie Mylroie, an eccentric scholar at the American Enterprise Institute who claimed that Saddam Hussein was behind the bombing of the World Trade Center in 1993. The author of a biography of Saddam Hussein with then-*New York Times* reporter Judith Miller—also a close friend of Wolfowitz and his then wife, Clare—she helped shape neocon thinking about terrorist conspiracies involving Hussein.

Then there was Michael Ledeen, an expert on Italian fascism who is also a resident scholar at AEI. Along with his wife, Barbara, a member of the neoconservative Independent Women's Forum, he makes up part of the neoconservative network. Ledeen, a student of the great European historian George Mosse at the University of Wisconsin, served on the Reagan administration's National Security Council and became embroiled in the Iran-contra affair. He went on to become an avatar of promoting democracy and smashing terrorism. In his 1996 book, *Freedom Betrayed*, he insisted that the right, not the left, should be the true heir to the radical, revolutionary tradition of upending dictatorships.[39] This was neoconservatism on steroids.

Despite these boisterous notes, Norman Podhoretz decreed in 1996 (somewhat perversely) that neoconservatism was dead—not because it had failed, but because it had succeeded. It was no longer necessary. It had become an accepted part of conservatism. Around this time, Irving Kristol published a history of neoconservatism in which he admitted that he was no longer sure what the term meant. For the older generation it had, of course, meant different things: for Nathan Glazer it had meant opposition to affirmative action; for Podhoretz and Kristol it had been rooted in an opposition to what they saw as a counterculture that threatened to subvert American values at home and abroad. But so successful had the neoconservatives become at aligning themselves with the GOP that they no longer saw much of a distinction between neoconservatism and conservatism. It simply seemed like the logical end of the war to embrace conservatism *tout court* and abandon the intellectual vanity of insisting on their special status. The younger generation seemed to concur with its elders that neoconservatism had in some sense outlived its usefulness. Thus Kristol fils had gone on record as saying that he thought of himself as "just a conservative."

Yet at the same time he and Kagan did all they could to revive neoconservatism as a distinctive force in American politics. Thus they attacked Jeane Kirkpatrick for stating that the United States could once again become a "normal" country. Instead, they argued that a true American foreign policy should seamlessly combine realism and idealism, national interest and national values. Wrote Kristol and Kagan in the *Washington Post* in 2000:

> Today, the absence of a Soviet empire does not alter the fundamental purposes of American foreign policy. Just as sensible Americans after World War II did not imagine that the United States should await the rise of the next equivalent of Nazi Germany, so American statesmen today ought to recognize that their charge is not to await the arrival of the next great threat. Rather, it is to shape the international environment to prevent such a threat from arising in the first place. To put it another way: The overarching goal of

American foreign policy—to preserve and extend an international order that is in accord with both our material interests and our principles—endures. Americans must shape this order, for if we refrain from doing so, we can be sure that others will shape it in ways that reflect neither our interests nor our values.[40]

Meanwhile, in *Foreign Affairs*, they laid out a neo-Reaganite foreign policy in 1996 that called for doubling the defense budget and converting the rest of the globe to American values, whether it wanted to or not. This essay became the foundation for the new neoconservative crusade. It argued, in effect, that traditional conservatives were not heirs to Reagan. To the traditional conservatives, Reagan was about caution and limited government rather than meddling in other countries' affairs. The neoconservatives saw it differently. They saw Reagan as, in essence, being like them—a New Deal Republican. So it was really they who deserved the Reagan mantle. They were going to bolster the U.S. military and unapologetically spread American values around the world.

Did they really think such a crusade could be launched? Perhaps not. But it was politically useful—the classic neoconservative category. What's more, their demand for doubling the defense budget was an inflammatory move that helped draw attention to their article. Almost more important than being right was being noticed. Kristol and Kagan were staking themselves out as the heirs of Reagan in the battle over his legacy between the realists and the neocons. What the neocons bitterly opposed was the idea of managed decline, which had started with Kissinger and continued with his intellectual heirs and protégés Brent Scowcroft, James Baker, and Richard Haass. This notion, that America had to accept that it was losing power, militarily and economically, was shared by almost all of the realists. As one insider puts it, "The neocons are more than anything anti-Kissinger. The critique of détente was more important in modern neocons than the Vietnam positions of the Democratic Party."

It was no accident, then, that the neocons found their allies among the liberal hawks at the *New Republic* and elsewhere. The ties had begun with Bosnia and continued with the battle over the expansion of NATO. The longtime neocon backer Bruce P. Jackson—a protégé, like Scooter Libby, of Paul Wolfowitz—who worked as a lobbyist at Lockheed Martin, established a group called the U.S. Committee on NATO that helped garner conservative support for the Clinton administration's move to include the Baltic States in NATO. The effort was spearheaded by Richard Holbrooke, who was, of course, instrumental in Balkans diplomacy. Jackson would go on to create the Committee for the Liberation of Iraq, which included liberal members like Will Marshall, head of the Progressive Policy Institute, and former senator Bob Kerrey. Indeed, though it has not received sufficient attention, Kerrey was instrumental in creating the coalition of liberal hawks and neoconservatives to justify support for attacking Iraq. Kerrey, in effect, provided important political cover for the endeavor.

On October 31, 1998, President Clinton signed the Iraq Liberation Act, which Senator Kerrey had cosponsored to funnel money to the Iraqi exile (and former Wohlstetter student) Ahmed Chalabi. Had the act been heeded, it might have helped avoid the chaos that the toppling of Saddam Hussein created. The act emphasized that the United States would provide Iraq with humanitarian assistance. Few of its supporters actually believed that the United States would invade Iraq. They were hoping for a successful version of the Bay of Pigs. Senator Kerrey played an important part. He said in 1998 in the Senate,

> This bill is a statement that America refuses to coexist
> with a regime which has used chemical weapons on its own

citizens and on neighboring countries, which has invaded its neighbors twice without provocation, which has still not accounted for its atrocities committed in Kuwait, which has fired ballistic missiles into the cities of three of its neighbors, which is attempting to develop nuclear and biological weapons, and which has brutalized and terrorized its own citizens for thirty years. I don't see how any democratic country could accept the existence of such a regime, but this bill says America will not.

Was this cheap and easy rhetoric, based on the notion that the United States would never actually go to war, or did it represent a sincere opposition to Saddam Hussein? There can be no doubting that the neocons reinforced the liberal hawks' doubts about failing to attack Iraq at every opportunity. In particular, they sought to overturn what has come to be called the Vietnam syndrome.

The liberal hawks were flocking to the interventionist camp. As *Salon*'s David Talbot declared,

> It's true, any liberal who came of age during the Vietnam War, as I did, feels some kinship with these implacable critics of American policy, even a lingering sense of alienation from our own country's world-straddling power. But most of us, at some point during the last two decades, made a fundamental break from this pacifistic legacy. For me, it came during the savage bombing of Sarajevo, whose blissfully multi-ethnic cosmopolitanism was, like New York would later become, an insult to the forces of zealous purity. Most liberals of my generation, however, feel deeply uneasy about labeling themselves hawks—to do so conjures images for them of Gen. Curtis "Bombs Away" LeMay, it suggests a break from civilization itself, a heavy-footed step backwards, toward the bogs of our ancestors. What I have come to

believe, however, is that America's unmatched power to reduce tyranny and terror to dust is actually what often makes
civilization in today's world possible.[41]

Unmatched power? Tyranny and terror to dust? Such language was
straight out of the neoconservative playbook. In fact, the neocon
strategy was outlined in a book by David Wurmser, who would become Dick Cheney's Middle East adviser, called *Tyranny's Ally:
America's Failure to Defeat Saddam Hussein.* In it, Wurmser, who
had already coauthored with Feith and Perle an extremely radical paper ("A Clean Break: A New Strategy for Securing the Realm") that
advised Israeli prime minister Benjamin Netanyahu to declare war
against and topple various Arab despotisms, championed the idea
of an insurgency led by Ahmed Chalabi and the Iraqi National
Congress. Chalabi, he said, would lead a popular rebellion rather
than the coups that had afflicted Middle East countries like Iraq.
This was supposed to be a reprise of the Reagan era, when insurgen-
cies were used to topple regimes unfriendly to America. Moreover,
Wurmser's mentor, Richard Perle, believed, in the Wohlstetter mode,
that the era of large armies was over. The United States would have
to rely on Chalabi to carry the burden.

Wurmser began to move in neocon circles at the U.S. Institute of
Peace during the Reagan era. "For Wurmser," says a Bush administration official who is friends with him, "Israel is the driving force.
He had ideas about Israel—we're both arsenals of democracy. He is
the son of two émigré Jews, Swiss and Czech. He met his wife,
Meyrav, in Israel and they are the dynamic duo of think-tank
Zionism. His wife writes about Israel losing its Zionist view. What
people describe in conspiratorial terms isn't true; it's an intellectual
connection." He adds, "They just believe this stuff. They're not
agents. David is completely without guile." At AEI, Wurmser was
"Perle's pen. Perle was too busy making money to write."

Perle boosted Wurmser's voice by installing Danielle Pletka, the wife of Steve Rademaker, a leading neocon. Pletka was going nowhere before she landed at AEI. "She's become infinitely more neoconservative after arriving at AEI," says one neocon. "Perle made her. Her job was to kick her stiletto heel into the academics and make them agitate. She met with Chalabi a lot; the Iraq Liberation Act was something that she helped put together. It was written by her husband, Steve Rademaker." Rademaker, who was on the House International Relations Committee before joining the current Bush administration, had also worked for Elliot Abrams at the State Department. At AEI Wurmser's job was to update the Reagan doctrine for Iraq.

Unfortunately, Wurmser's book was hopelessly overoptimistic, beginning with Perle's introduction, which claimed, "It is time we recognized that our Iraqi problem arose not because of incompetent application of ideas but rather because of flawed ideas about the region." Perle made clear his—and by extension neoconservatism's—contempt for the establishment professionals. He claimed that the U.S. approach toward the Middle East had failed and that "this failure stems from both the curious ideas about American leadership and the abysmal state of expertise that are held by many regional specialists, particularly in our intelligence community."[42]

This statement might well serve as an epitaph for the neoconservative movement itself. Wurmser and Perle were stuck in the past. Wurmser's conclusion that the "Middle East is rapidly becoming a battlefield that disgraces and undermines our victory in the cold war" was the sort of overheated statement that the neoconservatives were all too prone to make.

But many liberals bought it. Why? The liberal hawks had rightly fought to stop Serbian aggression in the Balkans. But their fervor to aid the Bosnians led to the hubristic belief, as Madeleine Albright put it, that America was "the indispensable nation." This morphed into the conviction that the United States could intervene anywhere it wished with impunity. A remarkable combination of arrogance and obtuseness characterized the liberal hawks, who flattered themselves on their higher morality. Similarly, the neoconservatives, militaristic idealists who never missed a chance to scorn the motives and assertions of their opponents on the left and right, were hopelessly naive about the Arab predicament.

One of the few observers to take into account the culpability of the liberal hawks has been Tufts political scientist Tony Smith, who noted in the *Washington Post* that "sources for many of the critical elements of the Bush doctrine can be found in the emergence of neoliberal thought during the 1990s, after the end of the cold war. In think tanks, universities and government offices, left-leaning intellectuals, many close to the Democratic Party, formulated concepts to bring to fruition the age-old dream of Democratic President Woodrow Wilson 'to make the world safe for democracy.' "[43] For both the neoconservatives and the neoliberals, promoting human rights and democracy would rest on using armed force. But the neoliberals such as the Brookings Institution's Kenneth Pollack and Will Marshall of the Progressive Policy Institute got it wrong.

Perhaps part of the problem was that they lacked the deep sense of historical irony that had distinguished Irving Kristol. His son William was genial, witty—and earnest. The skepticism and sense of detachment that characterized the elder Kristol were absent from the younger generation.

And for George W. Bush, the simplistic neoconservative credo would prove a perfect fit. Bush would weld together a new blend of optimism about spreading democracy and fear of the decline of the West if democracy failed to spread. Kristol and Kagan had reinvented Republican foreign policy. They believed the only way America could protect itself was by importing liberal doctrine and fusing it with militarism. Bush would agree.

Much has been written about the neoconservative "takeover" of the Bush administration. Most critics seem to think that Bush was incapable of formulating his own ideas—yet they also credit him with

Machiavellian cunning. In fact the story is much more straightfor-ward—and much more interesting than some backstairs White House conspiracy.

Bush came into office with no particular ideas about foreign pol-icy. But to the extent that he fancied himself the heir to Reagan, his worldview was generally more Reagan than Bush—which is to say an amalgam of cowboy unilateralism and social-values conservatism. After 9/11, he suddenly needed a policy framework. The neocons had been right about confronting the Soviet threat, and they had long been warning about the threat of Islamic fundamentalism. It is therefore natural for Bush to have turned to the neocons; yet it is also important to remember that by this time there was very little distinction between Reaganism and neoconservatism. After all, the neocons were in large measure the authors of what might be called the Reagan Synthesis. It is only later, with the failure in Iraq and the consequent need to point fingers, that the neoconservatives were pushed to the front of the stage by their foes on both the left and the right.

Return to Exile

It is easy to conquer any Arab country, but their natural inclination to rebellion makes it difficult and expensive for the invader to maintain his control.

Sir John Glubb, A Soldier with the Arabs

Often the moral thing to do is also strategically correct.

Paul Wolfowitz

On September 11, 2001, some of Secretary of Defense Donald Rumsfeld's closest advisers were scattered in Europe and the Middle

East. A day later they met in Frankfurt, Germany, to fly in a KC-135 Stratotanker back to Washington. Among the people on the plane were Douglas Feith and his aide William Luti, who was the head of the Pentagon's Near East South Asia department and is now a staffer at the National Security Council. As the Bush officials flew back, they discussed various ways to respond to the 9/11 attacks and kept coming back to flushing terrorists out of their safe havens. While their plane flew over New York, they saw the smoke emanating from the World Trade Center. It was an experience that Luti said was unforgettable. The 9/11 attacks fortified the conviction in him and others that the United States had to wrap up terrorist networks and go on the offensive rather than pursuing the hapless law enforcement policies of the Clinton administration.[1]

Such thinking could hardly have been further from the early days of the administration. When George W. Bush ran for the presidency in 2000, the last thing anyone expected was that he would trigger the most impassioned foreign policy debate since the Vietnam War. Not only was Bush mocked for his lack of ideas about both domestic and foreign policy, but he also promised a "humble" approach toward other nations in his October 11, 2000, debate with Al Gore. As the GOP establishment candidate, Bush seemed to epitomize caution, if not vacuity, when it came to foreign policy. There was no reason to think that he would break with the realist tenets of his father, who had warned Ukraine against a "suicidal nationalism," who had tried to prop up Mikhail Gorbachev, who had turned a blind eye to the massacre at Tiananmen Square, who had attempted to rein in Israeli settlements, and who had failed to aid the Kurds and Shiites as Saddam Hussein rained down poison gas on them in the aftermath of the Gulf War. There was no reason to think that he would embark upon two wars that have yet to be concluded. There was, moreover, no reason to think that he would end up embracing the neoconservatives.

Nor was there ever much reason to think that the neoconservatives would embrace him. When the primary season for the 2000

Republican presidential nomination kicked off, where was William Kristol and the *Weekly Standard*? Was Kristol backing Bush? Not a chance. In the 1995 inaugural issue of his magazine, Kristol had created a minor sensation by arguing that Colin Powell should be the Republican candidate in 1996. Four years later he supported John McCain rather than Bush, who was seen by many of the neoconservatives as representing continuity with his father's failed policies.

When Bush set out to choose his cabinet, there was much apprehension as well among the neoconservatives. The neoconservatives seemed, by and large, to have taken a backseat during the campaign. To be sure, some leading neoconservatives had participated in sessions educating Bush about foreign policy, including Richard Perle and Paul Wolfowitz. In August 1999 an excited Wolfowitz told me over lunch at I Ricchi restaurant in Washington, D.C., that Bush had the ability to penetrate the dense fog of foreign policy expertise to ask a simple question, "Tell me what I need to know?" Bush, Wolfowitz said, was "another Scoop Jackson."

Richard Perle saw it the same way. The first time he met Bush, he immediately sensed that he was different from his father. Two things were clear to Perle: one was that Bush didn't know much about foreign policy and another was that he wasn't too embarrassed to confess it. Like Wolfowitz, Perle admired Bush's ability, as he saw it, to cut to the heart of the matter rather than become mesmerized by Washington policy talk.

However ardently the neoconservatives may have tried to adopt Bush once he became president, he didn't seem all that inclined, initially, to accept their overtures. After all, Donald Rumsfeld, Dick Cheney, Colin Powell, and Condoleezza Rice were hardly neoconservatives. What the neocons received were, at best, second-tier positions: John Bolton, a protégé of former senator Jesse Helms, became undersecretary of state for arms control and international security; there was also Paul Wolfowitz as deputy defense secretary and Douglas Feith as assistant secretary of defense, plus a scattering of lower-level posts elsewhere in the Defense and State departments.

Rumsfeld didn't want a big thinker as a deputy. He had his own ideas about how to transform the U.S. military into a modern force that could strike quickly whenever and wherever he wished. Rumsfeld viewed Wolfowitz, who was staunchly supported by Vice President Dick Cheney, with some trepidation. Wolfowitz for his part may have cultivated the air of an abstract intellectual, but he could play hard-ball when necessary. Thus he told Rumsfeld that he had to make a decision about bringing him on board or he was going to become ambassador to the UN.

But as Rumsfeld's deputy, Wolfowitz became his loyal front man. As former dean of the School of Advanced International Studies, he would provide a veneer of academic respectability for the Iraq war, as well as a conduit to the neoconservatives. Rumsfeld had always been careful about tending to his right-wing allies, and Wolfowitz's appointment was a shrewd way of pleasing (and appeasing) them. But it wasn't in Rumsfeld's nature to commit to anything, and he continued to keep a wary eye on Wolfowitz.

"After several decades, I still don't know what he believes in," says the former national security adviser Brent Scowcroft in puzzled amazement about Rumsfeld. "He just stands there and says, 'Who me?' when things go wrong." According to a former senior State Department official, Rumsfeld cut Wolfowitz out whenever he felt like it: "Wolfowitz routinely goes to meetings, has no idea where Rummy is, can't give a Department of Defense position when it gets to principles levels because Rummy undoes it ... if you go to a deputy's meeting, he's not the one who drives the agenda or the issues ... and Wolfowitz isn't always on his brief...." Small wonder that the neoconservatives ended up being frozen out on their plans to install Chalabi as the new potentate of Iraq. Rumsfeld wasn't interested in having *any* plan for the postwar occupation. He just wanted a hit-and-run invasion.

Still, Wolfowitz had good reason to be satisfied with his new post. Never before had a neoconservative been so close to the top job. It even looked as though Wolfowitz himself might become defense secretary or secretary of state should Bush win a second term. All Wolfowitz had to do was prove his mettle over the next couple of years.

One of his first decisions was to choose Feith as his deputy after Richard Perle declined to return to government service, pleading that he couldn't sacrifice his business interests. It was a catastrophic mistake on Wolfowitz's part. Not a manager himself, he had appointed someone as his deputy who was utterly incapable of leading a meeting effectively. At the same time, Perle became head of the Defense Policy Board, a position that allowed him to advise Rumsfeld and parlay his access into even more lucrative opportunities. Perle's performance was slipshod: the meetings were run in chaotic fashion, and he failed to tap the expertise of pros such as former defense secretary Harold Brown.

Unlike Wolfowitz, Perle enjoyed Rumsfeld's total trust. Rumsfeld, after all, had leaked documents to Perle in the 1970s that undermined Kissinger's push for détente with the Soviet Union. He also knew that Perle had no government ambitions and posed no threat to his position at the Pentagon. Wolfowitz did. With his expansive way of talking and self-confidence, free from Wolfowitz's more labored manner, Perle became Rumsfeld's new Albert Wohlstetter. Many of the ideas that Wohlstetter had touted—an emphasis on surgical strikes and a reliance on high technology to substitute for land forces—were implemented by Rumsfeld in the Iraq war. As a former naval aviator, Rumsfeld was obsessed with bypassing the army, and Wohlstetter's ideas seemed to provide a perfect way to do it.

It was no accident that Feith's own deputy, William Luti, was also a former naval aviator who had flown numerous missions in the Gulf War. Luti, too, was a protégé of Wohlstetter. He had studied advanced warfare at Tufts University's Fletcher School, where he earned a Ph.D. under the neoconservative professor John P. Roche and befriended Wohlstetter in the early 1990s. Wohlstetter, in turn, introduced him to Perle and the neoconservative circle in Washington, D.C. It was a mutually beneficial arrangement. Luti, who went on to work as a congressional fellow for Newt Gingrich (himself bedazzled by the promise of high technology), provided a connection for the neoconservatives to the military establishment.

Even with numerous neoconservatives stashed away in his administration, Bush didn't follow their counsel immediately. To be sure, his foreign policy showed signs of unilateralism right from the beginning: he tossed aside the Antiballistic Missile Treaty that had originally been signed with the Soviet Union in 1972 and thumbed his nose at the Kyoto Protocol at the very moment that German chancellor Gerhard Schröder was traveling to the White House from Andrews Air Force Base—a snub that may help explain Schröder's later vehement opposition to the Iraq war. But he did little to placate the neoconservatives. Condoleezza Rice, who was then national security adviser, hewed to her stated course of leaving nation building to the Democrats. She saw China as America's big partner, and the administration was taken aback when on April 1 a Chinese fighter collided with a U.S. Navy reconnaissance plane. The U.S. plane landed at Hainan, a large Chinese island. The crisis was smoothed over, but the neoconservatives, who were staunch supporters of Taiwan, seemed to see anything short of warfare as a sellout to China. Bush's big idea was to get the United States out of the Balkans. He made it abundantly clear that he had nothing but contempt for the idea of peacekeeping. In July, during a visit to Kosovo, he told Brigadier General William David, the commander of U.S. forces in the area, "We've got to get you out of here."[2]

Iraq was off the radar screen. Even Wolfowitz believed, as he put it in a foreign policy volume edited by Robert Kagan and William Kristol, that managing China's "emergence as a major power in East Asia and the world is likely to be the biggest challenge to maintaining a peaceful world through the first part of this century."[3] This was a clear sign, at bottom, of how conventional Wolfowitz's thinking was about foreign policy. Far from being some kind of ideological mastermind, as he came to be portrayed in the press, he is most striking for his banality. Wolfowitz was no Kissinger, Brzezinski, or Samuel P. Huntington. Instead, he was a combination of Washington operator and plodding academic. But his outreach to the neoconservatives meant that he was a valuable pawn for Rumsfeld and Bush. He functioned as the interlocutor between the two camps. By the time of the run-up to the Iraq war, however, Wolfowitz had become such a controversial figure that, according to Gary Schmitt, the head of the Project for the New American Century, he actively avoided being seen publicly with any other neoconservatives.

Unlike Rumsfeld, Wolfowitz was genuinely obsessed with the Middle East. But Wolfowitz was a humanitarian, not a warrior. He relished the fact that he had become a kind of folk hero in Indonesia for championing democracy as ambassador. He wanted to do good, to help the weak, to bask in the applause of foreign populations. He was especially concerned with human rights. These were laudable impulses. But they also allowed emotion to outstrip analysis when it came to the Middle East.

In his new post Wolfowitz daydreamed about starting an American-backed insurrection against Saddam Hussein. One idea was that the Kurds could lead a revolt from the north. His former aide Zalmay Khalilzad drew up papers at the National Security Council maintaining that support for Iraqi exiles might help bring down the regime—a harbinger of the Chalabi strategy that the Pentagon cabal of neoconservatives would embrace. Wolfowitz, racked with guilt at the abandonment of the Kurds and Shiites at the end of the Gulf War, and enraged by Colin Powell's failure to do anything about it, was scavenging for ways to atone for America's great foreign policy failure. He wasn't going to let a second chance go by. The ghost of the Gulf War had to be exorcised.

But Bush himself wasn't focused on any of these ideas or causes. In fact, he was floundering in his first year in office, bereft of a purpose or cause. Even when warned in August 2001 about looming terrorist attacks, he merely told a CIA briefer that he had covered his backside. Bush, like the country, was on vacation. This insouciance about terrorism extended to Rumsfeld as well; he declared on the eve of the 9/11 attacks that the greatest threat to American security was the hidebound Pentagon bureaucracy. And the neoconservatives outside the administration? Were they any more prepared? In the first week of September 2001, the *Weekly Standard* ran a cover story by David Brooks that featured his musings on the cultural significance of the popular 1970s television series *Gilligan's Island.*

Then came September 11. When nineteen men hijacked four commercial airliners leaving from Washington, D.C., Boston, and Newark and piloted them into Manhattan's World Trade Center, and the Pentagon, and crashed the fourth in Pennsylvania, Bush's presidency was irrevocably altered. The change did not occur immediately. Bush looked chastened, unsure, and frightened when he appeared on national television that evening to deliver an address. But within days he recovered his footing and moved further and further into the web that the neoconservatives had woven around him.

At least this is the widespread view of how Bush ended up invading Iraq and launching a general war on terror. But is it true? Did the neoconservatives manipulate Bush? Was he instead using them as much as they sought to use him? Perhaps the full truth will never be known. But it seems clear that Bush ultimately became even more enamored of, or hostage to, the neoconservative vision than many neocons.

After 9/11

The neoconservatives and the conservative movement in general fell all over themselves to lionize Bush after 9/11. The stripling who had been elevated to the presidency by the Supreme Court was now hailed as a Churchillian figure. Bush himself made no secret of his worship of Churchill, even putting a bust of the great man in the Oval Office (a gift from the British embassy). The *National Review* published a collection of Bush's speeches on "war, terrorism, and freedom" as a major event—as though they couldn't be downloaded from the Internet. The *Weekly Standard* also viewed him as a new Churchill, and indeed no magazine would prove more important in puffing Bush and the war effort. As Scott McConnell—a former contributor to *Commentary* and editor at the *National Interest* who defected from neoconservatism to the isolationist *American Conservative* in the late 1990s—astutely observed:

> With the fledgling Fox News network, the *Standard* soon emerged as the key leg in a synergistic triangle of neoconservative argumentation: you could write a piece for the magazine, talk about your ideas on Fox, pick up a paycheck from Kristol or from AEI. It was not a way to get rich, but it sustained a network of careers that might otherwise have shriveled or been diverted elsewhere. Indeed, it did more than sustain them, it gave neocons an aura of being "happening" inside the Beltway that no other conservative (or liberal) faction could match.[4]

McConnell, who cut his teeth on Jimmy Carter's campaign for the presidency before migrating to neoconservatism, confessed that he even felt a certain wistfulness for the energy and zealotry that he had experienced as a member of the neoconservative movement. William F. Buckley Jr. puts it simply: "The neoconservatives have a flotilla in place in Washington. They fire off a lot of guns."

Before 9/11, Kristol's magazine and the neoconservative movement itself were adrift. Kristol and his comrades had bashed away at Bill Clinton, but it hadn't gotten the conservative movement very far.

Kristol didn't have close ties to Bush, either, because the administration had not forgotten (or forgiven) his support for McCain. It was the war that gave the neocons a new sense of meaning and purpose, as much as it did for Bush himself.

Yet the editors of the *Weekly Standard* didn't recommend attacking the Taliban in Afghanistan. War wasn't necessary, they argued. Aid to the Taliban's local enemies would suffice. The real target was Saddam. The magazine, led by its perfervid correspondent Stephen Hayes, would relentlessly tie together Saddam Hussein and Osama bin Laden. Hayes began—and continues—to claim that Saddam Hussein was working on weapons of mass destruction and that he had intimate ties to al-Qaeda. In the *Weekly Standard*, Max Boot called outright for an American empire, complete with jodhpurs and pith helmets. The magazine's editors opined that anything less than an attack on Saddam would constitute "surrender."

How much of this posture was dictated by concern for the fate of Israel, as many critics charged? The neoconservatives had devoted much of their energies to debunking the 1993 Oslo Accords signed at the White House by Yitzhak Rabin and Yasser Arafat. In 1994, for example, Yoram Hazony, a young Israeli neoconservative, established the Shalem Center, a Jerusalem-based think tank that was financed by Ronald Lauder and Roger Hertog (also a supporter of the Manhattan Institute who subsequently became a co-owner of the *New Republic*). The purpose of the center is to defend the idea of Zionism and to introduce neoconservative ideas about foreign policy and economics to Israel. Likewise, the Jerusalem-based Institute for Advanced Strategic and Political Studies (created by Robert Loewenberg in 1994) commissioned the famous 1996 "Clean Break" study, which advocated overthrowing Saddam Hussein and strikes on Syria as well as other Middle East regimes; this became the basis for later neoconservative dreams about reordering the Middle East. These maneuvers, the paper said, "could be the prelude to a redrawing of the map of the Middle East, which could threaten Syria's territorial integrity." So controversial did this paper become that Douglas Feith would write a weasely letter in September 2004 to the *Washington Post* distancing himself from it. He declared that "David Wurmser as the group's rapporteur, drafted the report. There were no coauthors, and the discussion participants were not asked to clear the final text of the paper."

Apprehensions about Israel's future were indeed rife among the neoconservatives. In 1998, for example, Charles Krauthammer wrote an article for the *Weekly Standard* ("At Last, Zion") in which he declared, "Israel is not on the edge. It is not on the brink. This is not '48 or '67 or '73. But Israel is a small country. It can disappear. And it knows it." In the aftermath of the Iraq war, the Yale professor David Gelernter promoted a tendentious Saddam-Hitler analogy in the *Weekly Standard*:

> I don't claim that Saddam resembles Hitler; I do claim that the world's indifference to Saddam resembles its indifference to Hitler . . . Saddam, like Hitler, murdered people sadistically and systematically for the crime of being born. Saddam, like Hitler, believed that mass murder should be efficient, with minimal fuss and bother; it is no accident that both were big believers in poison gas.[5]

But the neoconservatives did have a secret weapon: Elliott Abrams, who had spent the 1990s as the president of the Center for Ethics and Public Policy, and who had written two books. One was called *Undue Process* and attacked special Iran-contra prosecutor Lawrence J. Walsh and his assistants as "filthy bastards." The other, *Faith or Fear: How Jews Can Survive in a Christian Nation*, argued that conservative Jews and Christians needed to establish a closer alliance.

Abrams became a top aide to then national security adviser Condoleezza Rice in June 2001. Abrams did not need to be confirmed for the post. He worked assiduously on democracy promotion in the

Middle East and ties with Israel, but he never enmeshed himself in Iraq. In fact, Abrams, who had been burned by his high profile during the Reagan administration, shunned, and continues to shun, the spotlight. He has a measure of contempt for the officials in the Defense Department who didn't. If they were going to seek out the glare of publicity, he seems to suggest, then they should have been prepared to deal with the consequences.

Abrams worked to ensure that Israel's interests were catered to by the White House. Bush announced in November 2001 that he was endorsing a two-state solution to the Israeli-Palestinian conflict, and in April 2001 he laid out a roadmap. The Israeli government, led by Prime Minister Ariel Sharon, saw it as a generous plan that the Palestinians were foolish to spurn. Not surprisingly, Abrams took a hard line about any final peace deal, clashing with both Assistant Secretary of State Nicholas J. Burns and National Security Council Aide Flynt Leverett, who would become a thorn in the side of the Bush administration, accusing it of missing an opportunity to cut a deal with Iran in April 2003. Abrams prevailed. Bush never exerted serious pressure on Israel to give up settlements; instead, Sharon himself made the decision to exit the Gaza Strip and construct a wall that would amount to a de facto settlement. Abrams also made a secret trip to Israel with the then deputy national security adviser in May 2003; Stephen Hadley took a special helicopter tour with Sharon over the West Bank that was supposed to underscore the precariousness of Israel's borders. Despite Abrams's role, however, the neoconservatives were convinced that more—much more—needed to be done. Iraq remained on their hit list.

———

In 1981 Claire Sterling, a former writer for the *Reporter,* published a book called *The Terror Network: The Secret War of International Terrorism* that tied the Soviet Union to almost every terrorist act in the world. Reagan's CIA director William Casey held it up at a meeting with top officials and told them he had learned more from it than all of their analyses. Vincent Cannistraro, the former head of the CIA's counterterrorism center, told me that Dick Cheney, then a congressman from Wyoming,

> bought into and echoed what Reagan and Casey were saying. He came to Rome after visiting Saudi Arabia. He told us the Soviets were behind everything. Casey tried to get the analysts to go along. Most rejected it. The difference between the Reagan administration and the Bush administration was that the analysts could push back without being punished.

The book, which argued that from Italy to Ireland, Lebanon to Germany, groups of highly trained, fanatically dedicated terrorists were preparing to wreak havoc on Western society, had a big influence on the Reagan administration. Liberals claimed that Sterling failed to provide convincing evidence. The controversy anticipated the kinds of conspiracy arguments that the American Enterprise Institute's Laurie Mylroie would make about Arab terrorism in the 1990s. Indeed, Cannistraro says, "I assign tremendous culpability to her" for creating a fictitious link between Saddam Hussein and terrorism. "I went with Laurie to her first briefing with Paul Wolfowitz in 1998. Laurie wanted me to go. Paul asked me to stay after the meeting. I said she has a case that depends on a hypothesis that no one can prove." But Wolfowitz was captivated.

Mylroie, who attended Cornell as an undergraduate and earned a Ph.D. at Harvard, had been an adviser to the 1992 Clinton-Gore campaign. She taught at Harvard and the Naval War College and had been something of an apologist for Saddam Hussein, but after the invasion of Kuwait she performed a U-turn. She wrote a book with Judith Miller called *Saddam Hussein and the Crisis in the Gulf*. After the 1993 World Trade Center bombing, she became obsessed with the idea that Saddam was behind it. Among the people to whom she had given presentations on this theme was, of course, Wolfowitz. Her 2000 book, *Study of Revenge: Saddam Hussein's Unfinished War Against America*, was published by AEI Press and blurbed by Richard Perle and the former CIA director James Woolsey. In it, Mylroie thanked Wolfowitz for his assistance: "At critical times, he provided crucial support for a project that is inherently difficult."

Mylroie claimed that one Ramzi Yousef, involved in the first World Trade Center attack, was an Iraqi intelligence agent. In fact, he was an al-Qaeda agent. But in March 2001 Woolsey alerted several administration officials about her book, and she helped him prepare a briefing about Yousef. Months later, 9/11 occurred. Wolfowitz, an enthusiast for the Mylroie thesis, began pushing for an attack on Iraq almost as soon as 9/11 took place; in the famous September 15, 2001, meeting at Camp David, chronicled by Bob Woodward, Wolfowitz made the case to Bush for toppling Saddam Hussein. However, the State Department had it right in a 2000 counterterrorism report: "[Iraq] has not attempted an anti-western attack since its failed attempt to assassinate former President Bush in 1993 in Kuwait." As the terrorism expert Peter Bergen put it, "By the mid-'90s, the Joint Terrorism Task Force in New York, the F.B.I., the U.S. Attorney's office in the Southern District of New York, the C.I.A., the N.S.C., and the State Department had all found no evidence implicating the Iraqi government in the first Trade Center attack."[6]

After 9/11, however, Wolfowitz sent Woolsey on a special mission to Great Britain to investigate Mylroie's claims. Perle said that Mylroie should be put in charge of "quality control" at the CIA. Vice President Dick Cheney constantly asserted that Iraq was linked to al-Qaeda, as has George W. Bush. Despite the claims of critics of the administration that the war was simply "sold" to the American public, there was more to it than that. The administration was selling what it had sold to itself. It was, you could say, the dupe of its own propaganda about weapons of mass destruction. Given Saddam Hussein's years of defiance and, moreover, the fact that he had made much more progress on nuclear weapons, as the intelligence services discovered to their shock, in the 1980s, the CIA didn't want to commit the same error again. Small wonder that the CIA rejiggered its National Intelligence Estimate to include a worst-case assessment of Iraq after September 11. In addition, the neoconservatives—and Britain's prime minister, Tony Blair—were convinced that al-Qaeda was in league with Saddam Hussein. Just as in the days of the Soviet Union, a vast and implacable enemy was trying to subvert freedom and democracy. The *Weekly Standard* and other neoconservative outlets became mesmerized by the specter of al-Qaeda. They saw what they wanted to see—a new totalitarian movement that had to be stopped. In Cheney's case, this belief was reinforced not only by his (selective) reading of history books but also by his intense discussions with leading scholars such as Princeton University's Bernard Lewis. Cheney's confidence in his own judgment was also buttressed by aides such as Scooter Libby, who viewed his boss as nothing less than a new Winston Churchill. The basic problem was that by the 1990s, neoconservatism had become an echo chamber. As long as the neoconservatives were simply scribbling moralistic essays and op-eds, their stands were harmless enough.

Also almost completely forgotten in assessing the run-up to the Iraq war is the administration's success in liberating Afghanistan. The first flush of initial victory in Afghanistan convinced many liberals that it would be as foolish to oppose a second Iraq war as it had been the first. Recall that many Democrats were savaged for voting against the first Iraq war. Hillary Clinton and others who harbored presidential ambitions were convinced that they had to support a new war. Afghanistan, where the dreadful Taliban regime had quickly been toppled, seemed to justify Rumsfeld's confidence in a fast, mobile army. Iraq augured a repeat performance.

In the end, the neoconservatives adduced a number of reasons justifying war against Saddam. Their moralism stemmed less from imperial dreams than from something else—a firm belief in America's role as the only bulwark against a second Holocaust. As Jews, they (and their Catholic conservative allies) were haunted by the memory that the Allies had not stopped the Holocaust—and they strongly believed that it was America's obligation to act preemptively to avert another one. Their sense of historical mission lent their prognostications an air of moralistic fervor that grated, and continues to grate, on traditional conservatives who see this as a new form of Jewish political correctness and wish to purge the neoconservatives from the GOP. Traditional conservatives see no reason to attach any unique guilt or odium to the United States for its actions during World War II. Similarly, liberals such as Arthur Schlesinger Jr. have violently rejected the imputation that Franklin Roosevelt willfully abandoned the Jews of Europe to their terrible fate.

The insular nature of the neoconservative movement, comfortably inhabiting the institutional counter-establishment that Kristol and his partners had largely created, had begun to take its toll. In those rarefied precincts, the old immigrant resentment against the WASP establishment had mutated into a sophisticated contempt for the visionless bureaucrats who populated the State Department and other governmental redoubts. Laurie Mylroie was a prime exponent of this view. Shortly after the Iraq War, she offered a scathing depiction of the CIA and State Department in *Bush vs. the Beltway*. Her book, which featured an endorsement from Christopher Hitchens stating that "In the face of the glibly repeated slogan that America is 'in search of enemies,' Mylroie shows that many in our intelligence establishment are fatally unable to recognize an enemy even when they meet one," contained the standard neocon line about the "corporate mentality" of the CIA and State Department. Mylroie complained that CIA obduracy forced the Bush administration to base its case on weapons of mass destruction rather than on Saddam Hussein's likely involvement with 9/11: "When, for whatever reasons, the agency decides to leave key stones unturned, the inevitable result is policymaking in an information vacuum—with potentially enormous damage to national security interests and to broader national interests as well." It would be hard to think of a more fitting description of the Bush administration's own approach to the war on terror.[7]

Indeed, the neoconservative movement itself became professionalized in the 1990s. The think tanks, the magazines, the foundations—the movement became what Andrew Sullivan once referred to as a highly subsidized welfare hotel. The younger generation in particular was callow and opportunistic; they had never undergone the mental torments of their elders but had been neoconservatives almost since they were born, in many cases literally so. They had defined themselves on the basis of filial piety and hostility to their liberal opponents instead of developing their own ideas independently. Few of these neoconservatives had very impressive academic records; rather, they specialized in polemics. The most gifted neoconservative was Robert Kagan, but he, too, championed the binary simplicity of the neoconservative vision: the United States good, everyone else hopelessly bad.

The most basic problem was intellectual hubris. The neoconservatives had proven—to their own satisfaction at least—their prescience about both the danger of Soviet communism and the need to confront it aggressively. For many years—due mainly to their intense concern with the Holocaust and, by extension, Israel—they had also warned of the dangers of Islamic extremism. *Commentary* had been filled, as early as the 1970s, with warnings from the likes of Bernard Lewis about the growing threat of Islamic terrorism. Daniel Pipes (the son of the Harvard historian Richard Pipes) pounded away at this theme in the 1990s, suggesting that there was a dangerous domestic component as well. Far from being oblivious to the Islamic threat, as the liberal historian John Patrick Diggins would suggest in a lengthy denunciation of neoconservatism in the *American Prospect,* the neoconservatives were quite alarmed about it.[8] Did they see it as the principal threat to the United States? No. As we have seen, they were excessively preoccupied with looking for a new Soviet Union in the form of China. But they were certainly not inattentive to the noxious doctrines emanating from the Islamic world. This is why, when 9/11 occurred, the neoconservatives had an entire program that they could dust off and present to Bush, who eagerly signed on to the notion that terrorism could be fought and defeated by decisive military action.

With the attacks of 9/11, the neoconservatives once again felt like vindicated prophets. And they proceeded, with an even stronger sense of certainty about the "rightness" of their views, to propose a solution. Only this time they would not be standing outside the halls of power writing hand-wringing magazine articles and hortatory op-eds. Now they would be inside the government, helping to shape U.S. policy.

From the outset, both the liberal hawks and the neoconservatives occupied, or purported to occupy, the moral high ground by, in effect, accusing doubters and opponents of the war of being complicit with Saddam's dictatorship. Perhaps nothing captures the moralistic hubris of the neoconservatives better than *The War over Iraq,* a book published in 2003 by Lawrence F. Kaplan and William Kristol. This work has not received the attention it deserves. It offers a very revealing snapshot of neoconservative thinking on the eve of the war. Not surprisingly, Paul Wolfowitz attended the book party at the Washington, D.C., Metropolitan Club.

The book's title was a clue to the real stakes for the neoconservatives. It wasn't the war *for* Iraq but the war *over* it that concerned them. The neocons had always fought on two fronts, combating the communist enemy abroad and the liberals at home. The book by Kaplan and Kristol was aimed at the home front, intended to discredit the domestic traitors—namely, the practitioners of liberalism and, above all, realpolitik—who wanted to stand aside and allow Iraqis to expire in the mire of Saddam's dictatorship. It was the Scowcrofts, the Bakers, the paladins of the Bush I administration who earned the particular ire of neoconservatives such as Kaplan and Kristol. They weren't simply intellectual antagonists; they were enemies who had to be routed, driven out of the GOP, and replaced with a true fighting faith that would begin in Iraq to liberate the rest of the world. America shouldn't be a reluctant sheriff, as Richard Haass had put it, but eagerly seize the opportunity to become one for the rest of the world. If other countries didn't like America telling them what was in their best interest, they would soon learn to rue any opposition, whether it was the surrender monkeys in France or Saddam Hussein or any other Third World despot.

As a senior editor at the *New Republic*, Kaplan served as a vital bridge between the neoconservatives and the liberal hawks. Kristol and Kagan saw him as the key to disseminating ideas aired in the *Weekly Standard* to the wider and more respectable liberal audience reached by the *New Republic*, which had been mainstreaming neoconservative arguments for years. Irving Kristol himself often observed that ideas that had been considered outré only a few years earlier were now ventilated in places like the *New Republic.*

Like many of the younger neoconservatives, Kaplan, who had attended a Quaker school as a small boy, was rebelling against the legacy of the 1960s. He relished taking on the left wing of the Democratic Party, repeatedly assailing the "McGovernites" in *Wall Street Journal* op-eds. Kaplan studied with the noted European historian István Deák as an undergraduate at Columbia and went on to become the protégé of Eliot Cohen, himself a prominent neoconservative at the Johns Hopkins School of Advanced International Studies. Cohen (who leans toward the realist pole of the neoconservative spectrum) helped Kaplan land a job as executive editor of the *National Interest*, which was then run by Owen Harries. Harries gave Kaplan free rein, another sign of his intellectual catholicity. But it wasn't until Kaplan began to work at the *New Republic* under its former editor Peter Beinart that he became a kind of transmission belt for neoconservative thinking. Whether it was John Bolton, Richard Perle, or Douglas Feith, Kaplan effectively channeled their ideas in a series of articles that assailed, among other things, Richard Haass, the realist head of the State Department Policy Planning Staff, as a Scowcroft "mini-me."

One belief that the neoconservatives constantly attacked was the idea, first promoted by Henry Kissinger, that the United States was in decline. In essence, it held that the United States would have to accommodate itself to other nations. This notion, which the realists never abandoned, remained a red flag for the neoconservatives. They saw it as a kind of self-imposed, mental Treaty of Versailles that would permanently fetter the United States. In 2000, for example, Kaplan wrote, "The danger is precisely that the declinists will influence Republican policy and Republican presidents . . . Beneath the technocratic jargon, the urgent demands that the United States accommodate itself to hitherto indiscernible 'facts' . . . all betray a yearning to see US power erode."[9] Whether they yearned for it to erode or believed that it was simply inevitable, and that the United States had to make the best of a bad situation, the realists were coming into bad odor among both the liberal left and the hawkish right. By bashing traditional Republicans like James Schlesinger, Brent Scowcroft, Richard Haass, and Henry Kissinger, Kaplan helped create what might be called a Popular Front between the liberals and the neoconservatives. Soon enough, the traditional right was frozen out of polite discourse.

As Kaplan and Kristol depicted it in their book, the main issue that should unite the liberal and conservative hawks was the belief that American power, which had liberated the Balkans from Serbian oppression, should be redeployed against Iraq. Once again, morality was the key, as well as the putative link between Osama and Saddam. "The more one learns about the Iraqi dictator," wrote Kaplan and Kristol, "the clearer it becomes that he epitomizes—no less than Osama bin Laden—sheer malice ... He is at once a tyrant, an aggressor and, in his own avowed objectives, a threat to civilization."[10] This, of course, could be said about a number of rulers around the world—but that was Kaplan and Kristol's point: the war against Iraq was only the first shot in an extended campaign around the globe to establish freedom and democracy.

Such bellicose language was adopted by numerous liberal hawks, including Paul Berman, who published a best seller on the totalitarian thought of Sayyid Qutb. The militancy of traditional liberals such as Berman, who argued that radical Islam was the new face of fascism, did not go unremarked at the time. The liberal blogger Joshua Micah Marshall noted in the May 2003 *Washington Monthly* that Berman had succumbed to the temptation to become a new George Orwell: "The image he cast—or rather his ghost, or his shade—has ... become part of the pornography of the intellectuals. Berman has given way to this craving."

In March 2003 Leon Wieseltier declared, in debating the *New Yorker*'s Mark Danner at Swarthmore College, "There are two crimes, there are two heinous categories of acts, that I believe require, obligate, every civilized individual to oppose them, into doing something about them. They are genocide and the use of biological, chemical and nuclear weapons." Fine. But the stridency with which the *New Republic* attacked foes of the war as pacifists and dunderheads meant that it ended up losing much of its credibility, not to mention numerous subscribers. As the historian Ronald Steel observed in the *New York Review of Books*, the magazine had replicated its blunder during World War I, when it had detected a triumph of liberalism emerging from the Wilsonian crusade to end war forever. Instead, the stage was set for a second, and even more destructive, conflict.

The most ferocious attacks on the liberal hawks and the neoconservatives came from the traditional right. In March 2003 Patrick J. Buchanan declared:

> We charge that a cabal of polemicists and public officials seek to ensnare our country in a series of wars that are not in America's interests. We charge them with colluding with Israel to ignite those wars and destroy the Oslo Accords. We charge them with deliberately damaging U.S. relations with every state in the Arab world that defies Israel or supports the Palestinian people's right to a homeland of their own. We charge that they have alienated friends and allies all over the Islamic and Western world through their arrogance, hubris, and bellicosity.[11]

The interesting thing about such statements is that they don't amount to an intellectual dispute so much as a criminal indictment. No doubt Buchanan had a penchant, right from the beginning—to borrow from the title of his memoir—for strident invective. But the neoconservatives trigger his ire, and that of other old right members, to a startling degree. Far more than the left, the neoconservatives are the apostles of evil for the right. The overheated language suggests the extent to which the foes of neoconservatism sometimes become mirror images of it in their eagerness to debunk and expose the movement.

For their part, the neoconservatives were alarmed both by the rise of isolationism on the right during the 1990s and by the Clinton administration. The neoconservatives, led by Kagan and Kristol, saw themselves as waging a two-front war. As many liberal hawks and neoconservatives saw it, the Clinton years had been feckless, wasted ones. The neoconservatives, who had been reduced to circulating petitions during those years, wanted Bush to be different. They wanted him to enact what had earlier seemed like a pipe dream. Kaplan and Kristol thus claimed that polishing off Iraq would allow the United States to set an example for the rest of the world: "Duly armed, the United States can act to secure its safety and to advance the cause of liberty—in Baghdad and beyond."[12]

The neoconservatives were promoting the very themes that the Bush administration would put into action. Wolfowitz, Feith, Bolton, and a host of other Bush officials ensured that such themes became policy. On September 20, forty neoconservatives, including Podhoretz, Krauthammer, Kristol, and Perle, signed a letter from the Project for the New American Century. It advised Bush that he had no choice but to attack Iraq; a failure to do so "will constitute an early and perhaps decisive surrender in the war on international terrorism." Even if direct evidence tying Iraq to the World Trade Center attacks was lacking, it continued, Saddam Hussein needed to be toppled. The letter lauded Israel as "America's staunchest ally against terrorism."

This was essentially the message delivered by Richard Perle as head of the Defense Policy Board. In the past, the board had been run like clockwork. Participants were briefed on what to expect, and working groups were created. Perle, by contrast, winged it. But winging it meant that he could simply ram through his preferred policies. On September 19-20, 2001, the board, which included Henry Kissinger, met at the Pentagon in Donald Rumsfeld's conference room to listen to Bernard Lewis and Ahmed Chalabi, the director for the Iraqi National Congress, explain why Iraq had to be freed. Rumsfeld agreed. But in addressing the board, he talked not about democracy but about the need to demonstrate American power.[13]

Cheney, too, took a dim view of Chalabi. According to an adviser of Cheney's who worked closely with the Iraqi exiles, "Cheney was skeptical of Chalabi . . . We should have picked a horse and rode it. We are insane. The Iraqis were looking to us to lay down the law. We didn't. Now we're faced with no personal, strong connection." The thinking of this school of thought, which Cheney's adviser John Hannah supported, was that the United States needed to set up an interim government, a kind of constituent assembly, immediately in the Kurdish north. "This would have provided a center of gravity" and was being heavily pushed by officials in Cheney's office in January 2003. "Cheney," the adviser says, "did what all senior officials do"— he punted.

With so many conflicting agendas in the administration— Rumsfeld uninterested in Iraq itself, the CIA backing tribal sheikhs, and the State Department opposed to war—the administration focused on creating the case for war. Perle used the Pentagon as his base to foment the zeal for war. For instance, on July 10, 2002, Laurent Murawiec, a senior analyst at the Hudson Institute and former employee of Lyndon LaRouche, was brought in by Perle to brief the Defense Policy Board. He created a sensation by declaring, "The Saudis are active at every level of the terror chain, from planners to financiers, from cadre to foot-soldier, from ideologist to cheerleader . . . Saudi Arabia supports our enemies and attacks our allies." Murawiec dubbed the Saudis "the kernel of evil, the prime mover, the most dangerous opponent." The members of the board distanced themselves from Murawiec's remarks, which were first reported by the *Washington Post* in August 2002, but his mistake had been to spell out openly what the neoconservatives in the administration were actually thinking—an Iraq war would lead to a wider transformation of the Middle East, including the replacement of the Saudi monarchy by a democratically elected government.

It was no accident that Murawiec's briefing was held at the Pentagon. The champions of the neoconservatives were Vice President Dick Cheney and, to a lesser extent, Secretary of Defense Donald Rumsfeld, whom the neocons would ultimately turn on. It was an alliance of mutual convenience. Cheney, an old-fashioned nationalist, caught a bad case of the neocon virus, or "fever," as former president Gerald Ford later put it, while Rumsfeld did not. Rumsfeld used the neoconservatives to get the war that *he* wanted: a high-tech extravaganza, with no nonsense about Ahmed Chalabi or trying to democratize Iraq. Rumsfeld simply wanted to get in and out. Planning for the aftermath was a waste of time.

Cheney was different. Years of reading military histories, the powerful influence of Roberta Wohlstetter—the *Los Angeles Times* bureau chief Doyle McManus told one of his reporters, accompanying Cheney on his plane, to ask him about the "pleasures of self-deception"—and the opportunity to permanently cripple the Democratic Party on foreign policy proved all too tempting for Cheney. Cheney would regularly convene meetings at his home at Washington's Naval Observatory with eminences such as Bernard Lewis and the military historian Victor Davis Hanson to discuss remaking the Middle East. Unlike Bush, he was interested in the ideas that the neoconservatives were backing. For Cheney, it wasn't simply about demonstrating the latest whiz-bang military technology but about fundamentally reshaping the world in America's interest. Cheney, however, had himself changed markedly since the Gulf War. Back then, says one former colleague, "If you'd say, Dick, that's crazy, this, this, and this, he'd say, 'Okay.' He was very relaxed, very accessible. Now he cannot change his mind." In addition, Cheney was not mesmerized by Wolfowitz: "I remember he said, 'Oh, shut up,' to Wolfowitz. He was not in thrall to him."

For the neoconservatives, Cheney was of course the key to the Bush administration, creating a network of loyalists, including I. Lewis Libby, John Hannah, William Luti, and David Wurmser. Libby, a former student of Wolfowitz's at Yale University in the 1970s and a speechwriter for him in 1981 at the State Department, became Cheney's chief of staff. He would become the neocon martyr of the second Bush administration, mired in scandal and self-justifications. Cheney, who had published a defense of the Reagan administration's Iran-contra shenanigans while in Congress, tried to circumvent the bureaucracy, essentially following Richard Perle and David Frum's prescription in their book *An End to Evil*, which saw the U.S. government itself as a hostile force needing to be end-run or undercut if anything serious was to be accomplished.

This was not unprecedented. John F. Kennedy employed the CIA to run his foreign policy toward Cuba; Henry Kissinger and Richard Nixon used back channels to the Soviet Union to bypass the State Department; and Ronald Reagan employed the National Security Council to create a new, secret foreign policy toward Iran. Cheney established his own "shadow" National Security Council to ensure that he got whatever information and intelligence he needed to sell the Iraq war to a credulous Congress and public. Like Wolfowitz and Perle, Libby viewed the CIA as untrustworthy. Its analysts were "experts" whose expertise—not to mention their partisan loyalties—clouded their judgment and prevented them from reaching the obvious conclusions that the neocons had reached: enemies were out there and had to be fought by whatever means necessary. The neocons had seen nothing wrong with Iran-contra, and they saw nothing wrong with Cheney's backstairs operation. In fact, they privately applauded it.

The Straussian Abram Shulsky, deputy to Feith, headed much of the secret intelligence work that went on as a channel for Cheney. Shulsky believed that there had been an excessive preoccupation with social science methods—hence the false assumption had arisen that a methodology could be constructed at the CIA that would produce scientific results about regimes like Saddam Hussein's. The neoconservatives were skeptical of the CIA. According to Shulsky,

> As for the suggestion that a single center for information gathering and analysis, a center on which the government would place primary reliance in determining the entire range of its national security policies (including interna-

tional economic, environmental, and health issues, to say nothing of international terrorism and drug trafficking), we should recognize that for the utopia it is.[14]

Rumsfeld, who had trafficked in neocon circles as the chairman of Midge Decter's Committee for the Free World—and was later the subject of a fawning biography by her—signed on to the neoconservative crusade because it fit in with his plans for a new military. Iraq wasn't interesting to Rumsfeld in itself, as it was for the neoconservatives; he was neither a moralist nor a gentile "friend" of Israel; he simply saw Iraq as a proving ground for his own theories about the military. But the same could be said about the neoconservatives, who were interested in Iraq mainly as a testing place for their theories about democratization, or, in the case of Wolfowitz, expiating guilt about leaving the Kurds and Shiites in the lurch back in 1991, when Saddam Hussein gassed tens of thousands to death.

To provide the evidence that Cheney sought, Rumsfeld and Wolfowitz relied on Feith. Feith was one of the most peculiar members of the administration. A character out of a Woody Allen film, he relished lecturing his subordinates about the fine points of English grammar and the history of the Ottoman Empire. Some speculated that Rumsfeld sent Feith to State Department meetings because he knew that his penchant for rambling disquisitions would ensure that they went nowhere. Feith also famously earned mention from the retired general Tommy Franks, who saw him as a "master of the off-the-wall question that rarely had relevance to operational problems."[15] But this underestimates Feith. The fascinating thing about him isn't that he's stupid but that someone as intelligent as he could mess up so badly.

———

Feith's interest in the Middle East was long standing. On December 10, 1969, for example, the *New York Times* ran a letter critical of the Nixon administration's stance toward Israel. It read:

Secretary of State William Rogers's announcement urging Israeli withdrawal from occupied territory in return for something as insubstantial as an Arab pledge on peace demonstrates the lack of responsibility which has characterized the U.S. policy in the Mideast since John Foster Dulles. In 1956, after Nasser blatantly violated international agreement by closing the Suez Canal to Israeli ships, Israel occupied the Sinai Peninsula in an attempt to secure its rights to navigate through the canal. Through diplomatic coercion, similar to what Mr. Rogers has proposed, the United States forced Israel to withdraw upon the condition that Nasser open the canal to Israeli shipping. Immediately after Israel's withdrawal, Egypt renounced its promise and declared the canal closed to Israel. It is appalling the State Department can be so blind to historical precedent as to call for a withdrawal from the captured area. There is no evidence to indicate that Nasser's "pledge on peace" will prove any more sincere in 1969 than in 1956. Just as Dulles's actions in 1956 established conditions which led to the Mideast war of 1967, so Rogers's proposal is paving the way for another disastrous war between the Arab states and Israel in the near future.

The writer was Feith and he was fifteen years old. When I met with Feith in the Pentagon, he dismissed the letter as a piece of "juvenilia." To the contrary, however, this precocious piece of writing shows that his views were already set in stone as a youth.

Like Wolfowitz, Feith was powerfully shaped by the Holocaust.

Unlike Wolfowitz, however, he came to his hard-line views very early in life. Feith, who grew up in Elkins Park, Pennsylvania, was deeply influenced by his father, Dalck, who served heroically in World War II. Born in Galicia, Dalck grew up in Danzig, a "free city" located in the contested area known as the Polish Corridor, established after World War I as Germany's link to East Prussia. Dalck was captured by the Germans but escaped with British forces shortly after the United States entered the war. He promptly joined the U.S. merchant marine and participated in the invasion of Normandy. His family perished in the Holocaust.

After the war the senior Feith set up a metal-finishing company in Philadelphia. As a child, Douglas recalled, "a lot of my interest in history was a desire to understand his biography. He would give tantalizing glimpses, but he never laid it out in an orderly fashion." Feith notes that Danzig's status as a free city was established at Versailles by "people who wanted to run things rationally." Not only the dangers of totalitarian regimes but also the fragility of the Western democracies' attempts to create cartographic order out of messy European and colonial boundaries came home to him at a young age. It's not a stretch to argue that Feith's well-known contempt for diplomats and their geographical plans for peace in the Middle East derives from his father's experiences.

Still, it would be a mistake to think of the hawkish Feith as a Republican. According to him, "I grew up in a liberal Democratic Jewish household." Like Elliott Abrams, however, he was scarred by his experiences as an undergraduate at Harvard, where, he recalls, "I was at the end of the antiwar movement and was far less liberal than a lot of people." Feith was especially impressed by the courses he took with Richard Pipes. A summer internship at the Foreign Policy Research Institute in 1974 helped hone his writing skills. Feith also worked with Harvey Sicherman, who was a good friend of John F. Lehman. Lehman, a former Kissinger aide on the National Security Council and later secretary of the navy under Reagan as well as a member of the 9/11 Commission, arranged an internship for Feith at the Arms Control and Disarmament Agency, where he met the neoconservatives Wolfowitz, Carnes Lord, Francis Fukuyama, and Fred Iklé. In particular, Feith worked closely with Wolfowitz.

Another important experience was going to hear the dovish Leslie Gelb, then a correspondent for the *New York Times*, deliver a talk at Wellesley College on U.S.-Soviet relations. Feith drove Gelb back to Cambridge, talking the whole way about his speech, titled "Détente, Entente, and Irrelevant Diplomacy." Feith gave Gelb an earful. "With your views," Gelb exclaimed, "you should be working for Scoop Jackson!" "I'd love to," Feith responded. Gelb sent Feith's résumé to Perle, who arranged a summer internship for him. Decades later, Perle would arrange a new job for Feith—as undersecretary of defense in the George W. Bush administration.

Feith went on to work for Admiral Elmo Zumwalt in 1976, when he waged a quixotic campaign against the Virginia senator Harry Byrd. Zumwalt was a leading member of the Committee on the Present Danger and, as Feith recalls, "a real Scoop Jackson Democrat. He had a lot of liberal domestic views, but he was a critic of the Nixon-Kissinger détente." Feith grabbed the opportunity to befriend Zumwalt. After working up a fifteen-page memo blasting détente, he was hired on the spot. Zumwalt made Feith, who went on to work on arms control and Middle East policy. By 1981 Feith's undergraduate mentor Richard Pipes was working on the National Security Council. Feith joined him there before moving on to the Pentagon in 1982 to work as special counsel for Richard Perle.

Feith's positions in the Reagan administration had been relatively unimportant. But in the 1980s and 1990s he incessantly published articles in places like the *Washington Times* denouncing liberals. Perhaps his most sustained crusade was against the Geneva Conventions. Feith anticipated the arguments that the Bush administration would use to lock up suspected terrorists indefinitely without putting them on trial. In 1985, for example, he criticized negotiations that took place under the auspices of the International Committee for the Red Cross on reaffirming international humanitarian law in international conflict.[16]

Invited to join the Bush administration, he hesitated for a moment at becoming number three in the Pentagon. Was he really up to the job? he asked Wolfowitz. Reassured, he took it. Feith went on to set up in 2001 a small intelligence unit, which consisted of David Wurmser and Michael Maloof, that was supposed to vet raw CIA intelligence. It was called the Policy Counterterrorism Evaluation Group. Feith had his deputy, William Luti, help establish the unit to examine data about Saddam Hussein's ties to al-Qaeda—and it was here that neoconservatism went off the rails.

The shadowy figure at the center of the Iraq intelligence debacle was Ahmed Chalabi. Chalabi, the scion of a prominent Shia family (his father, Abdul Haydi Chalabi, served in the council of ministers of King Abdul Faisal II), was born in 1944. He studied as an undergraduate at MIT at the tender age of sixteen before becoming a protégé of Albert Wohlstetter's at the University of Chicago, where he earned a Ph.D. in mathematics. Wohlstetter ensured that Chalabi met both Richard Perle and Paul Wolfowitz. Chalabi went on to become active in exile circles and fled Jordan in 1989 in the trunk of Crown Prince Hassan's car after being accused of financial peculation. He headed the Iraqi National Congress, which gained influence in Washington during the 1990s. He would appear at places like the *New Republic* to make the case for overthrowing Saddam. Chalabi was—and, for some neocons, remains—a hero. In an April 10, 2003, editorial called "Smearing Mr. Chalabi," the *Wall Street Journal* denounced the State Department's Near East Bureau—"always a force for preserving the region's despotic status quo"—for failing to embrace Chalabi. On November 9, 2005—the anniversary of the day the Berlin Wall fell in 1989—Chalabi, in his role as deputy prime minister of Iraq, spoke at AEI, where he was feted by its president, Chris DeMuth, only to be decried as a kind of war criminal by the assembled journalists, including the *Nation*'s David Corn, whom DeMuth imprudently picked to ask the first question. Chalabi was central for the neocons because to them he represented the possibility of an enlightened leader bringing Iraq out of the dark ages. Whether it was Angola's rebel fighter Jonas Savimbi or Nicaragua's contra leader Adolfo Calero, the neocons always needed someone that they could trot out as a freedom fighter.

The official version of the Pentagon's ties to Chalabi goes something like this: The government had what Chalabi called the Information Collection Program, which had been started in the Clinton administration as a result of the Iraq Liberation Act. The act authorized the State Department to support Iraqi opposition groups. Chalabi's Iraqi National Congress was designated as the umbrella organization to carry this out. The State Department, a senior official says, "hated Chalabi. They didn't want to do anything. So a government decision at very high levels decided to bring it into the Defense Department." Furthermore, there was nothing wrong with dealing with Chalabi: "The President talked to Chalabi, the Vice President talked to Chalabi. The Secretary of Defense talked to Chalabi." What Chalabi ended up doing, of course, was corrupting the intelligence process by, among other things, insinuating a bogus Iraqi defector named "Curveball" into the intelligence agencies. "Curveball," a drunk and a liar, told the administration what it wanted to hear—that Saddam Hussein was beavering away on weapons of mass destruction, including nuclear technology.

Nor was this all. In essence, the Pentagon's own intelligence unit—which became the center of controversy after its existence was revealed by Seymour Hersh in the *New Yorker* and by Michael Isikoff in *Newsweek*—tried to depict a spiderweb of links between al-Qaeda and Saddam Hussein that either did not exist or were impossible to prove. Thus, in a 150-page report, Wurmser and Maloof portrayed the

9/11 attacks as an al-Qaeda operation rendered vital assistance by Baathists in Baghdad. This unproven assertion was sedulously repeated in the pages of the *Weekly Standard.* It was the "clean break" all over again.

Were Feith and others knowingly fudging the facts when they briefed an ecstatic White House? Not really. They fit the facts to conform with their own preconceived theories. In February 2007 Feith, in responding to a report by the Pentagon's inspector general that his assessments about al-Qaeda links were "inappropriate," passionately argued that he was not off base and that the CIA's estimates had to be challenged. On February 11, 2007, for example, Feith stated in an interview with Chris Wallace on *Fox News Sunday,* "There was substantial intelligence. I mean, evidence is a legal term, not really appropriate here. There was a lot of information out there . . . [T]he people in the Pentagon were giving a critical review. They were not presenting alternative conclusions. They were presenting a challenge to the way the CIA was looking at things and filtering its own information." Feith was right in theory but not in practice. The CIA had routinely gotten its estimates wrong, and there was no cogent reason not to take a second look at its Iraq reports. But whether Feith and his minions were the right officials to carry out that task is another matter.

Luti's office later became the focus of the belief that there was a Jewish, Straussian cabal behind the administration's foreign policy. Certainly there were numerous neoconservatives in Luti's office apart from David Wurmser, such as Michael Rubin, currently a fellow at the American Enterprise Institute; Ladan Archin, an Iranian expatriate and protégé of Paul Wolfowitz; and David Schenker, who was staffing the new Israel, Lebanon, and Syria desk. An Egyptian-American naval officer, Lieutenant (later Lieutenant Commander) Youssef Aboul-Enein, was also assigned to Luti to ferret out any news from the Arabic world that might be used to demonstrate Saddam Hussein's links to terrorists. Seymour Hersh played up the fact that the Straussian Abram Shulsky worked for Luti and that Strauss preached a kind of deception that his followers tried to employ when it came to intelligence matters as well. Whether Strauss was really a necessary ingredient in all of this is questionable; but the charge stuck.

One source for that charge was a former official in Luti's office named Karen Kwiatkowski. Mere mention of her name would send officials in Luti's office into conniptions. She was reviled for stating, among other things, that Luti had referred to retired general Anthony Zinni, a critic of the Iraq war, as a "traitor." A retired U.S. Air Force officer, she was a Ph.D. candidate in world politics at the Catholic University of America and worked for Luti from 2002 to 2003. Her anonymous articles, called "Insider Notes from the Pentagon," appeared on retired colonel David Hackworth's Web site. She went on to write "The New Pentagon Papers," declaring that Luti's office had fundamentally distorted prewar intelligence. Writing in *Salon*, she stated, "I saw a narrow and deeply flawed policy favored by some executive appointees in the Pentagon used to manipulate and pressurize the traditional relationship between policymakers in the Pentagon and U.S. intelligence agencies." She continued, "I witnessed neoconservative agenda bearers within OSP [Office of Special Plans] usurp measured and carefully considered assessments, and through suppression and distortion of intelligence analysis promulgate what were in fact falsehoods to both Congress and the executive office of the president."

Interestingly enough, the same charge had been made in a pamphlet titled "Children of Satan: The 'Ignoble' Liars Behind Bush's No-Exit War," drawn up by one Jeffrey Steinberg on behalf of the cult leader Lyndon LaRouche. LaRouche himself claimed that Strauss's vision had been fulfilled: "The categorical form of that widespread denial of the efficient existence of truth, is the central feature of the intentionally fraudulent life's work of that now-deceased Professor Strauss, the Nietzschean den-mother of today's Chicken-hawk brood."

In his exposé, Steinberg pored over the Straussian backgrounds of Wolfowitz and Shulsky. According to Steinberg, "For Leo Strauss and his disciples the ignoble lie—disinformation—was the key to achieving and holding political power. And raw political power was the ultimate goal. For Strauss and the Straussians, there were no universal principles, no natural law, no virtue." This kind of fevered conspiracy thinking migrated with astonishing rapidity from the LaRouchian fringe to the pages of the *New Yorker* and *Harper's* magazine. Indeed, a later edition of this pamphlet gloated, in a Note to Readers, that "Since the original publication, on April 9 [2003], significant Establishment news outlets around the world have responded by publishing exposés of their own. Most prominent was the coverage in the Sunday May 4 *New York Times*, followed by a major article by veteran investigative journalist Seymour Hersh and a long news wire by the Inter Press News Agency's Jim Lobe, who is often picked up in the international press." This, you could say, was the neocon filter technique in reverse.

The only Strauss whom Bush and Cheney had probably ever heard of was the jeans maker Levi Strauss. But most of the themes pounded home by the neoconservatives would be adopted by them: the unproven ties to al-Qaeda, the patriotic sanctification of the American homeland and the demonization of domestic critics, the claim that no time could be lost in toppling Saddam, and the fantasy that the Middle East would, in a modern reprise of the domino theory, be liberated from tyranny once Baghdad had fallen.

Bush and Cheney began with the argument that weapons of mass destruction justified the war before lurching to embrace the democratization argument as the occupation went sour. The first sign that the administration was in earnest came when Bush stated in his 2002 inaugural address, "I will not wait on events while dangers gather. I will not stand by as peril draws closer and closer. The United States of America will not permit the world's most dangerous regimes to threaten us with the world's most destructive weapons."

Cheney was no less sweeping. In an address to the Veterans of Foreign Wars on August 26, 2002, he sounded just like Kaplan and Kristol. He portrayed a cunning and ruthless despot who was very likely in league with bin Laden and would stop at nothing to create weapons of mass destruction that he could employ, directly or indirectly, against the United States. America would be in grave danger if it did not take preemptive action. The upside was that the United States would be greeted as a liberator. Extremists in the region would have to rethink their strategy of jihad. Moderates would take heart. And our ability to advance the Israeli-Palestinian peace process would be enhanced, just as it was following the liberation of Kuwait in 1991.

On March 20, 2003, the United States and its small coalition of allied forces launched an attack on Iraq. Bush declared, "American and coalition forces are in the early stages of military operations to disarm Iraq, to free its people and to defend the world from grave danger." The fact is that the administration made no real attempt to ensure that Saddam would step down. It willed the war. In the *London Review of Books*, the military expert Andrew J. Bacevich observed that Feith had declared that the United States couldn't afford to have Saddam step down peacefully; in Bacevich's view, "allusions to Saddam as a new Hitler notwithstanding, they [the neoconservatives] did not see Baghdad as Berlin but as Warsaw—a preliminary objective." This is putting it rather strongly. But there is no question that the neoconservatives saw Iraq not as an end in itself but as a means to a larger end of transforming the whole Middle East.

It is important to be clear about the nature of this utopian vision. Much has been said in hindsight about the neocons' agenda. Many accounts look for hidden motives such as advancing America's imperial ambitions or subordinating U.S. policy to Israeli security needs. Above all the neocons have been tarred as "ideologues." But what does this mean?

The Straussians invested a great deal of energy in trying to revive the study of classical political philosophy, along with the work of certain moderns who inspire their admiration. Foremost among these was Tocqueville. The neocons seem to have envisioned Iraq as a Tocquevillian experiment in the spontaneous regeneration of civil society. But the charge, lodged by Francis Fukuyama, that they were indulging in the kind of social engineering that they had repudiated in the 1960s doesn't quite stick. The neoconservatives didn't spend too much time thinking about social engineering; they spent too little. In effect, they weren't Tocquevillian enough. The culprit, in many ways, was Fukuyama himself, who had unleashed the giddy sense of triumphalism among the neoconservatives after the successful conclusion of the cold war.

Initially, the war seemed to justify the optimistic boasting about a "cakewalk" in Iraq. Rumsfeld's blitzkrieg worked. The United States took Baghdad within a few weeks. When Bush landed aboard the USS *Lincoln* on May 1, 2003, on a U.S. Navy S-3B Viking to announce the end of major combat in Iraq, the Democrats could only sputter impotently. Senator John Kerry complained, "The president's going out to an aircraft carrier to give a speech far out at sea . . . while countless numbers of Americans are frightened stiff about the economy at home." Congressman Henry Waxman called for a General Accounting Office investigation of the cost of the trip. Senator Robert C. Byrd said, "I am loath to think of an aircraft carrier being used as an advertising backdrop for a presidential political slogan, and yet that is what I saw." The Democrats didn't realize that Bush had handed them the greatest gift they could receive: the "Mission Accomplished" banner behind him as he spoke dogs Bush to this day. Step-by-step, the administration found itself embroiled in a guerrilla war whose existence it tried first to deny, then (in various unsuccessful ways) to defeat or suppress.

By June 2003 the facade of unity in the administration had started to crack. Wolfowitz gave a memorable interview to Sam Tanenhaus for *Vanity Fair*, in which he said, "The truth is that for reasons that have a lot to do with the U.S. government bureaucracy we settled on the one issue that everyone could agree on, which was weapons of mass destruction as the core reason." This little bombshell sent the neoconservatives into overdrive to tar Tanenhaus; William Kristol called the piece a "disgrace." Still, Bush himself was able to deny reality for some time. In his second inaugural speech he suddenly veered to embracing the democracy crusade. He declared that the United States must "seek and support the growth of democratic movements and institutions in every nation and culture, with the ultimate goal of ending tyranny in our world." He emphasized that "the survival of liberty in our land increasingly depends on the success of liberty in other lands." Yet the very next day his national security adviser, Stephen Hadley, was assuring reporters and nervous foreign diplomats, including the Saudis, that the president had not really meant what he said. But Bush did not really deviate from this message once he had adopted it. He thus became, in essence, not the tool of the neoconservatives but a neoconservative in his own right.

Take his November 6, 2003, speech to the National Endowment for Democracy, itself a Reagan-era creation that had emphasized peacefully helping to bring about democratization in Latin America and elsewhere. "Iraqi democracy will succeed," Bush said in the speech, "and that success will send forth the news, from Damascus to Tehran—that freedom can be the future of every nation. The establishment of a free Iraq at the heart of the Middle East will be a watershed event in the global democratic revolution." In a speech at the Library of Congress on February 4, 2004, Bush offered more of the rodomontade that had worked effectively during the presidential campaign against John Kerry. He declared,

> Today, we are engaged in a different struggle. Instead of an armed empire, we face stateless networks. Instead of massed armies, we face deadly technologies that must be kept out of the hands of terrorists and outlaw regimes. Yet in

some ways, our current struggles or challenges are similar to those Churchill knew. The outcome of the war on terror depends on our ability to see danger and to answer it with strength and purpose. One by one, we are finding and dealing with the terrorists, drawing tight what Winston Churchill called a "closing net of doom." This war also is a conflict of vision. In their worship of power, their deep hatreds, their blindness to innocence, the terrorists are successors to the murderous ideologies of the 20th century. And we are the heirs of the tradition of liberty, defenders of the freedom, the conscience and the dignity of every person. Others before us have shown bravery and moral clarity in this cause. The same is now asked of us, and we accept the responsibilities of history.

While Bush had adopted the rhetoric of the neocons, his second term would see a progressive move away from neoconservatives actually occupying positions in his administration. One exception was John Bolton, whom Bush nominated to become UN ambassador in March 2005. Bolton ran into fierce resistance on Capitol Hill and was never confirmed. Bolton himself rejects the term "neoconservative." A graduate of Yale, he loathed the student left of the late 1960s and cut his political teeth fighting campaign finance regulations. Bolton carried over his uncompromising stands into the arena of international affairs. He was a unilateralist who believed that the United States should not negotiate with Iran and North Korea, and did his best to stymie any negotiations during his tenure at the State Department. At the UN, Bolton cracked down on the American staff, insisting on vetting any cables leaving the building. A protégé of James Baker and former North Carolina Senator Jesse Helms, Bolton functioned as a bridge between the neocons and traditional conservatives. Today, he occupies Jeane Kirkpatrick's former office at AEI, where he is finishing a memoir and gives speeches denouncing the government bureaucracy.

The longer his presidency went on, the more of a neoconservative Bush became—and the less power the neoconservatives themselves exercised directly. Wolfowitz and Feith would leave the administration in disgrace. Perle was forced to resign from the Defense Policy Board because of perceived conflicts of interest, including his Israeli financial ties. I. Lewis "Scooter" Libby became embroiled in a perjury trial that ended with three out of four guilty convictions.

With the United States running into quicksand and the neocons exiting the Bush administration, a chorus of critics rushed to declare neoconservatism dead. "Long after the new fundamentalist thinking fades away," wrote G. John Ikenberry, "American diplomats will be repairing the damaged relations and political disarray it wrought."[17] The British philosopher Anthony Dworkin pronounced an obituary for neoconservatism in the May 2006 issue of *Prospect*. The editor of *Foreign Policy* magazine, Moisés Naím, scoffed that neoconservative ideas "lie buried in the sands of Iraq." On the right, Patrick J. Buchanan gloated that the "salad days" of the neocons would soon be over.

Once again, however, neoconservative ideas proved harder to extirpate than their critics hoped.

The neoconservatives received an apparent reprieve when the Iraqi elections took place in January 2005. The ink-stained fingers of Iraqis who took part in a genuinely free election were a moving sight. But the fresh optimism about Iraq didn't last. Soon enough, Iraqi politicians fell to bickering, and gang warfare kept increasing among the various religious factions in Iraq. Then came what looked like another bright spot. This time it was in Lebanon. The "Cedar Revolution" took place. In fact, Undersecretary of State Paula J. Dobriansky, a neoconservative, was the first to use the phrase in the Bush administration. The assassination of former Lebanese prime minister Rafik Hariri on February 14, 2005, triggered popular protests against some fourteen thousand Syrian troops stationed in Lebanon. The Syrians withdrew on April 27, and the pro-Syrian government dissolved itself. The neocons crowed about the events in Lebanon. A March 1, 2005, *New York Sun* editorial was not untypical:

> Freedom, as President Bush has said so often, is something that is hungered for by all human beings, no matter what their nationality or religion. Despite the view that seems to obtain on the left, even Arabs have a desire for freedom. And today, it is on the march, and at least some of the Lebanese have said publicly that they are inspired partly by events in Iraq.

But despite the Syrian withdrawal, Lebanon, like Iraq, remained fractured by religious divisions.

Neoconservative optimism about Lebanon, too, proved mistaken. But the neoconservatives refused to give up.

Bush himself never dropped the democratization angle, but he also maintained the line that it was necessary to stop terrorists from establishing a kind of caliphate in the Middle East. He luridly exaggerated the threat by taking the grandiose statements of al-Qaeda at their word rather than considering what its members could actually accomplish. On December 14, 2005, he declared:

> These acts are part of a grand strategy by the terrorists. Their stated objective is to drive the United States and coalition forces out of the Middle East so they can gain control of Iraq and use that country as a base from which to launch attacks against America, overthrow moderate governments in the Middle East, and establish a totalitarian Islamic empire that stretches from Spain to Indonesia.

This wasn't exactly a rational analysis of the problem posed by terrorism, but a revival of the domino theory that was discredited by Vietnam.

But as the U.S. casualties mounted, the neoconservatives began to feel the heat. They adopted several strategies to deflect responsibility or to urge a new course. One approach was to argue that there was no such thing as neoconservatism. Anyone who used the term was trying to turn it into a synonym for "anti-Semite." David Brooks claimed in the *New York Times* that only "full-mooners" could believe that the Project for the New American Century and similar organizations wielded any actual influence: "In truth, the people labeled neocons . . . travel in widely different circles and don't actually have much contact with one another." According to Brooks, "Con is short for 'conservative' and neo is short for 'Jewish.' " David Frum and Richard Perle repeated this point in their book, *An End to Evil*: "Most important, the neoconservative myth offers Europeans and liberals a useful euphemism for expressing their hostility to Israel."[18]

Brooks's latter argument had some validity but it didn't succeed in deflecting criticism from the neoconservative role in promoting the failed Iraq policy. The neoconservatives tried to turn the anti-Semitic charge into a general brief on behalf of their cause. Like good prophets, they wanted to confirm their "rightness."

The 2006 mid-term election might have been expected to deliver the final blow to the neoconservative movement. Charges of cynicism and corruption stuck to the GOP, but the Iraq war was clearly the biggest factor in stripping the Republicans of control of both houses of Congress.

The fallback position for neoconservatives was to pin the blame for what was going wrong in Iraq on Secretary of Defense Donald Rumsfeld. Former coalition provisional authority head Jerry Bremer had already been drubbed for numerous mistakes, including disbanding the Iraqi army. Now it was Rumsfeld's turn. Rumsfeld had earlier been praised to the skies by the neocons. Now everything he did and said was bad. It was Rumsfeld who had failed to send in enough troops. It was Rumsfeld who had glibly assumed that Iraq would not need to be occupied. This new neoconservative tack can be dated precisely to a December 14, 2004, *Washington Post* op-ed by William Kristol: "But surely Don Rumsfeld is not the defense secretary Bush should want to have for the remainder of his second term." With Kristol in the lead, the neoconservatives relentlessly pummeled Rumsfeld.

After the election Bush seemed to acknowledge his failures by replacing Rumsfeld with Robert Gates. The neoconservatives responded by attacking the realists at home and, abroad, the Iraqi people themselves. The Iraqis were ungrateful wretches who had failed to recognize the benefits bestowed upon them by the United States. Charles Krauthammer observed, "We have given the Iraqis a republic, and they do not appear able to keep it." David Brooks blamed the Iraqis for succumbing to innate "demons: greed, blood lust and a mind-boggling unwillingness to compromise . . . even in the face of self-immolation." Leon Wieseltier said much the same thing in the *New Republic*:

> The security situation is at bottom the social-cultural situation. It seems increasingly clear to me that the blame for the violence in Iraq, and for its frenzied recoil from what Fouad Ajami hopefully called "the foreigner's gift," belongs to the Iraqis. Gifts must not only be given, they must also be received . . . For three and a half years, the Iraqis have been a free people. What have they done with their freedom? . . . After we invaded Iraq, Iraq invaded itself.[19]

Despite such attempts to absolve themselves of responsibility for the Iraq fiasco, the most notable feature of the neoliberals and neoconservatives has been the recriminations that developed from inside. In each generation the sectarian schismatics of the Trotskyist past have been replayed as leading thinkers bailed out of the movement. In the 1970s it was Daniel Bell who bailed out when Kristol embraced Richard Nixon. In the 1980s it was Daniel Patrick Moynihan who recoiled at the Reagan administration's contempt for international law and exaggeration of the Soviet threat. Now it was Francis Fukuyama, whose "end of history" thesis can be viewed as the touchstone of the new foreign policy idealism displayed by the neocons during the Bush administration.

Fukuyama's own clean break began with a public indictment of the neoconservative columnist Charles Krauthammer. In January 2003, Fukuyama had led a group commissioned by the Pentagon's Office of Net Assessment to analyze how to conduct a war against terror. Its conclusions were that the United States should avoid overt military action and follow a "hearts and minds" strategy in the Third World. Wolfowitz attended a briefing, but, needless to say, he was championing the opposite course.

By 2004 Fukuyama had become so fed up with the Bush administration that he told his friends he was voting for John Kerry. He was also so appalled by Krauthammer's blatant triumphalism at an American Enterprise Institute award dinner that he ended up writing a book disavowing the neoconservative movement and proposing a return to realism in American foreign policy. (The dinner was typical of the incestuousness of the movement: Krauthammer received the Irving Kristol Award and was introduced by Vice President Dick Cheney. In 2007, with Cheney once again sitting at the head table, Bernard Lewis received the same award.) Krauthammer's bellicose speech sought to reconcile realism with idealism, but it was suffused with chest-thumping about the greatness of America and snide remarks about European passivity in the face of evil. In the *National Interest*, Fukuyama pointed to the delusional sense conveyed by Krauthammer that Iraq was a success when, in fact, it was accomplishing the very opposite of what the administration had intended. Fukuyama's diagnosis was largely correct. In the face of Krauthammer's accusation that he was engaging in anti-Semitism by offering a few words of caution about America's Israel policy, however, he backed off the subject in his book. Once again, it was a sign of the bullying tactics the neoconservatives often employ to avert any criticism of Israel, however mild.

Since then, the neoconservatives have begun to run pell-mell from the administration itself. Max Boot lamented the administration's refusal to chastise Egypt as a sign of the "apparent waning of the Bush administration's ardor" for democracy promotion. AEI's Michael Rubin concluded that the Bush Doctrine was all but a dead letter "in the face of Bush's reversal." The *New Republic* did a 180-degree turn, first asking, "Were we wrong?" then, at the end of 2006, saying "we deeply regret" supporting the war. The hard-core neoconservatives also flipped—and once again *Vanity Fair* was the outlet for the neocons to expose themselves. Richard Perle, Kenneth Adelman, and David Frum, among others, interviewed for an article by David Rose, complained that Rumsfeld had betrayed the neoconservatives. They would never have supported the war had they known how it would be conducted. It was a great idea that had been tarnished by lesser minds. And so on.

Perhaps the most outlandish charge the neoconservatives made was to complain about a lack of fervor in Israel itself for going to war in the Middle East. The neoconservatives had hoped that Israel would not stop at attacking Lebanon, as they did in the summer of 2006, but also pummel Syria. Meyrav Wurmser, an Israeli with close ties to the Likud Party and the director of the Center for Middle East Policy at the Hudson Institute, lamented that had Israel attacked Syria, the insurgency in Iraq would have been destroyed. "If Syria had been defeated, the rebellion in Iraq would have ended," she said. It was the efforts of the deputy national security adviser, Elliott

Abrams, as well as United Nations ambassador John Bolton that had helped hold off pressure and give the Israelis sufficient time to attack both Lebanon and Syria. In her words, "The neocons are responsible for the fact that Israel got a lot of time and space . . . They believed that Israel should be allowed to win." This hope was dashed by the failure of Israel's preemptive strike against Hezbollah.

David Wurmser and John Hannah, also a Cheney adviser, worked closely with Elliott Abrams to scuttle Secretary of State Rice's attempts to convince Bush to create a channel to Syria to end the war in Lebanon. As Daniel Levy, a negotiator at Oslo, noted in *Haaretz* on August 28, 2006,

> Israel and its friends in the United States should seriously reconsider their alliances not only with the neocons, but also with the Christian Right. The largest "pro-Israel" lobby day during this crisis was mobilized by Pastor John Hagee and his Christians United For Israel, a believer in Armageddon with all its implications for a rather particular end to the Jewish story. This is just asking to become the mother of all dumb, self-defeating and morally abhorrent alliances.

In other words, the Israelis should be rescuing the United States from the neocons rather than the neocons trying to rescue Israel.

Closer to home, Fukuyama is trying to rescue neoconservatism from the neoconservatives. He broke with the *National Interest* after its editor John O'Sullivan left. (Irving Kristol sold the magazine to a third party, which later turned it over to the Nixon Center.) But the main foreign policy grouping that might be able to accomplish this task would be the realists in Washington, D.C., rather than Fukuyama. Senator Chuck Hagel and a clutch of realists based at the Nixon Center and the *National Interest* might try to return the GOP to traditional realist principles. They see neoconservatism as anathema to traditional GOP principles of restraint, which it is.

But whether the realists can make a comeback is another question. It may take a reinvention worthy of Nixon himself for them to have an impact on the party. A December 14, 2006, Nixon Center dinner at the Four Seasons Hotel honoring General Brent Scowcroft and Senator Richard Lugar brought home the degree to which realists have been frozen out of the Bush administration. The audience consisted mostly of former eminences. There was hardly a passionate young realist to be seen. Unlike the neoconservatives, the realists have cultivated no successor generation.

For their part, the neoconservatives (like any well-oiled family enterprise that suffers a few reversals in the marketplace) are not about to go away. Bush may be making it difficult for them by continuing to espouse neoconservative principles, but they quickly moved to tie their fortunes to a new candidate, John McCain, who was pushing for a robust foreign policy and a bigger military. Meanwhile, Senator Joseph Lieberman has been the last apostle among the Democrats pleading for a muscular foreign policy.

It may have taken a few decades, but the neoconservatives have quite possibly not only destroyed conservatism as a political force for years to come but also created an Iraq syndrome that tarnishes the idea of intervention for several decades. After Vietnam, the United States became mired in a self-defeating and narcissistic mind-set. It was the neoconservatives who helped overcome it and set the stage for Ronald Reagan. Now the reverse is true. The neoconservatives have debauched the idea of intervention and created the environment for a new round of self-abnegation.

At the same time, the professionalization of the neoconservative movement, which has been its undoing as both an intellectual and a moral force, means that it will remain an institutional one. Whether it's the Foundation for Defense of Democracies or the National Endowment for Democracy, the *Weekly Standard* or the *New York*

Sun, the neoconservatives are battle-hardened fighters who have created a permanent base for themselves. They will not disappear. An elite caste, they will simply regroup, deftly detaching themselves from George W. Bush. Had Bush only followed the neoconservative prescription, they argue, Iraq could have been a success. For others, the prospect of permanent warfare in the Middle East is a welcome one. In this regard, the neoconservative vision has been not destroyed but fulfilled by the Iraq war. The menace posed by Iran's nuclear ambitions offers a further rationale for neoconservative demands that the United States remain on a perpetual war-fighting basis in the Middle East. Democrats such as Hillary Clinton have largely assimilated this message. In 2006, speaking at Princeton University, Clinton made no secret of her wish to challenge Iran. "Let's be clear about the threat we face now," she said. "A nuclear Iran is a danger to Israel, to its neighbors and beyond. The regime's pro-terrorist, anti-American and anti-Israel rhetoric only underscores the urgency of the threat it poses. U.S. policy must be clear and unequivocal. We cannot and should not—must not—permit Iran to build or acquire nuclear weapons."

Other liberal hawks have grappled somewhat helplessly with the Iraq war as well. Paul Berman adheres to the belief that the Bush administration cannot be permitted to taint the battle for spreading American, liberal ideas around the globe. In his view, "Democracy, in short, requires liberalism, and liberalism is, after all, an ism, and isms need to be presented, clarified, popularized, and defended. The Bush administration, with its belief in magic solutions, has failed to do this. But neither has anyone on the left taken up the job, which is a little strange, if you think about it."[20]

Then there is Israel. None of the Democratic candidates has uttered even a mild word of criticism of Israel. This, too, must be counted as a neoconservative success. Israel, formerly the whipping boy of the left, has become sacrosanct, at least for any Democratic or Republican politician intent on seeking the highest office of the land. Finally, another neoconservative success is that the movement has not been driven out of the Republican Party. The lack of accountability is, in fact, astonishing. The neoconservatives, in creating the greatest foreign policy disaster since Vietnam, may also duplicate its political effects—for the Republican Party. The Democratic coalition was shattered by the Vietnam War. The GOP may experience the same fate over Iraq. But so far, the neoconservatives have essentially gotten off scot-free. Robert Kagan continues to write his column in the *Washington Post.* William Kristol has become a columnist at *Time.* The *Weekly Standard* is thriving. The mea culpas briefly issued by Richard Perle and Kenneth Adelman in *Vanity Fair* were quickly disowned by most neoconservatives. Unlike the Vietnam-era generation of Democrats, the neocons show no signs of remorse for the disaster they have created. As Douglas Feith put it, he isn't going to make any "Oprah-like" confessions. In addition, Eliot Cohen, a former student of Harvard professor Samuel Huntington and a professor at the Johns Hopkins School of Advanced International Studies, became counselor to Secretary of State Condoleezza Rice in March 2007. Staunchly pro-Israel, Cohen wrote a vituperative piece in the *Washington Post* in 2006 that invoked his son's service in Iraq to decry John Mearsheimer and Stephen Walt's addled essay about the power of the "Jewish lobby" in America. Cohen's neoconservative bona fides could not be more pristine. Rice astutely protected her neoconservative flank by picking Cohen, much as George Shultz had used Elliott Abrams to buffer himself from criticism. Cohen has been a staunch proponent of what he dubbed "World War IV" in a November 20, 2001, *Wall Street Journal* essay. Not just Iraq, but also Iran should be a target: "The overthrow of the first theocratic revolutionary Muslim state and its replacement by a moderate or secular government, however, would be no less important a victory in this war than the annihilation of bin Laden." While Cohen was critical of the manner in which the administration conducted the Iraq war, he himself bears much intellectual responsibility for it. He was a member of the Committee for the Liberation of Iraq and has been a proponent of the so-called Revolution in Military Affairs, which was based on Wohlstetterian notions of clean, surgical, high-tech warfare. Cohen himself, as New America fellow Anatol Lieven has pointed out, grossly underestimated the perils of guerrilla warfare in his writings. Cohen also repeatedly claimed that Saddam Hussein had links to al-Qaeda in testimony before Congress and elsewhere. What's more, Cohen's book *In Supreme Command*, which appeared in 2002, emphasized the importance of civilian command over the military, which played well to George W. Bush's (and Donald Rumsfeld's) predilection for running roughshod over the military (before the Iraq war, Bush appeared in the Rose Garden holding a copy of Cohen's book). In any case, Cohen's appointment is further testimony to the continued sway of the neoconservative movement inside the GOP.

Perhaps the neoconservatives' greatest accomplishment was to persuade Bush, who had been under heavy pressure to adopt the recommendations of the Iraq Study Group led by James Baker and Lee Hamilton to reach out to Syria and Iran diplomatically, to go in the opposite direction. The idea of a surge in Iraq was devised by the neoconservatives and once more demonstrated the sway that they have in the Bush administration. Specifically, the AEI fellow Frederick Kagan—Robert's brother—and the retired general Jack Keane argued in their fifty-two-page presentation that bulking up the military and trying to subdue Baghdad could lead to victory. The usual suspects—the AEI fellows Michael Rubin, Reuel Marc Gerecht, and Danielle Pletka, among others—contributed to the plan. It was called "Choosing Victory: A Plan for Success in Iraq" and was released at AEI with both senators Joseph Lieberman and John McCain in attendance. The neoconservative publicity machine rolled into action immediately. "Alone among proposals for Iraq, the new Keane-Kagan strategy has a chance to succeed," wrote the *Weekly Standard*. Keane and Kagan promptly met with Bush to pitch their plan, and he bought it. The surge began in January 2007. Kagan's wife, Kimberly, was deputed by the *Weekly Standard* to offer a fortnightly assessment of the plan's accomplishments; she herself had participated in devising it. Robert Kagan promptly declared it a success in an op-ed in the *Washington Post. Salon*'s Glenn Greenwald observed, "In April 2003, Kagan declared the war over and said we won. Since then, he has continuously claimed that things were getting better in Iraq."[21]

What prompted Bush to reject the Baker plan? According to one former official in the first Bush administration:

> I think the president thinks Baker stabbed him in the back with the Iraq Study Group. Baker's meeting him regularly as the group progresses and says, "I think we can come out with a report that you can put your arms around and get some bipartisan support." Then came the [2006] election, and the Democrats on the commission insisted on getting some words in there about a date certain to start drawing down. Baker fought it. He had to compromise to get a consensus report. The report comes out and Bush thinks, "I'll show those bastards."

———

So it will take an insurgency inside the GOP itself to dislodge the neoconservatives. But whether the old guard in the GOP has the mettle for that battle is dubious. There has been no real attempt to create new generations of realists to replace the Scowcrofts and Bakers and Schlesingers. The contrast between the Nixon Center event honoring Brent Scowcroft in 2006 and the AEI dinner for Bernard Lewis was striking. At the former, elderly veterans of the Nixon, Ford, and Bush administrations reminisced about their glory days. Senator Chuck Hagel of Nebraska, one of the few realists left in the GOP, offered generalities about Iraq. Meanwhile, at the AEI dinner, none of the neoconservatives displayed much doubt about their own influence. *Slate*'s Jacob Weisberg, for example, was dumbfounded by neoconservative serenity, noting that "the overall mood of self-celebration was unabated. From the stage, one caught no hint that matters were not working out as anticipated. All rose to salute the arrival of Dick and Lynne Cheney, herself a longtime fellow at the institute." The *Weekly Standard* writer Matt Labash has summed up neoconservative influence this way:

> While all these hand-wringing Freedom Forum types talk about objectivity, the conservative media likes to rap the liberal media on the knuckles for not being objective. We've created this cottage industry in which it pays to be unobjective. It pays to be subjective as much as possible. It's a great way to have your cake and eat it too. Criticize other people for not being objective. Be as subjective as you want. It's a great little racket. I'm glad we found it actually.[22]

But it's more than a racket, Labash's jocularity aside. The sheer scale of the neoconservative network, which includes the AEI, the Ethics and Public Policy Center, the *Weekly Standard,* the Committee on the Present Danger, and the Foundation for Defense of Democracies, means that it has become part of the Washington establishment. In February 2007, at the Munich Conference on Security Policy, Senator Joseph Lieberman declared, "What we are fighting is an ideology—the totalitarian ideology of radical Islam, as brutal and hostile to personal freedom as the communism we fought and defeated in the last century." The problem with such apocalyptic statements is that they endow a disparate group of terrorists with an importance that they simply do not deserve. Owen Harries, the former editor of the *National Interest*, had it right when he said it trivializes the cold war to make such overblown comparisons. But Senator John McCain, a close friend of William Kristol's, has essentially the same message as Lieberman. No one could do more than McCain to revive the neoconservative cause. It's also the case, as a prominent New York neo-conservative observes, that being "beleaguered plays into all the old psychological reflexes. Everyone's decided the neocons are wrong. That's vindication." The neocons are thus unbowed. At the annual May 2007 *Commentary* dinner, John Bolton regaled a receptive audience about the need to engage in further regime changes around the globe. And Norman Podhoretz feted Henry Kissinger at the dinner, to the extent of bussing his erstwhile adversary. The neocons aren't breaking ranks; they're closing them.

The neocons' liberal detractors, however, persist in acting as though neoconservatism were a phenomenon that has run its course. They crowed, for example, when the Project for the New American Century closed down in the summer of 2006. But don't be fooled. Prophets are not easily dissuaded from their crusade. They may regroup, reassess, and retrench. But these reckless minds, to borrow a term from Mark Lilla, aren't going away. Quite the contrary.

Postscript: Prophets Unarmed

As George W. Bush prepared for his seventieth birthday festivities in July 2016, he was cautiously optimistic. His reputation, in shreds for years, was starting to look as though it might enjoy a distinct uptick. The reason was simple: revisionist historians, intent on making a name for themselves by flouting received opinion, were taking a fresh look at his presidency. They argued that, like Dwight Eisenhower, Bush had deliberately fooled the press into portraying him as a callow simpleton when, in reality, he had used his vice president, Dick Cheney, to absorb the brunt of public criticism for many years.

To be sure, as even his most stalwart defenders felt forced to acknowledge, Bush had left behind a record that was, at best, a mixed one. For one thing, as Richard Perle had already noted in 2007, Bush's detached managerial style was detrimental to his policies:

"He's had a method of operating in which he is the chief executive, and that he expects things to happen, and he doesn't superintend them very closely, and a significant number of people who are nominally working for him don't agree with him, don't work very hard to implement his policies and in some cases even work against him."[1] But how different, really, argued a new, younger generation of historians, was this from Ronald Reagan's corporate style of leadership?

Then there was the devastating reverse the GOP suffered in the 2008 presidential election. A second victory in 2012 seemed to have cemented the Democratic hold on the White House for the long haul. Liberal authors were now writing books called *The Strange Death of Conservative America*, while conservative publishers released titles such as *What's the Matter with Pennsylvania?* Former ambassador Joseph Wilson had become a populist radio talk-show host and remained a thorn in the side of the conservative movement. Meanwhile, traditional conservatives did not tire of observing that the party's woes were the fruit of the neoconservative war in Iraq.

Then again, despite the numerous promises of the Democrats to exit Iraq, they hadn't been fulfilled as quickly as their base expected. In 2012 fifty thousand troops remained stationed in Iraq. Others were based in Kuwait and Qatar. The notion that America could suddenly withdraw from Iraq proved to be a pipe dream. Democratic leaders didn't want a "who lost Iraq?" debate that could prove as poisonous as the aftermath of Vietnam. Like the ancient crusaders, American forces had hunkered down, operating mainly from the modern version of castles—large, fortified desert bases from which they periodically emerged to target leading al-Qaeda terrorists. The Democratic administration also had to send an additional fifteen thousand troops to Jordan to help King Abdullah II suppress a violent uprising. With Saudi Arabia and Egypt quietly insisting that America had to remain, Washington worked to maintain a balance of power in the region.

And Iraq? While the eventual outcome was hardly as rosy as its partisans had confidently predicted, it did not end up as a catastrophe, either. After Bush was replaced by a president eager to work with the United Nations and the international community, Washington was able to hammer out a deal that effectively partitioned the country into a federal republic. The insurgency never went away—Iraq came to resemble Northern Ireland during the British occupation—but the story gradually slipped off the front pages, and public interest, never very great, in the internal affairs of Iraq faded almost completely. As some Republicans had predicted, once the Democrats took the White House, they no longer had the luxury of assailing the GOP but had to deal with the poisoned chalice that Bush had handed them. In 2009 a spectacular, foiled terrorist attack in downtown Washington—a dozen al-Qaeda operatives attempted to detonate a dirty bomb near K Street—earned the Democrats hosannas but also underscored the fact that the terrorist threat had not disappeared. The attack prompted a new era of good feelings that strengthened the hand of internationally minded Republicans such as Senators Chuck Hagel and Richard Lugar, who positioned the GOP to adopt a bipartisan approach toward confronting terrorists and cooperating with other nations. They worked assiduously to bury the memory of the Bush presidency, as far as possible.

In 2010, Berlin, Paris, London, and Warsaw experienced a simultaneous wave of bombings that almost brought Europe to its knees. Public outcry led to a banning of the display of Muslim symbols, deportation of radical imams, and a draconian crackdown on civil liberties that made the Patriot Act look mild by comparison. With Europe desperately trying to deal with a large, restive Muslim population, America was starting to look like a kind of paradise. Once more, as in the 1990s, foreign journalists flocked to Washington to try to explain the American miracle. And once again, they tried to fathom the increasing power of the group known as the neoconservatives.

Indeed, to the astonishment of many, the neoconservatives not only had remained unrepentant but seemed relatively unaffected by the obloquy they had endured during the Bush years. "They're gone, but they're not gone," Steven C. Clemons, a longtime observer and fellow at the New America Foundation, had already marveled in 2007. But public memory, notoriously short, worked to their advantage. By 2012 their longevity in Washington had made them seem like a permanent part of the landscape. Christopher Hitchens, for example, became a senior scholar at the Hoover Institution, where he continued to denounce his former comrades on the left with the same ferocity that he had previously reserved for the right. He had recently written a book called *The Trials of George W. Bush: A Study in Valor* and was said to hope for an appointment as a kind of roving ambassador for the next Republican president.

And the rest of the neoconservatives? Though out of power, they had weathered bouts of exile before. They continued to write and review one another's books, deliver lectures, and award prizes to one another from their secure perches in the network of think tanks and policy centers that Kristol had continued to construct. While the younger generation had by now become the new "older" generation at the American Enterprise Institute, it was supplemented by a new wave of children. The sons of Krauthammer and Feith, among others, emerged to carry on the wars of *their* elders. Thus, Daniel Krauthammer, a graduate of Harvard and a self-described neoconservative, wrote on his blog, "The Right Stuff," "Though I don't fit all that well into any one category, if I had to pick an ideological title to peg myself with, it would probably have to be neocon. Why? At root, one basic reason: the best policies are those that pursue the loftiest ideals by practical, realistic means." Others spent their time making a renewed case for an American empire that required imperial managers deeply versed (like themselves) in Thucydides and in the histories of Britain and Rome.

Bush himself had never expressed any regret for the war. Instead, he spent much of his time clearing sagebrush on his ranch and granting occasional interviews to friendly reporters such as Brit Hume of *Fox News*. Bush continued to maintain that Saddam Hussein had posed a dangerous menace to the United States. But veteran Bush watchers did note a cooling in relations between Bush and his former vice president. Bush was spending more time with his father and had largely abandoned the neoconservative circle that surrounded him in the White House. Cheney for his part had retreated into isolation in Jackson, Wyoming, where he was said to host a parade of former energy executives who enjoyed shooting quail and reminiscing about the old days.

Whatever lingering hostilities might have remained among Bush's followers, his birthday proved an occasion for the scattered members of his administration to reunite. Even former CIA director George Tenet, who many thought had burned his bridges with his self-exculpatory memoir, made an appearance. Bush had reportedly shown his forgiveness by sending Tenet a pair of Converse high-tops along with a note saying, "George, we all thought it was a slam dunk!"

A central part of the festivities was the dedication of a George W. Bush presidential library. The mere proposal that it be situated at Southern Methodist University had triggered protest back in 2006. A letter from the "Faculty, Administrators, & Staff" of the Perkins School of Theology to R. Gerald Turner, president of the board of trustees, announced:

> We count ourselves among those who would regret to see SMU enshrine attitudes and actions widely deemed as ethically egregious: degradation of habeas corpus, outright denial of global warming, flagrant disregard for international treaties, alienation of long-term U.S. allies, environmental predation, shameful disrespect for gay persons and their rights, a pre-emptive war based on false and misleading premises, and a host of other erosions of respect for the global human community and for this good Earth on which

our flourishing depends . . . [T]hese violations are antithetical to the teaching, scholarship, and ethical thinking that best represents Southern Methodist University.

But with tenure having been abolished at most universities across America, Bush's donation of several million dollars to establish a George H. W. Bush theology chair had stifled most faculty complaints.

The same could not be said for the major news outlets and academics across the country who had initially complained that the library would offer a grossly distorted version of history. Some critics said that it was bound to serve less as an oasis of dispassionate contemplation than as an ideological training ground for a new cadre of conservative activists intent on recapturing the territory that had been lost to liberals. Indeed, a number of commentators noted the irony that the true legacy of the Bush presidency had been to revive liberalism.

The display opened with a tribute to the Bush patriarch Prescott Bush. It alluded only briefly to Bush 41 before extolling the accomplishments of Bush 43. Bush's youth and career as Texas governor were treated as a warm-up to his presidency. Highlights included a mock-up of the fighter plane he flew in Texas during the Vietnam War and quotations attesting to his collegiality from his friends at Yale and the Harvard Business School.

What stirred the ire of critics, however, was the depiction of the Iraq war as part of a larger (and longer) struggle to export freedom and democracy to every part of the globe. Ahmed Chalabi and the Iraqi insurgency had largely been airbrushed out of the library's history. Instead, the exhibits praised the toppling of Saddam Hussein, the dissolution of the Baath Party, and the creation of an Iraqi parliament. Huge photos of purple-fingered voters put a cheerful face on Iraqi democracy. At the dedication ceremony, Bush said that he viewed himself as a "freedom fighter" in the mold of Abraham Lincoln and Winston Churchill.

Yet most Americans, left and right, greeted the library's opening with something of a yawn. To the public at large, the Iraq adventure seemed almost as remote as the Spanish-American War. Most of the characters involved had long since shifted gears. Wolfowitz, who resigned from the presidency of the World Bank over allegations of impropriety involving his companion, Shaha Ali Riza, now held forth in the Wohlstetter Room at AEI. Feith had become dean of the Georgetown School of Foreign Service, where he had instituted a new course on the British Empire and Winston Churchill. Kristol, dissatisfied with AEI's drift back toward Ripon Society values, was rumored to be setting up a new think tank called the Project to Restore American Principles in Washington, D.C. Its president was supposed to be the *New York Times* columnist David Brooks, who had taken a leave of absence from the *Times* and was now a professor in media and culture studies at the University of Chicago. Drawing on older conservative traditions, Brooks was calling for a new "fusionism" to unite neoconservatives and realists, splitting the differences between the two camps.

To be sure, Patrick J. Buchanan observed that he wanted to be a divider, not a uniter; but his was an isolated voice. In fact, a general reconciliation had taken place between the neoconservatives and the realists, who had fought one another immediately after the Democrats captured the presidency only to be united by their mutual hatred of what they perceived as the left's excesses. Meanwhile, the liberal hawks, recruited by the new Democratic administration, found themselves embroiled in a conflict with the new—or was it the old?—Democrats. A best-selling book by a young aide to Senator Nancy Pelosi charged that they were really neoconservatives.

The worsening situation in Iran had also bolstered the standing of the neoconservatives. Despite the efforts of the Western powers,

Iran had succeeded in its drive to develop nuclear weapons, prompting Saudi Arabia and Egypt to accelerate their own atomic programs. The neoconservatives used this grim development to argue that their larger view of foreign policy had proven correct and labored mightily to pin the blame on Bush's Democratic successor, who had become bogged down in brokering seemingly endless talks and parleys between Hamas, the Palestinian Authority, and Israel. Indeed, the neoconservatives had already begun to make a comeback shortly after the Democrats took the White House by alleging that they were dangerously weakening America's defenses—proving once again that the neocons were always more comfortable in opposition. "Appeasement by Any Name" was the title of a long essay, which became a best-selling book, by the Carnegie Endowment fellow Robert Kagan about the passivity of Republican realists in the face of dire dangers.

But in a seeming reversion to their origins in Alcove 1, the neoconservatives had experienced something of a schism; Kagan and several other neoconservatives were flirting with the Democratic Party in hopes of influencing it to take a firmly internationalist stand, coupled with a readiness to use force, while Kristol remained firmly entrenched in the GOP. Some even wondered if the neoconservative history of defectors leaving the movement—Daniel Bell, Walter Laqueur, Daniel Patrick Moynihan, Michael Lind, Mark Lilla, Francis Fukuyama—was about to repeat itself, as it seemed that the most talented members, at some point, always bolted. But overall, the neoconservatives sought to sound a new reveille; they believed that America was dangerously complacent about the gathering storm abroad.

Christian evangelicals, who had tired of the GOP's failure to deliver the goods when it came to issues such as abortion, had largely abandoned the party and were uninterested in Israel as well. Still, after eight years of Democratic dominance, the Republican Party's electoral fortunes looked as though they might be on the mend. The Democrats had banned SUVs in the new president's first term and were now contemplating a national conservation system based on fuel ration cards, a move that the GOP hoped would arouse sufficient public anger to permit it to regain power. Meanwhile, Bush, who had not been invited to attend the previous Republican convention, was being repositioned. To help burnish the family image, Laura Bush had launched a national campaign to modernize public and school libraries, though her husband was careful never to appear reading books to children. His appearance at the George W. Bush library was the first step in a carefully calibrated campaign to reintroduce him to the public in a flattering light. (If Nixon could retrieve his fortunes, why not Bush?) A speech at the Republican National Convention was supposed to be the turning point in the rehabilitation of his image. With Jeb Bush preparing to accept the GOP's presidential nomination in August in a rebuilt New Orleans, the stakes could not be higher.

Notes

PROLOGUE: NOW IT CAN BE TOLD: BUSH LOOKS BACK

1. www.csmonitor.com/specials/neocon/neocon101.html.
2. Irving Kristol, "The Neoconservative Persuasion," *Weekly Standard,* Aug. 25, 2003.
3. Douglas Murray, *Neoconservatism* (New York: Encounter Books, 2006), p. 223.
4. Charles Krauthammer, "Democratic Realism: An American Policy for a Unipolar World," speech to the American Enterprise Institute, Feb. 4, 2004.
5. Peter Steinfels, *The Neoconservatives: The Men Who Are Changing America's Politics* (New York: Simon and Schuster, 1979), p. 294.
6. Anatol Lieven, "A Trap of Their Own Making," *London Review of Books,* May 8, 2003.
7. James G. Muhammad, "Farrakhan: Jews, Zionists Making America Weak," *Chicago Defender,* Feb. 27, 2006.
8. David Biale, *Power and Powerlessness in Jewish History* (New York: Shocken Books, 1987), p. 203.
9. www.melaniephillips.com/articles-new/?p=285.
10. Norman Podhoretz, "Letters: the Bush Doctrine," *Commentary,* Dec. 2006.

EXODUS

1. Niall Ferguson, *The War of the World: Twentieth-Century Conflict and the Descent of the West* (New York: Penguin, 2006), p. 62.
2. Simeon Strunsky, "Abraham Cahan—an American Democrat," *New Leader,* June 13, 1942, p. 5.
3. Bill King, "Neoconservatives and Trotskyism," www.enterstageright.com, March 22, 2004.

4. Irving Howe, *World of Our Fathers* (New York: Harcourt Brace Jovanovich, 1976), p. 251.

5. Cited in Alexander Bloom, *Prodigal Sons: The New York Intellectuals and Their World* (New York: Oxford, 1986), p. 16.

6. Ruth Wisse, "The New York (Jewish) Intellectuals," *Commentary*, Nov. 1987.

7. Cited in Peter Drucker, *Max Shachtman and His Left: A Socialist's Odyssey Through the "American Century"* (Atlantic Highlands, N.J.: Humanities Press, 1994), p. 23.

8. Gerald Sorin, *Irving Howe: A Life of Passionate Dissent* (New York: New York University Press, 2005), p. 12.

9. Daniel Bell, "The Moral Vision of 'The New Leader,' " *New Leader,* Dec. 24, 1973.

10. Cited in Bloom, *Prodigal Sons*, p. 29.

11. William Barrett, *The Truants* (New York: Anchor Press, 1982), p. 23.

12. James Yaffe, *The American Jews: Portrait of a Split Personality* (New York: Random House, 1968), pp. 222-23.

13. Philip Selznick, "Irving Kristol's Moral Radicalism," in *The Neoconservative Imagination: Essays in Honor of Irving Kristol,* eds. Christopher DeMuth and William Kristol (Washington, D.C.: AEI Press, 1995), p. 20.

14. William Phillips, "How 'Partisan Review' Began," *Commentary*, Dec. 1976.

15. Gertrude Himmelfarb, "The Trilling Imagination," *Weekly Standard*, Feb. 14, 2005.

16. Tess Slesinger, *The Unpossessed: A Novel of the Thirties* (New York: New York Review of Books, 2002), p. 280.

17. Lionel Trilling, "On the Death of a Friend," *Commentary*, Feb. 1960.

18. Sidney Hook, *Out of Step: A Life in the Twentieth Century* (New York: Harper and Row, 1987), p. 214.

19. Alan M. Wald, *The New York Intellectuals* (Chapel Hill: North Carolina University Press, 1987), p. 63.

20. Lionel Trilling to Sidney Hook, Dec. 10, 1937, Hoover Institution Archives, box 28, folder 56.

21. Cited in Bloom, *Prodigal Sons*, p. 125.

22. Ibid., p. 138.

23. Max Shachtman, "Only Socialism Can Bring Peace and Freedom," *Labor Action*, Feb. 28, 1944.

24. Irving Howe, "Liberals State Their Program of Bankruptcy," *Labor Action*, Dec. 29, 1941.

25. Shachtman, "Only Socialism Can Bring Peace and Freedom"; Philip Selznick, "The Dilemma of Social Idealism," *Enquiry*, Nov. 1942.

26. William Ferry, "Other People's Nerve," *Enquiry*, May 1943.

27. Jessie Kaaren, "Jews of Europe Face Doom," *Labor Action*, Feb. 28, 1944.

28. *The Collected Essays, Journalism, and Letters of George Orwell: In Front of Your Nose*, ed. Sonia Orwell and Ian Angus (New York: Harcourt Brace and World, 1968), vol. 4, pp. 168-69.

29. For a superb discussion of the *New Leader*, see Hugh Wilford, "Playing the CIA's Tune? The *New Leader* and the Cultural Cold War," *Diplomatic History*, Jan. 2003.

30. See Peter Coleman, *The Liberal Conspiracy: The Congress for Cultural Freedom and the Struggle for the Mind of Postwar Europe* (New York: Free Press, 1989).

31. Barrett, *The Truants*, p. 244.

32. "America and the Intellectual: The Reconciliation," *Time*, June 11, 1956.

33. Stefan Collini, *Absent Minds: Intellectuals in Britain* (Oxford: Oxford University Press, 2006), p. 67.

WILDERNESS

1. Walter Goodman, "When Black Power Runs the New Left," *New York Times Magazine*, Sept. 24, 1967.

2. "Two Rich Young Activists," *Washington Post*, Feb. 2, 1969.

3. Martin Peretz, "The American Left and Israel," *Commentary*, Nov. 1967.

4. Irving Kristol, "Comment: New Right, New Left," *Public Interest* (Summer 1966), p. 7.

5. Cited in Merle Miller, "Why Norman and Jason Aren't Talking," *New York Times Magazine*, March 26, 1972.

6. Charles Peters, "I Was a New York Snob," *Washington Monthly*, June 1988.

7. Norman Podhoretz, *Making It* (New York: Random House, 1967), p. 35.

8. Midge Decter, *An Old Wife's Tale: My Seven Decades in Love and War* (New York: Regan Books, 2001), p. 39.

9. Ibid., pp. 41–42.

10. Norman Podhoretz, "The Cold War and the West," *Partisan Review* (Winter 1962).

11. John Leo, "Some Scholars, Reassessing Cold War, Blame U.S.," *New York Times*, Sept. 24, 1967.

12. Lionel Trilling, "Young in the Thirties," *Commentary*, May 1966.

13. Cited in Miller, "Why Norman and Jason Aren't Talking."

14. Cited in Warren Bass, *Support Any Friend: Kennedy's Middle East and the Making of the U.S.-Israel Alliance* (New York: Oxford University Press, 2003), p. 248.

15. Cited in Judith A. Klinghoffer, *Vietnam, Jews and the Middle East: Unintended Consequences* (New York: St. Martin's, 1999), p. 172.

16. Douglas Robinson, "New Carmichael Trip," *New York Times*, Aug. 19, 1967.

17. Geoffrey Kabaservice, *The Guardians: Kingman Brewster, His Circle, and the Rise of the Liberal Establishment* (New York: Henry Holt and Company, 2004), pp. 419–20.

18. Homer Bigart, "Faculty Revolt Upsets Cornell," *New York Times*, April 25, 1969.

19. Nathan Glazer, "Blacks, Jews, and Intellectuals," *Commentary*, April 1969.

20. Catherine Zuckert and Michael Zuckert, *The Truth About Leo Strauss: Political Philosophy and American Democracy* (Chicago: University of Chicago Press, 2006).

21. Leo Strauss, *The City and Man* (Chicago: Rand McNally, 1964), p. 1.

22. For the best discussion of Strauss and Kristol, see Nina Easton's *Gang of Five: Leaders at the Center of the Conservative Crusade* (New York: Simon & Schuster, 2000).

23. Eugene R. Sheppard, *Leo Strauss and the Politics of Exile: The Making of a Political Philosopher* (Waltham, Mass.: Brandeis University Press, 2006), p. 98.

24. An Interview with Albert Wohlstetter (July 5, 1985), "The Development of Strategic Thinking at RAND 1948-1963: A Mathematical Logician's View," Interviewers Jim Digby and Joan Goldhamer (RAND, 1997), p. 6.

25. Ibid.

26. H. H. Arnold, "Air Power in the Atomic Age," in *One World or None*, ed. Dexter Masters and Katharine Way (New York: McGraw-Hill, 1946), p. 31.

27. Albert Wohlstetter, letter to Michael Howard, Nov. 6, 1968, copy in author's possession.

28. Fred Kaplan, *The Wizards of Armageddon* (Stanford, Calif.: Stanford University Press, 1983), pp. 117-18.

29. " 'Terror' Is Declared No Bar to Atom War," *Washington Post*, Dec. 17, 1958.

30. Chalmers M. Roberts, "Rising Red Peril Seen in ICBMs," *Washington Post*, Dec. 28, 1958.

31. Khurram Husain, "Neocons: The Men Behind the Curtain," *Bulletin of the Atomic Scientists*, Nov./Dec. 2003.

32. Roberta Wohlstetter and Albert Wohlstetter, proposal to the Ford Foundation, June 30, 1989, p. 11, copy in author's possession.

33. Albert Wohlstetter, "National Purpose: Wohlstetter View," *New York Times*, June 16, 1960.

34. "Failure at Geneva," *New York Times*, Dec. 20, 1958.

35. Andrew J. Bacevich, *The New American Militarism: How Americans Are Seduced by War* (New York: Oxford University Press, 2005), p. 154.

36. Interview with Elliott Abrams, Jan. 10, 2004.

37. "History's Pallbearer," *Guardian*, May 11, 2002.

38. Robert G. Kaufman, *Henry M. Jackson: A Life in Politics* (Seattle: University of Washington Press, 2000), p. 39.

39. "Jamil the Irrepressible," *Time*, Dec. 13, 1971.

40. J. K. Mansfield, "The Early Years," in *Staying the Course: Henry M. Jackson and National Security*, ed. Dorothy Fosdick (Seattle: University of Washington Press, 1987), pp. 25-26.

41. Kaufman, *Henry M. Jackson*, p. 33.

42. Mansfield, "Early Years," p. 26.

43. Patrick Glynn, *Closing Pandora's Box: Arms Races, Arms Control, and the History of the Cold War* (New York: Basic Books, 1992), p. 124.

44. Walter Isaacson and Evan Thomas, *The Wise Men: Six Friends and the World They Made* (New York: Simon and Schuster, 1986), p. 488.

45. Glynn, *Closing Pandora's Box*, p. 229.

46. William Beecher, "Acheson Group Seeks 'Balanced' Defense Debate," *New York Times*, May 27, 1969.

47. William Chapman, "ABM Dispute Spurs Partisan Activity," *Washington Post*, June 16, 1969.

48. Paul Nitze, *From Hiroshima to Glasnost: At the Center of Decision* (New York: Grove Weidenfeld, 1989), p. 295.

49. Kaufman, *Henry M. Jackson*, pp. 214-15.

50. Jay Winik, *On the Brink* (New York: Simon and Schuster, 1997), p. 55.

51. Henry A. Kissinger, *Years of Upheaval* (Boston: Little, Brown, 1982), p. 250.

52. Henry A. Kissinger, *A World Restored: Metternich, Castlereagh, and the Problems of Peace, 1812-22* (Boston: Houghton Mifflin, 1957), p. 200.

53. David E. Rosenbaum, "Firm Congress Stand on Jews in Soviet Is Traced to Efforts by Those in U.S.," *New York Times*, April 6, 1973.

54. Cited in Stephen Isaacs, *Jews and American Politics* (Garden City, N.Y.: Doubleday, 1974), p. 39.

55. Joseph Albright, "The Pact of Two Henrys," *New York Times Magazine*, Jan. 5, 1975.

56. Peter Ognibene, *Scoop: The Life and Politics of Henry M. Jackson* (New York: Stein and Day, 1975), p. 202.

57. Raymond L. Garthoff, *A Journey Through the Cold War: A Memoir of Containment and Coexistence* (Washington, D.C.: Brookings Institution, 2001), p. 274.

58. Interview with Peter Rodman, Nov. 21, 2003.

59. Kissinger, *Years of Upheaval*, p. 256.

60. See Andrew Cockburn, *Rumsfeld: His Rise, Fall, and Catastrophic Legacy* (New York: Scribner, 2007), pp. 44-45.

61. Anonymous interview.

62. Richard L. Madden, "Harvard Lecturer Buys New Republic for $380,000," *New York Times*, March 13, 1974.

63. Michael C. Kensen, "Young Millionaires Are Big Contributors to McGovern," *New York Times*, Aug. 23, 1972.

64. Stephen Klaidman, "Conflict Rages over Policies of the New Republic," *Washington Post*, Sept. 2, 1975.

65. Edward Luttwak, "The Defense Budget and Israel," *Commentary*, Feb. 1975.

66. Norman Podhoretz, "Now, Instant Zionism," *New York Times Magazine*, Feb. 3, 1974.

67. Steven Rattner, "New Republic Is Seen Shifting Liberal Outlook," *New York Times*, Jan. 29, 1979.

68. Tom Buckley, "Brawler at the U.N.," *New York Times Magazine*, Dec. 7, 1975.

69. Daniel Patrick Moynihan with Suzanne Weaver, *A Dangerous Place* (Boston: Berkley Books, 1980), p. 217.

70. Frances FitzGerald, "The Warrior Intellectuals," *Harper's*, May 1976.

71. Anthony Lewis, "The Brooding Hawks," *New York Times*, Feb. 10, 1977.

72. See *Alerting America: The Papers of the Committee on the Present Danger*, ed. Charles Tyroler II and introduction by Max M. Kampelman (New York: Pergamon-Brassey's, 1984).

73. Albert Wohlstetter, "Can We Afford SALT?" *New York Times*, May 25, 1979.

74. Arthur Schlesinger Jr., "Human Rights and the American Tradition," *Foreign Affairs* 57, no. 3 (1978).

75. Terence Smith, "Opinion in U.S. Swinging to Right, Pollsters and Politicians Believe," *New York Times*, Dec. 4, 1977.

76. "Simon: Preaching the Word for Olin," *New York Times*, July 16, 1978.

REDEMPTION

1. Decter, *Old Wife's Tale*, p. 161.

2. Earl Shorris, *Jews Without Mercy: A Lament* (New York: Anchor Press/Doubleday, 1982), p. 36.

3. Irving Kristol, "Room for Darwin and the Bible," *New York Times*, Sept. 30, 1986.

4. Nicholas Lemann, "The Republicans: A Government Waits in Wings," *Washington Post*, May 27, 1980.

5. Bernard Weinraub, "Mondale Woos His Party's Conservative Wing," *New York Times*, Nov. 15, 1983. Similarly, the Coalition for a Democratic Majority would attempt to resuscitate itself. See David Shribman, "Democrats of 'Mainstream' Regroup to Try Again," *New York Times*, May 23, 1983.

6. Jeane J. Kirkpatrick, *The Reagan Phenomenon, and Other Speeches on Foreign Policy* (Washington, D.C.: American Enterprise Institute, 1983), p. 17.

7. Irving Kristol, "The War of Ideology," *National Interest* (Fall 1985), p. 12.

8. Sara Diamond, "The Thread of the Christian Right," *Z Magazine*, July/Aug. 1995.

9. Robert Gates, *From the Shadows: The Ultimate Insider's Story of Five Presidents and How They Won the Cold War* (New York: Simon and Schuster, 1996), p. 149.

10. Eric Alterman, "The Teflon Assistant Secretary," *Washington Monthly*, May 1987.

11. Richard Perle, *Hard Line* (New York: Random House, 1992), p. vii.

12. Wolf Blitzer, *Between Washington and Jerusalem: A Reporter's Notebook* (New York: Oxford University Press, 1985), p. 246.

13. Richard Pipes, *Survival Is Not Enough: Soviet Realities and America's Future* (New York: Simon and Schuster, 1984), p. 280.

14. Cited in Bernard Weinraub, "On the Right: Long Wait for Foreign Policy Hero," *New York Times*, July 12, 1985.

15. Elizabeth Kastor, "And Now 'National Interest,' " *Washington Post*, Sept. 10, 1985.

16. Cited in Sidney Blumenthal, "The Ultimate Neoconservative Weapon," *Washington Post*, Oct. 9, 1985.

17. Ibid.

18. Norman Podhoretz, "The Fantasy of Communist Collapse," *Washington Post*, Dec. 31, 1986.

19. Jay Winik, "The Neoconservative Reconstruction," *Foreign Policy* (Winter 1988-89).

20. Cited in Christopher Hitchens, "How Neoconservatives Perish," *Harper's*, July 1990.

21. www.abc.net.au/worldtoday/content/2005/s1304344.htm.

22. Jeane J. Kirkpatrick, "A Normal Country in a Normal Time," in *America's Purpose: New Visions of U.S. Foreign Policy*, ed. Owen Harries (San Francisco: ICS Press, 1991), pp. 156-57.

23. Joshua Muravchik, "At Last, Pax Americana," *New York Times*, Jan. 24, 1991.

24. George Bush and Brent Scowcroft, *A World Transformed* (New York: Vintage, 1998), p. 464.

25. A. M. Rosenthal, "Why the Betrayal?" *New York Times*, April 2, 1991.

26. William Safire, "Bush's Moral Crisis," *New York Times*, April 1, 1991.

27. www.jinsa.org/articles/articles.html/function/view/categoryid/109/documentid/289/history/3,653,109,289.

28. Michael Kelly, "Though Advisers Differ, Clinton's in Tune with All," *New York Times*, Sept. 11, 1992.

29. Peter Rosenblatt to Samuel R. Berger, Sept. 14, 1992.

30. Irving Kristol, "Defining Our National Interest," in *America's Purpose*, p. 73.

31. Irving Kristol, "My Cold War," *National Interest* (Spring 1993).

32. Kevin Sack, "Quayle's Right Hand: A Contrarian Tries to Remold Boss's Image," *New York Times*, Sept. 9, 1992.

33. Cited in Sidney Blumenthal, *Pledging Allegiance: The Last Campaign of the Cold War* (New York: HarperCollins, 1990), p. 277.

34. "Dan Quayle v. Murphy Brown," *Time*, June 1, 1992.

35. E. J. Dionne, *They Only Look Dead* (New York: Simon and Schuster, 1996), p. 185.

36. William Kristol and David Brooks, "What Ails Conservatism," *Wall Street Journal*, Sept. 15, 1997.

37. Robert Kagan, "Why I Am Not a Straussian," *Weekly Standard*, Feb. 6, 2006.

38. Fareed Zakaria, "Malcontext," *New Republic*, Aug. 18, 2003.

39. In *The War Against the Terror Masters* (New York: St. Martin's, 2002), Michael Ledeen declares:

> Creative destruction is our middle name, both within our own society and abroad. We tear down the old order every day, from business to science, literature, art, architecture, and cinema to politics and the law. Our enemies have always hated this whirlwind of energy and creativity, which menaces their traditions (whatever they may be) and shames them for their inability to keep pace. Seeing America undo traditional societies, they fear us, for they do not wish to be undone. They cannot feel secure so long as we are there, for our very existence—our existence, not our politics—threatens their legitimacy. They must attack us in order to survive, just as we must destroy them to advance our historic mission. (pp. 212-13).

40. Robert Kagan and William Kristol, "The Burden of Power Is Having to Wield It," *Washington Post*, March 19, 2000.

41. David Talbot, "The Making of a Hawk," *Salon*, Jan. 3, 2002, dir.salon.com/story/books/feature/2002/01/03/hawk/index.html.

42. Richard Perle, foreword to *Tyranny's Ally: America's Failure to Defeat Saddam Hussein*, by David Wurmser (Washington, D.C.: AEI Press, 1999), pp. xii-xiii.

43. Tony Smith, "It's Uphill for the Democrats: They Need a Global Strategy, Not Just Tactics for Iraq," *Washington Post*, March 11, 2007.

RETURN TO EXILE

1. See also Evgenia Peretz, David Rose, and David Wise, "The Path to War," *Vanity Fair*, May 2004.

2. See Michael R. Gordon and Bernard E. Trainor, *Cobra II: The Inside Story of the Invasion and Occupation of Iraq* (New York: Pantheon Books, 2006), p. 14.

3. Paul Wolfowitz, "Statesmanship in the New Century," in *Present Dangers*, ed. Robert Kagan and William Kristol (San Francisco: Encounter Books, 2000), p. 324.

4. Scott McConnell, "The Weekly Standard's War," *American Conservative*, Nov. 21, 2005.

5. David Gelernter, "The Holocaust Shrug," *Weekly Standard*, April 5, 2004.

6. Peter Bergen, "Armchair Provocateur," *Washington Monthly*, Dec. 2003.

7. Laurie Mylroie, *Bush vs. the Beltway: How the CIA and the State Department Tried to Stop the War on Terror* (New York: Regan Books, 2003), p. 127.

8. John Patrick Diggins, "The -Ism That Failed," *American Prospect*, Dec. 1, 2003.

9. Lawrence F. Kaplan, "Guess Who Hates America? Conservatives," *New Republic*, June 15, 2000.

10. Lawrence F. Kaplan and William Kristol, *The War Over Iraq: Saddam's Tyranny and America's Mission* (San Francisco: Encounter Books, 2003), p. 3.

11. Patrick J. Buchanan, "Whose War?" *American Conservative*, March 24, 2003.

12. Kaplan and Kristol, *The War Over Iraq*, p. 125.

13. See Gordon and Trainor, *COBRA II*, pp. 18-19.

14. Abram Shulsky, "What Is Intelligence? Secrets and Competition Among States," in *U.S. Intelligence at the Crossroads: Agendas for Reform*, ed. Roy Godson, Ernest R. May, and Gary Schmitt (Washington, D.C.: Brassey's, 1995), p. 27.

15. Tommy Franks with Malcolm McConnell, *American Soldier* (New York: Regan Books, 2004), p. 330.

16. Douglas J. Feith, "Law in the Service of Terror—the Strange Case of the Additional Protocol," *National Interest* (Fall 1985).

17. G. John Ikenberry, "The End of the Neo-Conservative Moment," *Survival* (Spring 2004).

18. David Frum and Richard Perle, *An End to Evil: How to Win the War on Terror* (New York: Random House, 2004) p. 163.

19. Leon Wieseltier, "Try Anything," *New Republic*, Nov. 27, 2006.

20. Paul Berman, "Symposium," *Dissent* (Spring 2007).

21. Robert Kagan, "The 'Surge' Is Succeeding," *Washington Post*, March 11, 2007; Glenn Greenwald, "Why Would Any Rational Person Listen to Robert Kagan?" *Salon*, March 11, 2007, www.salon.com/opinion/greenwald/2007/03/11/kagan/index.html

22. Jacob Weisberg, "Party of Defeat: AEI's Weird Celebration," *Slate*, March 14,

2007; "Interview with Matt Labash," May 2003, www.journalismjobs.com/matt_labash.cfm.

POSTSCRIPT: PROPHETS UNARMED

1. Alan Riding, "A Theater Holds a Hearing on Blair, Then Stages It," *New York Times*, April 27, 2007.

Index

236, 240, 258-59, 260, 266, 271, 278-79

American Federation of Teachers, 29

American Israel Public Affairs Committee (AIPAC), 128, 205, 207

American Jewish Committee, 40, 77

Americans for Democratic Action (ADA), 51, 109, 175

Americans for Intellectual Freedom, 52

Amitay, Morris J., 128-29, 207

Anatomy Lesson, The (Roth), 75

Andropov, Yuri, 168

Angola, 167, 183, 259

antiballistic missile systems (ABMs), 121-22, 129, 168

Anti-Ballistic Missile Treaty (1972), 129, 233

anticommunism, 51-64, 76-81, 85, 113, 128, 163, 178

   see also communists, communism

anti-Semitism, 10, 14, 20, 24, 25, 67, 152, 156, 162, 269, 271-72

appeasement, 15, 16, 59, 117, 120, 128, 151, 171, 192, 194

Aquino, Corazon, 179

Arabs, Arab states, 66, 82-83, 84, 123, 150-52, 180, 202, 226, 249, 268

   Gulf War and, 203-5

Arafat, Yasser, 237

Archin, Ladan, 260

Arendt, Hannah, 37, 80

Argentina, 153, 173

arms control, 85, 105, 110, 117-22, 129-32, 136, 147-48, 169, 185, 186-87, 191-93, 200

Arms Control and Disarmament Agency (ACDA), 120, 130, 147, 211, 257

Arnold, H. H. "Hap," 101

Aron, Raymond, 53, 219

ASAT tests, 19

Atlas, James, 197

Atomic Energy Commission, 118

Augenstein, Bruno, 103

B

Bacevich, Andrew J., 106, 263

Baghdad, 2, 4, 203, 204, 208

Baker, James, 160, 194, 203, 221, 266, 277-78

Baldwin, James, 84

Balfour, Lord, 60

Balkans, 99, 207, 208, 214, 222, 225, 226, 233

Ball, George W., 83

Baltic States, 25, 51, 194, 204, 222

Banfield, Edward, 111

Baroody, Jamil, 116

Baroody, William, Jr., 158

Barrett, William, 34, 56

Barthes, Roland, 110

Bartley, Robert, 106

Barzun, Jacques, 62

Baumann, Fred, 107, 157

Bawer, Bruce, 210

Beat generation, 76-77

Bechtel Corporation, 180

Beer, Samuel, 108

Beinart, Peter, 114, 247

Bell, Daniel, 31, 32, 34, 51, 52, 56, 63, 69, 77, 88, 100, 114, 159, 196, 210, 271, 288

Bellow, Saul, 27-28, 37, 75, 85, 89, 90, 97, 147

Bennett, William J., 14, 158, 163

Berger, Samuel R., 207-8

Berkeley Free Speech Movement, 88

Berlin, 17, 61, 82

Berlin, Isaiah, 218

Berlin blockade and airlift (1949), 53-54

Berlin CCF conference (1950), 53-54, 55

Berlin Wall, 193-94, 258

Berman, Paul, 248, 275

Berns, Walter, 87, 109

Beyond Culture (Trilling), 67

Biale, David, 11

bin Laden, Osama, 237, 263, 276

Birobidzhan, 140

Black, Barbara Amiel, 5

Black, Conrad, 5

black radicals, 66, 67, 84-85

Blair, Tony, 3, 7, 242

"blame America first movement," 79, 170

Blaming the Victim (Ryan), 138

1970s neocon vs. liberal views on, 137–38

nuclear weapons and doctrine in, 55, 79, 97–106, 117–22, 129–32, 136, 144, 147–49, 163, 186–87, 191–92

post-Vietnam Democrats' view of, 142–44

triumphalist view of, 20, 195, 200, 264

U.S. imperialism blamed for, 78, 79

U.S. linkage tactics in, 127–29

Collini, Stefan, 63

Columbia Law School, 99

Columbia University, 40, 41–42, 72–74, 88, 100, 153, 246

Commentary, 11, 16, 28, 40, 42, 57, 66, 71, 74–81, 84, 92, 130, 136, 146, 151, 153–55, 175, 176, 189, 193, 210, 216, 244

Committee for Peace and Security, 204

Committee for the Free World, 52, 131, 176, 254

Committee on the Present Danger, 52, 146, 166–67, 176, 179, 257, 279

Committee on U.S. Interests in the Middle East, 206

Committee to Maintain a Prudent Defense Policy, 121

Communist League of America, 30

communists, communism, 8, 11, 16, 25, 30–31, 32, 56, 68, 77, 110, 147, 244

Carter on "inordinate fear" of, 144, 150

in Central America, 137, 152–53, 174–79

human rights and, 169, 173–74, 177–84

neocon vs. Reagan view of, 184–92

post-Vietnam culture and, 148–49

Congress, U.S., 114, 121, 122, 128, 181–82, 261

see also House of Representatives, U.S.; Senate, U.S.

Congress for Cultural Freedom (CCF), 52, 53, 55, 56, 198

Conquest, Robert, 115, 123

conservatives, traditional, 13, 17, 50, 169, 211, 219–20, 243, 274, 282

containment policy, 49–51, 55, 126

Coors, Joseph, 156

Copland, Aaron, 52

Corn, David, 259

Cornell University, 87–88, 89, 95, 107, 109–11, 215, 216, 240

Costa Rica, 182–83

Council on Foreign Relations, 125, 191

counterculture (1960s), 67, 77–78, 220

Cropsey, Seth, 108

Cuba, 167, 181, 253

Cuban missile crisis (1962), 100, 120, 121

culture war, 20, 209–14

origins and precedents of, 58, 74, 86, 149, 158–60, 165, 209–11

"Curveball," 259

Czechoslovakia, 43–44, 193

D

Daniel Deronda (Eliot), 60

Danner, Mark, 248

Dannhauser, Werner J., 87

Darwinism, Christian right and, 165

Dayton peace talks (1995), 214

Decter, Midge, 18, 75–76, 98, 114, 131, 143, 149, 163–64, 165, 166, 190, 194, 254

Defense Department, U.S., 5, 131, 182, 185, 228–29, 231, 234, 235, 239, 251, 257, 259, 260

Office of Net Assessment of, 271

Defense Planning Guidance (1992), 217

Defense Policy Board, 232, 250, 251, 267

defense spending, 154, 192, 200

"Delicate Balance of Terror, The" (Wohlstetter), 104, 124

democracy, democratization, 4, 8, 21, 58, 95, 98, 112, 145, 163, 171, 173, 177–84, 189, 195, 208, 209, 217, 265, 268, 272

Democratic Party, 7, 17, 64, 86, 108, 116, 120, 142, 181, 226, 275–76

Clinton's rightward turn in, 206–7, 214

in culture war, 210, 213

Lind, Michael, 20, 288
Lipset, Seymour Martin, 36, 63, 111
little magazines, 39-40, 209
Lloyd George, David, 198
Lobe, Jim, 262
London Review of Books, 10, 263
Lortzing, Albert, 94
Los Angeles riots (1992), 212
Los Angeles Times, 252
Lowry, Rich, 214
Lugar, Richard, 274, 283
Luti, William, 229, 232-33, 252, 258, 260-61
Luttwak, Edward, 122, 201

M
McCain, John, 230, 236, 274, 277, 279-80
McCarthy, Eugene, 109, 133
McCarthy, Joseph R., 56, 61, 110
McCarthy, Mary, 14
McCarthyism, 55, 141
Macaulay, Lord, 60
McConnell, Scott, 236
Macdonald, Dwight, 37, 44, 52
McGovern, George, 68, 78, 79, 113-14, 121, 133, 147, 156, 170
McLaughlin Group, The, 203
McManus, Doyle, 252
McNamara, Robert, 120-21
McPherson, Harry, 175
Mailer, Norman, 78, 80
Making It (Podhoretz), 73-74, 79-80
"Making the World Safe for Communism" (Podhoretz), 131
Malamud, Bernard, 75
Maloof, Michael, 258, 259-60
Malraux, André, 37
Managerial Revolution, The (Burnham), 49, 50
Manchester Guardian, 55
Mansfield, Harvey C., 92, 111, 112
Marcos, Ferdinand, 179
Marcuse, Herbert, 66
Marshall, Joshua Micah, 248
Marshall, Will, 226
Marshall Plan, 117
Marx, Karl, 25

Marxists, Marxism, 9, 13, 21, 25, 27, 33, 36, 44, 49, 62, 64, 108, 152, 159, 191
"end of ideology" and, 196-97
Meany, George, 29, 128
Mearsheimer, John J., 276
Menorah Journal, 38-39, 41
Metternich, Klemens von, 126
Middle East, 66, 67, 80, 81-86, 110, 140, 150-52
in neocon scenario, 1-4, 21, 22, 234, 251, 263-66
neocon views on U.S. policy in, 225, 255-56, 263, 268, 271-73, 274-75
after 9/11, 237-39
peace process in, 150, 205, 237, 239, 249, 256, 263, 273
Middle of the Journey, The (Trilling), 42-43
Militant, 30, 49
military, U.S., 231
Milošević, Slobodan, 207
missile defense, 99, 101-5, 118-22, 129
missile gap, 104-5, 119
"Mission Accomplished" banner, 264
modernism, 36-37, 39-40
Modern Monthly, 42
Molotov-Ribbentrop pact (1939), 25, 35, 44, 51
Monat, Der, 54
Mondale, Walter, 18, 154, 167
Moore, Barrington, 66
Moose, Richard, 143
Morgan, Edmund, 101
Morgan, Edmund S., 216
Morgenthau, Hans J., 216
Moscow show trials, 25, 35
Moscow summit (1988), 192
Moynihan, Daniel Patrick, 14, 110, 111, 115, 126, 135, 138-41, 146, 155, 167, 171, 175, 176, 271, 288
background of, 138-42
in shift to center, 146, 148, 159, 187, 191
Mr. Sammler's Planet (Bellow), 85
multiculturalism, 31, 42, 218
Munich agreement (1938), 16
Munson, Naomi, 176

Shachtman, Max, 13, 29-31, 35, 36, 45, 47, 49, 96, 148, 171
Shalem Center, 237
Shanker, Albert, 29
Sharon, Ariel, 4, 239
Sheppard, Eugene R., 95
Shermanites, 32, 57
Shiites, 3, 188, 205, 229, 234, 254
Shorris, Earl, 164-65
Shulsky, Abram, 97, 108, 253-54, 261
Shultz, George, 160, 171, 174, 179-80, 182, 190, 216, 276
Sicherman, Harvey, 256
Silone, Ignazio, 53
Simon, William E., 156, 157
Sinai Peninsula, 84
Six-Day War (1967), 67, 80, 81-84, 151
Slesinger, Tess, 39
Smith, Tony, 226
Socialist Party, 31
Socialist Workers Party, 31
Socrates, 22, 90, 92, 96
Solarz, Stephen, 204
Solzhenitsyn, Aleksandr, 123, 126, 162
Sonnenfeldt, Helmut, 131
Sorin, Gerald, 31-32
South Africa, 18, 87, 171
South Korea, 55
Soviet peace conference (Waldorf Astoria; 1949), 52-53
Soviet Union, 7, 16-17, 25, 32, 35, 49-56, 66, 78, 82, 86, 104, 233
    Afghanistan invasion by, 154, 167, 180-81
    Carter policy on, 144, 145, 146, 148, 152, 154, 180-81
    collapse of, 173, 185, 188, 189, 192-93, 202, 204
    containment vs. rollback of, 49-51, 55, 125, 191
    hard-line stance on, 115, 125-32, 136, 144, 160, 218, 244
    Jews in, 117, 127-29, 139-40, 205
    as neocon dilemma, 50-51
    Nixon-Kissinger policy on, 106, 121, 125-31, 142, 146, 166, 253
    in Reagan era, 18-19, 115-16, 136-37,
147, 163, 166, 167-69, 171, 172, 181, 184-87, 188, 189, 190-93, 240, 271
    terrorism and, 239-40
    totalitarian history of, 123
    see also cold war
Spanish civil war, 25, 35
Spender, Stephen, 53, 57
Spock, Benjamin, 65
Stalin, Joseph, 13, 17, 25, 27, 32, 43, 44, 45, 49-50, 53, 79, 95, 123, 188
Stalinism, 25, 33, 35, 36, 37, 45
    liberals accused of, 55-56
Staples, Brent, 93
Starr, S. Frederick, 17
Star Wars initiative, 19, 168
State Department, U.S., 70, 73, 81, 82, 83, 130, 131, 142, 179, 185, 190, 191, 197, 216, 225, 231, 241, 243, 252, 253, 254, 255, 258, 259
    Policy Planning Staff of, 118, 123, 142, 247
Steel, Ronald, 218, 248-49
Steeves, Harrison Ross, 72-73
Steinfels, Peter, 5, 8-9
Stennis, John C., 121
Sterling, Claire, 239-40
Stevenson, Adlai E., 114, 122
Strachey, Lytton, 59
Strategic Air Command (SAC), 102, 104
Strategic Defense Initiative (Star Wars), 19, 168, 187
Straus, Roger, 80
Strauss, Leo, 14, 15, 16, 33, 58, 90-97, 98, 107, 110-12, 210, 215, 260-62
Straussianism, 87, 89, 90-97, 108, 111, 112, 158, 212, 213-14, 215, 260-62
Struggle for the World, The (Burnham), 50
Strunsky, Simeon, 25
Student Nonviolent Coordinating Committee (SNCC), 84
student protests, 87-89, 109, 126, 215
Students for a Democratic Society (SDS), 86, 87, 109
Study of Revenge (Mylroie), 241
Sullivan, Andrew, 244

Walsh, Lawrence J., 183, 238
Walt, Stephen, 276
Walzer, Michael, 66
Warnke, Paul, 143, 146-48, 175
war on terror, 7, 235, 243-44, 245
War Over Iraq, The (Kaplan and W. Kristol), 245-46
Warshow, Robert, 76
Washington Group, 127, 129
Washington Monthly, 72, 182-83, 248
Washington Post, 122, 133, 166, 190, 212, 238, 251, 276, 278
Washington Times, 218, 257
WASPs, WASP establishment, 14, 37, 61, 68, 86, 243
    Jewish social exclusion by, 11, 12, 14-15, 30, 33, 38, 40-42, 58, 71, 72-73, 75
Wattenberg, Ben J., 143, 148, 157
Waxman, Henry, 264
weapons of mass destruction (WMDs), 2, 241, 244, 248, 259, 262, 264-65
Weekly Standard, 4, 6, 38-39, 213-14, 218, 219, 230, 235, 236, 237, 238, 242, 260, 274, 276, 277, 278, 279
Weinberger, Caspar, 180, 185
Weinstein, Kenneth R., 97
Weisberg, Jacob, 279
Weiss, Paul, 34
West, decline of, 15, 64, 92, 93, 98, 162, 163, 195, 226
West Bank, 4, 84, 150, 151, 205
Who Paid the Piper (Saunders), 55
"Why the Soviet Union Thinks It Could Fight and Win a Nuclear War" (R. Pipes), 16, 136
Wieseltier, Leon, 20, 218, 219, 248, 270
Wildschütz, Der (Lortzing), 94
Wilhelm II, Kaiser of Germany, 22
Wilkerson, Lawrence B., 24
Will, George F., 5, 214
Wilson, James Q., 111
Wilson, Joseph, 282
Wilson, Peter, 122
Wilson, Woodrow, 46, 83, 226, 249
Wilsonian internationalism, 15, 169
Winckelmann, Johann Joachim, 94

Winik, Jay, 6, 124
Wisse, Ruth, 28
Wohlstetter, Albert, 97-106, 115, 120, 121, 124, 131, 136, 148, 149, 179, 180, 224, 232, 233, 258
Wohlstetter, Roberta, 98, 100-101, 216, 252
Wolfowitz, Clare, 219
Wolfowitz, Jacob, 107
Wolfowitz, Paul, 2, 4, 5, 24, 92, 97, 99, 104, 106-8, 110, 115, 121, 122, 136, 155, 166, 179-80, 195, 200-201, 208, 218, 219, 222, 228, 230-34, 240, 241, 245, 250, 252, 255-56, 257, 267, 271, 287
    attacking Iraq urged by, 241
    conventional thinking of, 233-34
    on WMDs, 264-65
Woodward, Bob, 241
Woolsey, R. James, 207, 241
Workers' Party, 35
World Bank, 287
World of Our Fathers (Howe), 27
World Restored, A (Kissinger), 126
World Trade Center:
    9/11 attack on, 229, 235, 250
    1993 bombing of, 219, 241
World War I, 44, 99, 249, 256
World War II, 2, 13, 15, 17, 18, 28-29, 54, 82, 99, 100, 104, 119, 125, 256
    neocon view of, 15, 116, 120, 143, 199, 243
    Trotskyist view of, 45-48, 56
Worsthorne, Peregrine, 57
Wurmser, David, 224-25, 238, 252, 257, 259-60, 273
Wurmser, Meryav, 224, 272-73

Y
Yale University, 34, 38, 42, 61, 86, 89, 137, 141, 147, 200, 215-16, 217, 238, 252, 266, 286
Yalta Conference (1945), 16, 130
Yemen, 82
Young, Andrew, 144
Young Communist League, 32
Young People's Socialist League (YPSL), 31, 32, 59, 171